Praise for...

On My Own Terms
A Journey Between Two Worlds

An elegant memoir that delicately recreates a vanished Indian world while charting the growth of an individual sensibility on the margins of cultures.

Pankaj Mishra
Indian essayist and novelist
Winner of the 2014 Windham–Campbell Prize for non-fiction

It is beautifully written and the prose flows with liquid ease. I particularly enjoyed the weaving of personal details and the social milieu that you portray—Sampurna Sastry, National Leather works, the sharp eye of Muslim tailors, Luz Avenue and Nageshwar Rao Park, and societal protocols of the time. Of course, the nuances of the epistolary romance were captured with such finesse—a delight to read.

Radha Sarma Hegde
Professor of Media, Culture and Communication
New York University

T0204633

On My Own Terms

A Journey Between Two Worlds

A Memoir

by

Vasu Varadhan

Mediacs
New Paltz, New York

Mediacs
151 State Route 32 S #14
New Paltz, New York 12561
www.mediacs.com

On My Own Terms — A Journey Between Two Worlds / Vasu Varadhan
ISBN 978-0-9994664-4-5
Also available as an eBook

Cover design by Chloe Annetts
www.chloeartdesign.com
Cover Photo Caption:
Standing left to right: The author's younger brother, Ranga; her paternal cousin Gopal, and the author at age 12.
Seated left to right: The author's paternal cousin, Rama, and her sister, Kalyani.
The photo was taken in the front yard of the author's paternal grandfather's house, No.3 Mahalakshmi Street.

For Raghu, Ashok, and my
grandchildren, Gavin, Stella and Liam.

May my memories become yours.

In loving memory of my son, Gopal, who died too young in the September 11, 2001 attacks on The World Trade Center. Your spirit continues to be my guide.

My Soul Is Dark

by

Lord Byron

My soul is dark – Oh! quickly string
The harp I yet can brook to hear;
And let thy gentle fingers fling
Its melting murmurs o'er mine ear.
If in this heart a hope be dear,
That sound shall charm it forth again:
If in these eyes there lurk a tear,
'Twill flow, and cease to burn my brain.

Closed Path

by

Rabindranath Tagore

I thought that my voyage had come to its end
at the last limit of my power—
that the path before me was closed,
that provisions were exhausted
and the time come to take shelter in a silent obscurity.
But I find that thy will knows no end in me.
And when old words die out on the tongue,
new melodies break forth from the heart;
and where the old tracks are lost,
new country is revealed with its wonders.

Preface

I came to write my memoir in the aftermath of losing my older son, Gopal, who was killed in the September 11 attacks on The World Trade Center. In the days, months and years that followed, family and friends, colleagues and acquaintances, described me as being strong, resilient, dignified and gracious in the midst of such an immense loss. That was the self I presented to the outside world but, deep inside me, there lay another self begging to be discovered and defined and brought to life. Writing this book allowed me to bring that being alive on the page.

No longer able to imagine a future or deal with the persistent sorrow that invaded the present, I circled back to my past, to touch the places and events of my childhood and re-create their particular texture with all its tensions and conflicts. Perhaps my childhood self could shed light on my adult self. My life had been blown off course but if I ever hoped to go forward, I had to peel back every layer of my self, confront each one head on, and re-orient myself by reckoning with my past.

What began as a process of healing evolved over time into a journey of self-discovery as I grappled with the nature of my own identity. It was an identity culled from a life that originated in America during the late 1940's to the late 1950's followed by a sudden and unexpected migration to India. My coming-of-age story is more than a crossing of geographical boundaries. It is the story of an Indian girl living in two different worlds where tradition, language, culture, and politics pose challenges to the process of assimilation. On a more intimate level, it provides a psychological portrait of the mother-daughter relationship, its tensions and contradictions, and my struggle to claim an identity on my own terms. My story ends with my arranged marriage at the age of sixteen and my impending return to America, the land of my childhood, where what was once familiar, now appeared foreign.

As a long time academic at New York University, I've encountered and had the privilege to teach several young Indian American women, many of them old enough to be my daughters. Sitting behind my desk, dressed in a sari, and looking very "traditional," I found it surprising that these young women would share intimate details of their lives with me. They sought me out as a mentor, as a role model, as someone who was able to crisscross two cultures and integrate the best of both worlds. These were American born girls facing conflicts with their Indian parents, particularly their mothers, which were eerily similar to mine. It was a bit disheartening to know that not much had changed over generations. All I could offer were snippets from my own life, the pain and loss of not fully belonging to any one culture, yet, the power and determination within to emerge stronger and in full command of one's destiny. With this memoir, I can now give a more complete account of my odyssey. In telling my story, I'm also telling their stories.

One last note. The rise of South Asian performers in television, movies, and most notably, stand-up comedy, has brought to the fore issues of racism, exclusion, and cultural appropriation. The voices of protest that erupt among these young professionals often situate these injustices in the here and now. I would urge them to take a more historical, cross-generational approach. The racism I experienced in 1950s America sadly persists today. We need to travel together and hear other people's stories beyond telling our own. This is the shared humanity of literature.

Vasu Varadhan
New York, 2018

Contents

Janaki and T.G. Narayanan
My Parents' Wedding Photo

CHAPTER 1

In The Name of Independence

Much was expected of me before I was even born. My parents, both Freedom Fighters in India's struggle for independence from centuries of British rule, willed that I should be born on August 15, 1947, a momentous day when Jawaharlal Nehru, the first Prime Minister, proclaimed in his "Tryst With Destiny" speech, that "at the stroke of the midnight hour, when the world sleeps, India will awake to life and freedom." My parents were equally convinced that I would be a girl and in their patriotic zeal settled on the one and only name that would do justice to their convictions--Swatantaralakshmi, Goddess of Freedom. I satisfied their craving by being born a girl, but proved to be a disappointment as far as their nobler aspirations were concerned. After ten days of a rather difficult labor due to the premature breaking of my mother's water, I was delivered on a rubber mat in my maternal grandparents' home.

There would be no fanfare to accompany my arrival into the world, only relief that the ordeal was over. My maternal uncle, Raghu Mamma, who coached my mother through the delivery, would never cease to point out that I was destined to cause my mother much pain. Cloaked as a joke, with a slight hint of seriousness, it was enough to make me wonder if somehow his prophecy would ring true. My father, in what would become a characteristic ritual of my childhood, was absent at the time of my birth. His acknowledgement came in the form of a telegram that read: "Delighted, it's a girl," dispatched while aboard the USS Renville, anchored in Jakarta Bay, Indonesia. He had been appointed Secretary of the United Nations Commission on Indonesia, with a mandate to broker a resolution to end the dispute between Indonesia and its Dutch colonial masters. The Renville Agreement, as it was known, bore the signature of my father, T.G. Narayanan. Three months later in November, 1947, my mother, older brother and I flew to Jakarta to be with him. It was there my father laid eyes on me for the first time.

No longer eligible to go by the name, Goddess of Freedom, my maternal grandfather dubbed me Vasundara, still a Goddess but one whose realm was the beautiful earth. As was the custom, the naming ceremony which took place ten days after I was born required two additional names which were of no significance and usually forgotten. It took many years to jog my mother's memory and learn that Sengamalam meaning Red Lotus and Kodhai meaning Beautiful Girl had been added to the roster. Ultimately, all these pretty names mattered little. I answered to Vasu, a common abbreviation of my given name, Vasundara, as well as that of a couple of others such as Vasudha, and Vasumati. I was a Goddess in name only.

The claim I had over my birthplace, the home of my maternal grandparents at 20 A Mandavalli Lane, Mylapore, Madras, proved to be short-lived. In a matter of months, as India took its initial steps to build a sovereign nation, my family found itself taking a giant leap across the oceans to the distant shores of America. My father was compelled to make his own tryst with destiny, a life-altering decision that would mark me permanently with a hyphenated identity.

Starting off as a journalist for India's national newspaper, The Hindu, my father quickly took on the role of war correspondent and was given his own by-line, a first in the history of the paper. An activist who had been jailed for joining Gandhi's Quit India Movement, my father was now an eyewitness to the momentous events that led to India's independence. To chronicle this history as it unfolded in the present was a dream come true for a journalist of his ilk. He pleaded with the editor for a transfer from Madras, where he was currently stationed, to Delhi, the capital and threatened to quit if his request was denied. My father was passed over in favor of another journalist, the scion of a famous and well-connected family, who exerted pressure on the editor to give their son the assignment. Angry and defeated by his less than privileged background,—a casualty of birth—my father kept his promise and quit his job thereby closing the chapter on his life as a journalist. It was a part of his past he hardly spoke about; for most of my life I knew him only as "My Dad, the diplomat."

Yet, the legacy he left in his journalistic career was not to be easily dismissed. His war dispatches from Imphal in the North-East part of India and later from Burma where the Japanese were forced to retreat from the Allied Invasion, had caught the attention of Vijaya Lakshmi Pandit, sister of India's first Prime Minister, Nehru. In addition, the publication of his book, A Famine Over Bengal in 1944 had earned her admiration; she wrote its Foreword. My father's embrace of humanitarian causes was not lost on Mrs. Pandit. When she was appointed to lead the Indian delegation to the newly founded United Nations, she approached my father and suggested he join the organization. He readily accepted and assumed the position of Personal Representative of the first Secretary-General of The United Nations, Trygve Lie. On the completion of his first assignment, the ratification of the Renville Agreement in January, 1948, my father was to return to America, but this time he wanted his family to accompany him. Thus began a journey, the politics of the time framing our future, particularly, my future. Born in a free India, I would know nothing of its early struggles; that part of its history would be gleaned from textbooks. The beautiful earth for which I was named had shifted tectonically beneath my feet, spawning a second birth at the age of five months when I was transplanted to America, reincarnated in its fecund soil, the karma of my existence about to take root.

The United Nations, founded in San Francisco in 1945, moved into its first home in Lake Success, Long Island, a year later. It was a move not without controversy. The community of fewer than 1,200 residents were initially opposed to the idea of a group of foreign nationals invading their neighborhood, in particular, the non-white delegates. The mayor, afraid that such attitudes would tarnish his image, interceded, and after a series of hard fought battles with the local citizens, he managed to get approval. Lake Success' official history stated: "The people of the Village were acclaimed all over the world as progressive, liberal Americans interested in the furthering of peace." Nothing could have been farther from the truth. It was one thing to welcome the UN as an organization and quite another to welcome its personnel. Racism ran deep and the UN was forced to develop its own housing projects which led to the construction of 600 units in Parkway Village, in Queens, New York, the new home for UN families. I spent the first twelve years of my life there.

I was five months old in 1948 when we moved into our first apartment, and though it was home to the first five years of my childhood, the only proof of my existence is in a handful of old black and white photographs. I in a playpen, clad in a baby bunting, staring into the eye of the camera, and another one of my mother in a striped sari cuddling my infant brother in her arms. Over the years, I could only rely on hearsay to fill in the gaps.

The origin of my own childhood memories took root when I was six years old, at which time we had moved into another apartment on 144--67 Charter Road in Parkway Village. Apartment B was a duplex, with the living and dining areas downstairs and three bedrooms with two bathrooms (one attached to the master bedroom), upstairs. The living room was a melange of East and West. A Castro-Convertible sat solidly on the burgundy Bukhara carpet, its pattern dating back to the Mogul rulers of India. An idol of Shiva, in the fiery form of Nataraja, Lord of the Dance, stood in sharp contrast under a portrait of a serene-looking Buddha. Small statues of the different gods in the Hindu pantheon stood in the niches staring out at the black and white Zenith television that occupied center place in the living room. A credenza in the dining area stored the good china that would be trotted out for the many dinner parties my parents hosted. The thalis, or stainless steel plates we ate on daily, had their own cupboard in the kitchen. The rosewood dining table with its protective felt pads was covered with a plastic red and black checkered tablecloth, to be replaced by one of damask linen for special occasions. There was never a time it lay naked, the beauty of the rosewood buried permanently under a shroud. Nevertheless, it was the hearth of our home. We did our homework, ate our meals, had our spats, chatted with our friends, and communed as a family around that table.

The kitchen, sole domain of my mother, was distinctively Indian. She had gone to great pains to replicate, in whatever way she could, the kitchens familiar to her past. Two megalithic stone grinders, an ammi, to grind her pastes to the right consistency, and a kaloral, to grind the rice and lentils for dosas and idlis, (the crepes and rice cakes of South Indian cuisine), had been shipped from Madras in huge steel steamer trunks. They took up an entire wall of our already small kitchen and I often stubbed my toe against the sharp stone edges. Gunny sacks of Indian rice were propped up among the boxes of Brillo pads and tins of Babbo cleansing powder in the cabinet under the kitchen sink. My mother's spice rack was an array of Sanka and Chock Full O'Nuts coffee cans filled with lentils from a provision store in Madras. Mason jars of coriander, cumin, fenugreek, and red chili peppers lined another shelf in the cupboard—all imported from the same provision store. She used only stainless steel utensils for cooking, all bearing the label of the manufacturer, "K. Ramanathan and Co., Mylapore, Madras." Adamant that her morning coffee be South Indian in flavor, she attached a Lovelock grinder on the wall to grind the coffee beans shipped periodically from Madras.

To insure the authenticity of her South Indian cuisine, my mother was not one to cut corners. Her own mother, a reputable cook, slavishly obeyed her husband, my maternal grandfather, who was a stickler when it came to food. Aviyal, a yoghurt-based stew, had to be made with fourteen specific vegetables, to suit his palate. The lack of a single ingredient let alone a substitute sent him into a paroxysm of anger. Coming as she did from such a household, it was not surprising that my mother would abjure the use of frozen vegetables, instant mixes or anything that was pre-prepared. She was fond of recounting her quest to find yoghurt, a key ingredient in many South Indian dishes. It was traditional to end one's meal with a mixture of rice and yoghurt accompanied by hot pickles, usually mango or lemon. In India, the name for yoghurt was curds; in fact, no one knew that a word like yoghurt existed. My poor mother, fluent in English, would go into supermarket after supermarket asking for curds to the puzzlement of the manager. She peeked into containers of sour cream and ricotta cheese on the sly, wondering if they were yoghurt but perhaps made of a different consistency in America. The ricotta was tossed out but the sour cream, though a poor substitute, was tolerable. One day she chanced to buy a container of Dannon yoghurt and her joy knew no bounds as if she had hit the jackpot. She quickly called her small coterie of South Indian women friends to announce her discovery. In quick succession, they emptied the store shelves of Dannon yoghurt, and collectively heaved sighs of relief, hailing my mother as their savior. How Mrs. Janaki Narayanan discovered yoghurt was curds became an oft repeated story as more families from the Indian subcontinent arrived in Parkway. More tales of success followed. While shopping for vegetables in Chinatown and Spanish Harlem, my mother learned that "lady fingers" were called okra, "brinjal" was eggplant, and "coriander leaf" was cilantro. With no Indian grocery stores around, these finds were a treasure trove for the Indian community for whom food served as a vital link to the country they left behind. Much like an old wives tale, (in this case a UN wife), my mother became a suburban legend, part of the lore that would seep into the next generation of UN children curious about the life their parents had led when they first arrived.

The process of adaptation was both painful and difficult for UN families, particularly for the South Indian Brahmin families like mine. Hailing as they did from a lineage of rigid orthodoxy steeped in ritual, their very act of crossing the ocean, was considered an act of pollution in the minds of the elders, a blight on the family name. Having committed this transgression, which was beyond atonement, it became all the more imperative that they preserve as many aspects of tradition as they possibly could.

The onus of carrying this out fell squarely on the shoulders of the wives while their husbands, preoccupied with more worldly matters, played a perfunctory role. Whether it be religion, food or dress, there was nothing accessible in the immediate environs: no Hindu temples, no provision stores and no sari shops. The rich diversity created by the UN in Parkway Village was a unique phenomenon for its time. But it was a self-contained diversity restricted to the perimeter of the surroundings. It was assumed the needs of the community could be met from within. The tug of home, and the fear that their heritage would be lost if the children became too Americanized, bred a certain recalcitrance in many of these Brahmin mothers, including my own. As a necessary first step, they brooked no compromise when it came to food, dress, and ritual worship. Many homes became microcosms of an imagined India, mine being no different.

I always called my mother "Amma," the Tamil appellation for mother, eschewing the American terms, Mom or Mommy. True to tradition, she wore a sari no matter what the season. Left on her own, she would have traipsed through the snow in her Indian sandals, but a stern warning from my father about the likelihood of catching pneumonia, was enough to make her wear a pair of shoes—the only one she owned and had expressly made in India for her trip to America—and pull on knee-high stockings which inevitably resulted in static cling as they rubbed against her silk sari. A Bonwit Teller coat, a birthday gift from my father, and a pair of gloves, helped her weather the bitter cold. She refused to wear hats or boots. Such accoutrements, she complained, would only be further affronts to her already compromised image of an Indian woman.

My mother's bindi, a small black dot in the center of her forehead, and her single studded diamond nose ring, raised many stares when we rode the subway together. Invariably, an American, would summon the courage to approach her with a barrage of questions: What does the black dot mean? Does it come off? How did you get the ring in your nose? Is it screwed on? Did it hurt? Proudly and at times, defiantly, she answered them all while I looked on with a mixture of embarrassment and admiration. I was glad to be attired in a dress during these encounters and not in a pavadai, (the traditional long skirt worn by South Indian girls), which my mother insisted I wear inside our home. Unlike my mother, I saw no reason to flaunt my ethnicity in public and was equally guarded among my friends in Parkway Village. I divided the UN families we knew into neat categories: the Tamil Brahmins; the North Indians and Pakistanis; the Europeans; and Others (a miscellaneous group from the Middle-East, and the Caribbean). The Viswanathans, the Narasimhans, and the Vaidyanathans along with my family, the Narayanans, constituted the core of the South Indian community. The Oberois, the Dalals and the Ahmeds (Pakistanis) were our other Indian neighbors and the Malinowskis from Poland along with the Roberts' and the Brands from England completed our circle of friends. We had but a passing acquaintance with two families, the Hassans from Jordan and the Desires from Haiti.

There was precious little to distinguish one South Indian home from another. Guests were asked to take their shoes off in the hallway before entering the living room as was the custom back home. The unmistakable pungent and somewhat acrid smell of asafetida—a dried resin, and an essential ingredient in rasam and sambar, regional dishes of South India—wafted from the kitchen. Joss sticks in varying fragrances of jasmine and sandalwood were lit to mask the smells of the day's cooking to little effect; it was enough to make you puke. The same Hindu gods with their consorts, albeit in myriad forms, stared at you from the niches—Rama and Sita, Shiva and Parvati and Vishnu and Lakshmi. Ganesha, the Elephant-God, Remover of Obstacles, and a divine source of inspiration, held a singular position. Krishna, an avatar of Vishnu, was often depicted either as a mischievous child taking stolen licks from a butter ball arduously churned by his mother from buttermilk or as a young lad surrounded by beautiful maidens called Gopis. Except for a few distinctive curios picked up by our fathers on UN-related travel, the rest of the furnishings, with minor variations, had all been bought from either Macy's or Gimbels, the two stores most frequented by our mothers.

Holidays specific to the South Indian community like Pongal, the Harvest Festival, were celebrated with much fanfare among the handful of Tamilian families. On such occasions, at my mother's insistence, I usually wore a brightly colored, richly woven, silk pavadai. She assured me that the daughters in the other families would be similarly attired and indeed they were. While our parents chatted downstairs, we retreated upstairs and could not help but giggle seeing one another in our native costume. It was a strange departure from our usual getup of dresses and pants and we felt as if we were playing dress up. As the day progressed, it became increasingly cumbersome to move around in the long skirt and we all wished we could be outdoors riding our bikes or swinging from the jungle gym. There was little we could do except to content ourselves with card games like Old Maid or Go Fish. For my Tamilian girl friends and me, the only significance we attached to these South Indian holidays was the opportunity it presented to parade around in our pavadais; anything deeper than that was completely lost on us.

Iterations of these communal get-togethers took place as the Bengalis gathered together for Durga Pooja and the Muslims observed Ramadan and Id. It was possible to layer one's identity in the UN community. We united as Indians on national holidays like Deepavali, the Festival of Lights, and on India's Independence Day, and we just as easily splintered into our sectarian groups for regional festivals. The rituals of home, dutifully re-enacted in spirit and faithful to form to the extent possible, insured the preservation and transmission of Indian culture to the next generation.

Parkway Village crafted with artifice and the promise of a global utopia, lulled its inhabitants into a false sense of security. My parents were no exception. In this rarefied atmosphere and idyllic surroundings a certain kind of myopia took hold which blinded them to the injustices that lurked beyond the periphery of home. They assumed the world outside was as hospitable as the one they lived in, an assumption that belied their own past beset as it was by the indignities heaped on them under British rule. My father's dogged pursuit to end the nuclear conflict between the United States and the Soviet Union became an obsession. Little did he realize that another type of conflict mired in racist attitudes would literally hit home. In this frame of mind, without giving it a second thought, my parents decided to enroll me in the local public school. It was a fateful decision as it turned out. My childhood was scarred forever. I came to learn in terms, more real than all the traditions of home, what it meant to be an Indian girl in America.

To recall those years in first and second grade at Public School 117 in Queens, is to excavate memories partially shrouded in a veil of amnesia. I was six years old in 1953 and knew for certain that my older brother, Ramu, had been sent away to boarding school in India at the tender age of eight. I distinctly remembered picking up my three-year old brother, Ranga, from his nursery class at the United Nations International School (UNIS), every day after school. When it came to the building that housed P.S. 117, and the faces of my teachers and classmates, my mind drew a blank. The only images that survived are the interior of the cafeteria with its long wooden tables and long wooden benches and the schoolyard boxed in by gray barbed wire. I see myself sitting in a corner, a forlorn look on my face, clutching an unopened book, while a group of girls jump rope and another group play hopscotch. I hope against hope for an invitation to join in only to hear the alarm bell signal that recess is over.

I should have known better given the contempt they held towards me. How could I have forgotten the daily taunts on the school bus where no one would sit next to me yelling, "brown-faced monkey!" as they walked up the aisle? On a dare, a boy, and it was always a boy, would be exhorted by the others to spit on my skin to see if the color rubbed off. He was shocked that the color of my skin held fast and barely noticed my own shock as I hastily wiped away his slimy saliva with the sleeve of my coat. Lunchtime was a nightmare as they passed the cucumber-cheese sandwich packed by my mother, around the table, taking turns to spit on it before returning it to me.

I endured it all without complaint not wanting to be called a tattle-tale on top of all the other epithets hurled at me. I was not one to bring home tales out of school and I seriously doubted if my parents would have listened anyway. I chose to suffer in silence that first year until one day well, into my second year, I could take it no more.

The nasty group of boys on the bus cornered me as I got off. I was pushed to the ground and stomped on. Someone tore at the green pompoms of my brand new scarf-like hat sending me into an uncontrollable rage. It was a present from my mother and I had worn it for the first time that day. The way they clawed at it felt like a violation of her love for me. It was enough to bring me to my feet and fight back making them flee. My knees all wobbly, I managed to make it home. I stumbled into the arms of my mother who grew alarmed by my appearance—cuts and bruises on my legs, my brand new scarf missing its pompoms. I shed two abominable years worth of tears repeating again and again how much I hated school.

This time I kept nothing back. Every taunt, every contemptible act was described in detail. "I'd rather be stupid the rest of my life than go back to that school," I cried out surprised at my own outburst. "Learn to adjust Vasu," my mother said, as she bandaged my knees. " No violence, Vasu, just turn the other cheek," my father sagely advised in a Gandhi-like manner. "Remember," he continued, "sticks and stones can break your bones but words can never harm you." Their tepid reaction infuriated me all the more and made me feel as if I had done something wrong. The next day, I begged to stay home, but my mother felt compelled to drag me along to the principal's office to get to the bottom of things. I was asked to sit outside. A little while later, my mother emerged with a look that was hard to read. "Mrs. Axelrod feels you don't mix with the other children and that you prefer to sit by yourself with a book. She thinks you are maladjusted," she said in a tone that sounded accusatory. I got the gist of the message without knowing what maladjusted meant but continued to protest: " No one wants to play with me. They won't let me in their games." The school year ended; I remained an outcast. The only memories that have prevailed were the cruel ones; the rest has been sucked into a black hole of oblivion.

The ugly countenance of racism had forced itself into our home like the snake in the Garden of Eden. It rattled my parents and assaulted their sensibilities. In India, their Brahmin pedigree denoted a higher status among all the other castes, a status that embodied characteristics of purity and virtue which made them immune to the more pernicious traits assigned to the lower castes. To arrive in America and bear witness to the opprobrium heaped on their Brahmin daughter was unthinkable. They could tolerate being different; they would not tolerate being inferior. As far as they knew, racism in America was reserved for "Negroes." Indians were in another category, so they thought. Fearful that even direr consequences would follow, I was taken out of P.S. 117 and enrolled at the United Nations International School (UNIS) the very next year.

I was given a hearty welcome by Mrs. Brown, my third grade teacher. To be Indian in her class was to be the subject of much curiosity among my classmates. In a matter of weeks, everyone knew where India was on the world map, what food I ate, what my native costume was, and what language was spoken at home. I finally got to play hopscotch and jump rope Double-Dutch style. An international food festival and a cultural program featuring the music and dance of different nationalities rounded off the school year. Above all, that first year at UNIS, made me proud to be Indian. The traditions of home, many of which I had come to tolerate without question became a source of ethnic pride and something to be shared in the universe that was UNIS. Even the pavadai I wore ceased to be merely a costume and for the first time an occasion presented itself where I, much like my mother in her sari, was proud to proclaim my identity in the homespun fabric of my native land.

It was October 24th, United Nations Day, commemorating the enforcement of the UN Charter in 1945, and I had been selected along with a few other children of different nationalities to be on the Perry Como Show. We were to appear in our native dress and along with the puppets, Kukla, Fran and Ollie, sing "Getting to Know You," from the play, The King and I. Mrs. Brown kept us after school to rehearse the lyrics until we were pitch perfect. She was careful to remind us that as poster children of the school we epitomized its mission statement of unity in diversity. We reveled in the excitement of being on one of the most popular television shows in mid-1950's America with an audience of millions. We gladly posed for the studio photographer, I in my silk pavadai and velvet blouse, flanked on one side by Illya Quimper, clutching her Peruvian sombrero precariously atilt on her head, and by Danuta Malinowski, in an elaborately embroidered Polish dress and bonnet, on the other. There we stood, on display, one big happy family, beseeching the audience to get to know us as we belted out the song. Much like Anna's hard won acceptance by the Siamese, we enjoined the audience to follow suit. For those of us who had seen the movie, the cultural clashes between the King and Anna were sources of much amusement; the imperial underpinnings were completely lost on us. Much as we wished for a happy ending, we ended up crying our eyes out upon the death of the King.

Living in Parkway Village and attending UNIS, housed in the same neighborhood, was akin to living in a bubble. My generation served as specimens in some kind of an experiment where we were developed like carefully cultivated organisms in a petri dish, protected from the contamination inhabiting the world outside. Lessons in history and geography were always of distant cultures other than the one we lived in. There was no mention of Jim Crow and the word, Negro, was never uttered. The only dark-skinned kids we knew were all from Haiti until Jessica Harris became the first "Negro girl" to be admitted. She was taunted mercilessly by the other children, who always accosted her in the bathroom, safely out of sight and earshot of the teachers. I immediately came to her defense, still smarting from the wounds inflicted by the kids at P.S. 117. We became fast friends soon after and it would take a few years before she gained acceptance among our peers.

I thought of Anna's song in the King and I, a paean to the harmonious co-existence that was possible among strangers, and knew it was a lie. Yet our school's credo made us believe it was true. I began to fall prey to this notion despite my horrible two years at P.S. 117 and the more recent racist attitudes I witnessed towards Jessica. My debut on the Perry Como Show allowed me to wallow in a fantasy world where a deep and abiding love was possible among all people no matter what their race or creed. It had such a palliative effect on me that I almost believed the racism in P.S. 117 was nothing more than an anomaly in an otherwise embracing world. But no matter how hard I tried, those voices, hissing words of scorn, refused to stay silent. It would remain an ugly memory throughout my life, half-buried in my subconscious, only to resurface when conversations centered around my childhood. I would then find myself recounting every excruciating detail as if it had happened only yesterday.

My sense of who I was and where I belonged was in constant flux depending on which world I inhabited, its locus either drawing me in or consigning me to its borders. My earlier hostile encounters at P.S. 117 shocked me into the realization that to be born with brown skin was to be cast in the role of a pariah. UNIS, on the other hand, celebrated my Indian heritage as a novel phenomenon. Much like an exotic curio I was put on display along with other equally exotic curios. Out of school, this bond of internationalism, common to my classmates and me, held but a tenuous grip over us. We were only too eager to rid ourselves of the labels affixed to our identities. The daily diet of American pop culture held us in thrall and turned us into avid consumers. We became fans of Archie and Veronica, devouring every comic book we could lay our hands on. We spent a penny from our allowance on Bazooka bubble gum, holding contests to see who could blow the largest bubble. We splurged by spending a whole nickel on Likamaid candy, biting into the wax bottle to get at the fruity liquid which left an ugly stain on our mouths. Not that we cared. We adopted the families in TV shows like Father Knows Best, Leave It to Beaver, and Ozzie and Harriet, and wished our families could be like them. We began to build another world for ourselves, away from home and the prying eyes of our parents, a world in which my compatriots and I saw ourselves, at least briefly, as Americans.

I would have gladly embraced the Indianness in me had it been on my own terms. My mother, unlike the other Tamilian mothers, insisted I strip myself of Western attire and don the Indian pavadai every evening. She made it seem I could not be Indian or become one while wearing American dresses and pedal-pushers. Yet, I wanted to be both Indian and American, free to select the traits of each culture to create an amalgam I could call my own. My parents' attempts to enforce a dichotomy between the two cultures as a defense against assimilation, only succeeded in making me feel less than whole. I gave birth to different selves, each like a Russian nesting doll, encased in its own shell. At school, my identity was tied to my nationality as if I were an ambassador for my country, India. At home and among other South Indian families, I was expected to behave like a good Tamilian Brahmin girl. I felt most free to be what I wanted to be when indulging in American pastimes. At times, I wished I were an orphan, accountable to no one but myself. Unwilling to plant both feet firmly in American soil, my parents chose to straddle it with one foot permanently anchored in India. It was an unequivocal indication that their sense of place was inextricably tied to their motherland. I, on the other hand, felt rootless, the ground beneath my feet shifting with each step.

CHAPTER 2

An *Indian* American Childhood

I discovered I had an older brother around the time I started at P.S. 117. Though he was born in 1945, two years before me, I was hard pressed to remember what he even looked like. His ghost-like presence wafted into our living room each time an imprint of an Indian postal stamp addressed to my parents in childish handwriting. Though its contents were a mystery to me, I saw the effect it had on my parents. My father with his well-trained journalistic eye, grimaced and muttered aloud at Ramu's misspelling. "What is this tin of 'bicuits' he wants us to send? Can't he spell biscuits properly?" He dismissed the letter — and along with it my brother—as he handed it over to my mother. She caressed the aerogramme, held it close to her heart, savoring each word, re-reading the letter to savor it yet again. "I'll buy the biscuits today," she said aloud. In the next two years, many more aerogrammes arrived, each one ending with a plea for more "bicuits." Ramu never corrected his spelling and I soon came to christen him my "bicuit brother." Once, my younger brother, Ranga, was born in 1950, three years after me, I considered him my only sibling. Ramu remained a discarnate spirit, an intermittent presence, manifesting itself only when an aerogramme arrived.

It was my mother who kept him alive. Forcing Ranga and me to share a bedroom, she appropriated the spare one upstairs calling it "Ramu's room," and turned it into a sanctuary for her ritual morning prayers and occasional afternoon sewing. It was in this very room that I got to observe our Hindu form of worship. My mother had set up a small altar: a framed picture of Lord Rama, (after whom Ramu was named), standing prominently in the center, flanked by Sita, his consort, to his left, and Lakshmana, his brother, to his right, while Hanuman, the Monkey-God, knelt in reverence at his feet. Reed-thin joss sticks, ceremoniously lit, fanned out from a silver perforated censer perfuming the air with sandalwood. A small silver bowl freshly filled with Domino's Sugar was Amma's daily offering to God. Freshly bathed, draped in nothing more than a towel, head bowed in prayer, eyes closed, Amma chanted words I found incomprehensible. The ritual ended with her sprinkling a pinch of sugar on her tongue and on mine and with a look of wonder she would utter, "Doesn't it taste sweeter now?" Far-fetched as it was, my mother truly believed that God had imbued the sugar with an added dose of sweetness which I barely discerned. It seemed like an offense both to her and to God to disagree. Once dressed, Amma took out a notebook and wrote in Sanskrit, "Sri Rama Jayam," (Victory to Lord Rama) a hundred and eight times, a number said to have mystical properties in Hinduism.

After two years worth of notebooks, Amma felt her prayers had finally been answered. My older brother, Ramu, now age ten, would be returning home. It was a shameful exit from India. He had been kicked out of the prestigious St. Paul's School in Darjeeling barely a year after he transferred there from the Lovedale School in the southern part of India. St. Paul's boasted a distinguished alumni, many of whom served in the British Army during World Wars I and II. It held its students to high standards and enforced a strict disciplinary code. Its mission to educate boys to fulfill their duty to one's fellow man, country and God epitomized for my father the highest ideals attainable. How could he deny his first born son such an opportunity? It was a short-lived dream that would soon become a nightmare. Ramu's repeated efforts to run away by hiding among the gunny sacks of a potato truck, prompted the headmaster to write a series of letters to my father expressing concern not only for my brother's welfare but also the additional burden placed on the school to constantly monitor his whereabouts. Despite the reprimands, Ramu's escapades continued. His patience sorely tested, the headmaster had no choice but to expel him from school and send him packing to America.

Ramu's return had a catalytic effect on my childhood ushering in radical changes in the existing family dynamics. Ranga and I, no longer the center of attention, saw Ramu as an interloper, worming his way into Amma's affection with a downright sense of entitlement. We envied all the new clothes Amma bought him, which made us appear shabby in comparison. The Singer sewing machine, one of the very few items in an otherwise sparsely furnished room, was moved to my parents' bedroom to make way for a brand new bed, a new wooden chest of drawers and a new work desk, the latter seen as a real luxury considering Ranga and I were forced to do our homework on the dining table. New toys filled the closet in Ramu's room: an Erector set; a Chemistry kit; a baseball bat and ball; and a Swiss bicycle, that had been especially imported from Geneva. Ramu gloated over his new possessions while Ranga and I enviously looked on. We took revenge by excluding him from our games but it had a negligible effect. It was clearly evident that Ramu wanted no part of us either.

The more my mother lavished her attention on Ramu, the less time she had to attend to my needs or that of Ranga's. By the time I was eight years old, I found myself in the role of surrogate mother to my five-year old baby brother. A day's chores included: fixing him breakfast, escorting him to and picking him up from school, bathing him, and generally keeping an eye on him. To make matters worse, Ramu's return coincided with my father's increased and prolonged absences from home. His new position as Personal Representative of the UN Secretary-General for Disarmament necessitated frequent travel to the Palais De Nations in Geneva. It was the height of the Cold War period and the United States and the Soviet Union were at loggerheads. Once again, events in the world arena impinged on our lives. Given the enormity of the stakes involved and my father's very public role as an arbiter of peace, my mother, who more and more had to manage the household alone, refrained from complaining lest she sounded petty. I, too, adopted her attitude and tried hard to be the best daughter I could be. In what became a routine farewell lecture, my father exhorted my brothers and me to be good and obedient children and to do well in school. "I'm working for world peace," he said, his voice filled with such earnestness that even the slightest hint of sadness in my eyes would have been seen as an act of betrayal.

Throughout our time together, until his death, I could not help but look up to my father. At six feet tall, his imposing stature loomed over me even when I reached my maximum height of five feet and four inches. The grandeur of his presence was equally matched by the grandeur of the ideals that became his life's work. In the early days of the UN, he was one of the few Indians to be given a top post, earning him much respect in the Parkway community. Seldom seen by my friends, who often thought I was fatherless, I was quick to quell their false impression by telling them that my father wasn't around because he was on a crusade for world peace. In public, I adopted his sacrifice of family as a sacrifice of my own while privately I ached for what I had forsaken. His sojourns, mainly to Geneva, grew longer, and we kept in touch through letters. I addressed him as "Dear Daddy," in writing and for some reason could not bring myself to call him "Appa" as I always did when he was home. Somehow, the intimacy I attached to "Appa" was lost, separated as we were by two continents.

I clung stubbornly to the times when I could genuinely be a child at home, free of the responsibilities and drudgery imposed by my mother. I found release in my father's company, grasping at the chance to reclaim my childhood spirit which threatened to disappear given the adult-like role I was forced to play. Rising early to grind the coffee beans, (a daily chore assigned by my mother), left me with enough time to do another chore I took on willingly—polishing my father's shoes. While my mother sipped her coffee downstairs and my brothers slept, I raced upstairs to my parents' bedroom to catch some alone time with my father. Perched on the bed, his Oxford shoe in a tight grip between my knees, I smeared the black Kiwi polish making sure to leave the laces untouched. I let the polish dry while I tackled the other shoe. Then came the part I liked best—the vigorous wiping, back and forth with the chamois cloth, adding a spit of saliva for good measure, until I saw my face reflected in the sheen. I proudly displayed my handiwork to Appa eager to receive his approval which readily came in the form of a big smile. During these moments, though short and fleeting, I was transfixed by my father's daily etiquette as he got dressed for work. Fresh from his shower, his tall frame clad only in boxer shorts, he would stoop in front of the dresser mirror and carefully brush the already thinning hair over his shiny bald spot. After a few splashes of Yardley's after-shave lotion, he meticulously buttoned his crisp white long-sleeved Oxford dress shirt, and once the cuff links were in place, he donned a dark-colored suit, custom-made by the English tailors of Savile Row. He tucked a neatly folded starched white handkerchief into his breast pocket, pulled on a pair of matching socks, and slid his feet into the newly polished shoes, a shining symbol of my love for him. Were it not for his brown skin, he could have easily passed for a proper Englishman.

My father's embrace of all things British extended not only to his favorite brand of cigarettes- Players- but to his literary tastes as well. He was quick to adopt me and only me, not my brothers, as his student. I often thought Ramu's bad spelling, which by now had expanded beyond the word, "biscuit," disqualified him in Appa's eyes and perhaps he thought it was premature to have Ranga join in given his tender age. On an earlier visit, Appa had waxed enthusiastic at my penchant for composing poems, and took great pains to have one of them published in the United Nations Newsletter. He took pride in my nascent talent and saw it as a genetic trait I had inherited from him. After all, he was a former journalist and student of English Literature. Encouraged as I was, my "poems" were actually more like ditties, banal in content with a simplistic rhyme scheme. I spent hours staring out my bedroom window, pencil and notebook in hand while the words danced playfully in my mind. My love for the English language, its power to shape meaning, the phonetic cadence and lilt of pronunciation—all these aspects became part and parcel of the legacy bequeathed to me by my father.

On Sunday afternoons, Appa and I engaged in what became my favorite ritual, namely, a magical tour of the British Romantic poets—Byron, Shelley, Wordsworth and Tennyson. Refreshed and energized after a tumbler of Amma's special South Indian coffee,

Appa opened the book of poetry and in an accent that was more British than Indian, began to read,"I met a traveller from an antique land, who said: Two vast and trunkless legs of stone stand in the desert…"

"It's Shelley's Ozymandias," he announced when done.

In rapt attention, I sat by Appa's feet, while his voice, raspy from his pack a day cigarette habit, caressed me with its undulations and marked pauses.

" So what do you think it means?" he asked peering into my eyes.

I stalled for time by asking a question of my own.

"Appa, what does visage mean?"

Not one to let me off lightly, Appa, in true Socratic fashion, re-read the lines where the word appeared and asked me to figure out its meaning through the context.

" …half sunk a shattered visage lies, whose frown, wrinkled lip and sneer of cold command…," he intoned.

"Does it mean face?" I ventured

"Very good Vasu! Correct, yes, visage means face," Appa replied, beaming with pride.

I asked him to read the poem again to give myself a bit of extra time to mull over its meaning.

With an air of confidence, I began to answer, " It's about this king, Ozymandias, who is very proud and wants to be remembered long after his death. But he's cruel so everyone forgets him."

Appa, impressed by my interpretation, elaborated further.

"You see, Vasu, people should not use their power to hurt others. Like the poet says, 'nothing beside remains.' People will remember you forever for the good things you do." We ended our session as always with Appa drawing me onto his lap in an affectionate cuddle, cooing I was the apple of his eye. "Next week, we'll tackle Lord Byron's, "She Walks in Beauty," and I'll teach you about the use of metaphors," he promised. By the time next Sunday arrived, Appa had already left on assignment. I bookmarked the poem in antici-pation of a quick return but Appa's absences only grew longer. I tried to tackle the poem on my own, but without Appa, I felt empty inside and just gave up.

My Sunday afternoon poetry sessions with Appa were usually followed by a spelling quiz that included my brothers. He liked to challenge us with a tough word like "pneumonia," which I alone was able to spell correctly unlike my brothers who did not know it began with a silent 'p.' Every now and then, he gave them a chance to spell an easy word, shushing me with a finger to his lips and a sly wink of the eye. My brothers and I reveled in these moments when we put aside our petty squabbles so Appa would see us as the good, obedient, children he expected us to be. My father's parenting skills were limited to these literary interludes. His constant travel to broker a nuclear test ban treaty freed him from the obligation of caring for us on a day to day basis. Though we were too young to comprehend the enormity of his mission, my father let it be known, whenever he could, that he was working for world peace. In doing his bidding, my brothers and I felt we were contributing to something larger than ourselves. Yet, I could not bear to sacrifice the shared intimacy of those Sunday afternoons and I often wished the world would go to hell so I could have Appa all to myself.

Appa's literary competitions reached its apogee during our Sunday dinners when we played the proverb game. Appa started off with an easy proverb like: "a stitch in time saves nine," and asked us to give examples that would elucidate its meaning. He progressed to harder ones such as "necessity is the mother of invention," where I won out over my brothers. Appa didn't believe in light-hearted banter. With missionary zeal he was intent on making us fall in love with the English language. To possess, let alone read comic books like Archie and Superman, was an act of moral turpitude in his eyes. Though banned at home, I managed to read them on the sly when I visited my friends. Reluctant at first, Appa finally gave in to my request for Classic Illustrated Comic books featuring the stories by Dumas, Defoe and Dickens among others, but not without first extracting a promise that I also read the original works. Just to be sure, he never failed to buy me the books, their title pages bearing his standard inscription, "Happy Birthday, Vasu. Love, Dad."

Amma exempted herself during these literary banters over which my father held court and either busied herself in the kitchen or perusing the New York Times for the latest sales in gadgets and cookware. Although my mother was well-educated and a college history teacher before she married my father, I rarely saw her read anything except for leafing through Life magazine and, on occasion, I would catch her poring over a Tamil literary magazine, Ananda Vikatan, which she subscribed to via air mail. The publication was highly popular in Madras and featured articles by budding writers along with political cartoons and a section devoted to horoscopes. Amma was not the least bit curious about what I read in school or about the assignments I was given. Her only concern was that my homework be done on time. While Appa was away, I continued my hand at crafting ditties. I knew it was a far cry from the lyric poetry of Byron and Shelley so beloved by Appa but it was my small foray into the world of words and the only way I knew to preserve the sweet memories of our Sunday sessions. I read and re-read the ditties to myself and with a sense of smug satisfaction admired my witty turns of phrase. I imagined Appa as my audience, beaming with pride at his budding poet of a daughter. It was a temporary antidote to assuage the sadness within and it would have to do for now.

My mother's down to earth attitude jarred with the quiet refuge I sought in the loftiness of the printed word. Her demands were many and the only way I knew to gain her love was by doing her bidding. Apart from taking care of Ranga, I assisted her in household duties. We waxed the floors twice a month on Saturdays, getting down on our hands and knees as we smeared the Butcher's Paste Wax on the wooden tiles. A half hour later, we were crouched down again, buffing them to a high gloss with the remnants of a frayed bath towel. Amma scrutinized my handiwork, peering at each wooden square from every angle possible, to make sure I had not missed a spot. By the time I was eight, I had been taught to use the double-boiler to make rice and snip the green beans close to the tip to avoid wastage. I rose earlier than anyone else (including weekends) to grind the coffee beans and pour the boiling water into the stainless steel filter just up to the right mark. Only then was I allowed to awaken Amma. That first tumbler of coffee set her mood for the day and it was my job to see it was off to a good start. My mother was not one to preface or end her requests with words like "please" or "thank-you." She tacitly assumed I would comply without complaint, which I did. As time passed, I realized that my mother's love for me was not unconditional. In essence it was a barter system where love was traded for services rendered.

My father's idealism was offset by my mother's pragmatism. I watched her no nonsense approach to the vicissitudes of life as she assumed the role of single parent during my father's absence. Out of sheer necessity, she learned how to drive and cajoled my father into purchasing an Austin car. She widened her circle of friends beyond the rim of Parkway Village to include the European and American wives of UN personnel who lived in the suburbs of Long Island. Together they formed a Bridge club which made her loneliness easier to tolerate. She assiduously collected the Green Stamps from our local Grand Union and, during my spare time, it was my job to paste them in the special books provided. Depending on the number of books collected, one could redeem them for any one of the gift items listed in a special catalog. Amma's first choice was a plastic poker chip dispenser. It was a colorful circular contraption, with rotating columns of red, white and blue chips that could be released one at a time by pressing a trigger mechanism on top. I often sneaked downstairs way beyond my bedtime to catch a glimpse of my mother and her friends playing poker. Seated around a large white bed sheet spread over the carpet, they would toss in the red, white and blue chips to up the ante. Faces were scrutinized to determine who held a good hand and players either folded or continued until a winner emerged. Amma, resplendent in her silk sari, looked radiant, happier than I had ever seen her without my father. The sound of her laughter trailed behind me as I crept up the stairs.

I viewed my mother through a kaleidoscopic lens. With a slight turn, the elements of her personality rearranged themselves to reveal yet another facet. Unlike most of the South Indian women in Parkway who confined their socialization to a tight-knit circle, my mother thirsted for amusement that went beyond the usual exchange of gossip, recipes and department store bargains. She found an outlet in the company of the American wives of UN personnel where she was introduced to the movies of Alfred Hitchcock and American theatre, particularly the more serious plays like "Tea and Sympathy." The get-togethers that traditionally followed these outings engendered spirited conversations during which every detail of the diabolical plots and every trait of the psychologically flawed characters were parsed in great earnest. I watched with much admiration as my mother weaved between these two vastly different circle of friends with such ease.

The image of my mother, in her sari and bindi, epitomized a sense of tradition and, by extension, a conservatism that to a large extent camouflaged the feistiness I chanced to observe. There was a derring-do aspect to her which surfaced now and again as in the bold bets she made while playing poker with a weak hand, or in being the first Indian woman in Parkway Village to drive a car. Influenced by her American friends she expanded her culinary repertoire to include dishes like vegetable casseroles, salads, and Betty Crocker brownies. Suddenly and inexplicably, she began to test recipes for chicken curry after consulting with her North Indian friends. The very presence of meat in a Brahmin household was considered sacrilegious and it was nothing short of a miracle that my mother, who would never forsake her vegetarianism, could churn out such a savory dish without ever tasting it. Moreover, it became her signature dish at the diplomatic soirees held in our home. I suppressed an urge to laugh as I watched my mother don a pair of Playtex gloves as she skinned and deboned the chicken breasts, her face contorted in disgust as the blood seeped onto the cutting board.

A similar kind of intrepidness fueled her decision to teach me how to ride a bicycle. It threw me off guard as I could not imagine my mother, in her sari no less, running behind me while clutching the end of the bike in the way I had seen some fathers in Parkway run while teaching their children. I should have been grateful to have had a mother who filled the role that I vainly hoped would one day be filled by my absentee father and was ashamed at the embarrassment I felt. Amma had intuited my long-held desire to ride a bike. She had watched my attempts to mount Ramu's bike and heard the squeals when my crotch slammed against the steel rod that ran through the center. Repeated attempts yielded similar results with little hope of success. But Amma, in keeping with her seize the bull by the horns temperament, was not to be deterred. She took me to one of the lawns in Parkway Village, hitched her sari up a few inches, and propelled me forward with a strong push from the back. She answered my pleas not to let go with a reassuring, "I'm right behind you, Vasu. Keep pedaling." In a matter of minutes, I experienced a sensation of sheer euphoria, a moment of total control and balance, the beast of a bicycle like putty in my hands, when I chanced to look back. The last thing I saw was Amma clapping from afar as I hurtled into a prickly bush. I stood up, bleeding from the scratches, massaging my sore crotch, looking down at the bike, its handlebars in a grotesque twist as Amma approached crying triumphantly, " See, see, Vasu, you did it!" I hobbled home, a bit weak-kneed from the whole experience, and begged her to buy me a girl's bike. Before long, I was the proud owner of a turquoise blue Schwinn bike with white tassels hanging from the handlebars.

The bike gave me the mobility to explore the environs beyond Parkway Village. On weekends when the weather was nice and while my mother napped with strict instructions that she not be disturbed, I escaped to Alley Pond Park and Cunningham Park with Ranga who was still at the stage where he needed training wheels on his bike. Together we discovered the joy of scooping up tadpoles into our Mason jars hoping they would turn into frogs as the days passed, but they never did. We returned again and again to the park unwilling to forsake this new found taste of freedom brought on by a short bike ride. I continued to keep a watchful eye on Ranga by force of habit but, during our jaunts, I began to see him more as my sibling than my child. Whether by design or by chance, my mother, by teaching me how to ride a bicycle, allowed me to reclaim a small part of my childhood.

A few years later, when I was around ten years old, my mother enrolled me in swimming lessons. "It's a skill you need to survive," she said with dead seriousness. My fear of drowning in a tidal wave was enough of an impetus to coerce me into joining the swim class at UNIS. I was also dying to see how I looked in a swimsuit.

I had seen Betty and Veronica clad in bikinis in some of the Archie comic books but had never laid eyes on a real person wearing one. The bikini was too skimpy for my taste and I knew full well that Amma would never consent to it. I had in mind a sleek one-piece with perhaps a few tiny ruffles in front and a little piping on the sides. Amma, however, had something else in mind. While all of us were vacationing with my father in Geneva, she took a short break to do some shopping in Paris. Amma's command of the French language was extremely limited save for two phrases, "Comme ci," and "Comme ca." Still, she somehow managed to buy me a one-piece mauve-colored swimsuit with sleeves. She took great pride in telling me how she had drawn a picture of the type of swimsuit she wanted and had combed all the big department stores in Paris until she had found it. I could barely say the words "thank you," and could not help but ask, "Why the sleeves?" "It's unladylike to reveal your armpits," Amma responded as if she were citing a rule out of an etiquette manual.

My swimsuit invited unwanted scrutiny by my classmates and I became the laughing stock of the swim team. I could not stand to see myself in the mirror and raced to the pool to plunge into the water. As soon as practice was over, I rushed to the bathroom stall and hurriedly peeled off the offensive suit hoping it would tear. Unfortunately, the lycra was too resilient. Eventually, the stares died down and, once I graduated to the deep end, I felt confident enough to show off my diving skills. The alacrity of my strokes made me a fast swimmer and the coach offered me a spot on the UNIS swim team. The news did not sit well with my mother. When she learned I would be swimming in contests held in schools other than UNIS, she refused to give permission as required by school policy, and I was dropped from the team. " There will be strange boys in those places, not ones I know," she said by way of explanation. "It won't be safe," she added, lowering her voice to an ominous whisper. On top of my disappointment and anger, I suddenly felt afraid. Of what or whom escaped me.

The notion that boys could be dangerous rattled my nerves. My experience at P.S. 117 had revealed how cruel they could be; their racial taunts saddened and confused me but I did not fear them. Many of the boys at UNIS lived in the neighborhood and some were siblings of my girlfriends. The camaraderie amongst us ran deep. I had no idea what my mother meant by "strange boys." My ten-year old mind could not fathom this allusion to danger. After all, I was anchored in the safe harbor of Parkway Village and saw no reason to tread on unfamiliar waters. Besides, I could always cheer my swim team on from the sidelines.

That summer, as if to atone for my disbarment from the swim team, my mother planned an outing to Jones Beach. It was the first time we engaged in a fun activity without my father and our first trip to the beach. Amma lovingly prepared a picnic basket filled with cheese sandwiches, bags of Wise Potato Chips, and Hostess Cupcakes. We stuffed the trunk of our Austin car with bright new beach towels, plastic buckets and shovels and an inflatable beach ball. Jean Das, a Britisher, and wife of an Indian UN diplomat, joined us at the beach with her three children. A close friend of my mother's, they shared much in common—both saddled with three children and an absentee husband. Thanks to Mrs. Das, who was a strong swimmer, I dove fearlessly into my first wave while riding piggyback. Awash in triumph in that ever so wonderful brief moment, I pressed my body against Mrs. Das, clasped her neck in a loving embrace, and wished she were my mother. I gazed across the sand and spotted Amma sitting in the hot sun. Several beach-goers strolling by in their trunks and bikinis, suddenly stopped to gawk at the sight of a woman draped in fine silk from head to toe in the scorching heat. Unfazed, Amma stared right back. I slithered down Mrs. Das' back as she carried me to shore and felt the thrill of the moment rapidly ebb as I walked towards my mother.

Chapter 3

An *American* Indian Childhood

The ubiquitous presence of television ushered in certain aspects of American culture, much to my parents' consternation. My father exercised his parental authority during the short periods that found him home, by monitoring the TV westerns that had become part of our regular fare. Wild Bill Hickok with his popular utterance, "shoot first and ask questions afterwards," was anathema to a man who feared the consequences of such advice in matters of nuclear warfare. The show was summarily banned from our list of favorites. Well-spoken heroes, like Hopalong Cassidy, Gene Autry, and Roy Rogers, received approval for their reserve and high sense of fair play. We accepted these restrictions more amused than intimidated as a quirk of my father's nature and as soon as he left, Wild Bill Hickok resumed his rightful position in the pantheon of American cowboys. My mother, left again to fend for herself, was grateful to have the TV as her babysitter. She assumed its influence to be contained within the screen and hence harmless. When I turned eleven, she came to realize just how mistaken her judgement had been.

It was the era of rock n' roll. The music of Elvis Presley, Bobby Darin, the Platters, the Monotones, Jerry Lee Lewis, Danny and the Juniors filled the radio waves. No one was immune to the infectious beat and plaintive melodies, not even my father who could be heard crooning to the lyrics of Sonny James' "Young Love" while he shaved. My brother, Ramu, by now a teenager, hogged our small record player spinning his budding collection of 78's and 45's of the latest hits. The music created a bond between us for the first time since he came home from boarding school. It was a communal partaking of American popular culture quite different in its effect from our watching TV together. Tapping our feet and wriggling our bottoms as we belted out the lyrics, we looked at each other with conspiratorial delight as we tacitly acknowledged the thrill of feeling very American in our Indian home.

Rock n' roll fever gripped me hard and I became an avid watcher of Dick Clark's American Bandstand which had premiered a year earlier in 1957 on the ABC network. Rock n' roll idols appeared in the flesh to the adulation of fans all over the country. The dance couple contest taught millions how to do the Lindy, the Stroll, and the Box Step. My girl friends and I spent our lunch hours in school speculating on the off-screen love life of these couples, taking votes on which pair would wind up at the altar and which pair never stood a chance. I sneaked whatever opportunity I could get to watch the show which conveniently aired at 4:00 pm after the close of school. My mother would have been mortified had she seen me dance and twirl around in our living room grasping the curtain string as an imaginary partner. It would have made matters worse had she known that I longed for a real-life American boy to hold me in his arms as we slow danced to "Only You" by The Platters.

As it turned out, the only dance partner I ever had was my best friend Shikha, a Bengali girl, who lived nearby, and was my closest friend both in and out of school. Eager to practice the latest dance steps we set up a secret tryst which required a bit of planning on my part. Between household chores and taking care of Ranga, I was hardly alone except on Saturday mornings when the task of doing the laundry fell on me. We only had a small washer at home and for bigger loads Parkway Village had installed laundry rooms with coin operated machines in old bomb shelters. The one we used was right across Shikha's apartment making it a convenient place for us to meet. We could guarantee on being alone as most people slept late on the weekends preferring to do their laundry in the late afternoons. I buried our record player along with the records in the folds of the dirty sheets and smuggled them out in the laundry cart.

As I hurried towards the laundry room, Shikha was able to spot me easily through her living room window and join me soon after. While the washer spun through its various cycles, our heads reeled with fantasies of our own. A shade taller than Shikha, I assumed the male lead. We wrapped our left hand around each other's waist, the fingers of our right hand in a tight clasp as we dipped and spun each other to the pulsating rhythm of "At the Hop" by Danny and the Juniors. I danced with such frenzy and abandon, my long black braid whipping the air, the once musty smell of the basement now redolent of Ivory Snowflakes. We took a break to load the dryers adding extra coins to prolong the cycle. We gained thirty minutes of dance time before the dryers tumbled to a stop. The record player and records were buried anew under the clean stack of laundry. I was in no rush to get home and wished the morning would last forever. The unmistakable smell of roasted cumin, coriander, and fenugreek, the holy triumvirate of South Indian spices, seeped through the door as I rang the bell. I had arrived just in time for lunch.

To the extent possible, I balanced the demands of home with my increasing appetite for American pop culture. My secret rendezvous' with Shikha continued with my mother none the wiser. But when I sought her permission to go to the movies with my girlfriends, there were a few rules I had to follow: Only matinees, no evening shows; I had to be accompanied by at least two girlfriends, (the first time, it was Shikha and Ann Wald), known to my mother. As they stood before her, she issued a stern warning, " Vasu, can only go if you promise she sits between you two. I don't want her sitting next to some boy in the dark. That's how things get started." I wasn't quite sure what Amma meant by "things," other than a boy's hand brushing against mine but I was sufficiently embarrassed even as I managed to stifle a smile as Shikha and Ann, each with a look of feigned seriousness, nodded in assent. "But it's the Ten Commandments," I whined, "it's about the Bible and the sins we shouldn't commit." But when it came to protecting her daughter, the only faith my mother had was in herself. I could have easily disobeyed my mother and counted on my friends not to tell but I lacked the temerity to do so. Besides, it would be a sin to tell a lie. As the lights dimmed, I eased into the middle seat, safely ensconced between my friends.

Birthday parties where boys would be in attendance or what my mother referred to as "mixed parties," were taboo. It effectively shut me out from the emergent social scene of my peers and I was soon dropped from the invitation list. With the quickening darkness of the fall season, the time I spent outdoors was shortened more so than in previous years. Immured in the apartment for longer periods of time, I took to staring out my bedroom window as the light began to fade. All these restrictions whether they had to do with the type of company I should keep or where I could go, came without warning or explanation. I had promised my father to be an obedient girl in his absence, a promise I simply could not break. I performed what was expected of me when home and grew into my role as the good Indian daughter. But the blinking eye of our television had cast an American shadow over our very Indian home seducing me with its pixilated images of happy families like the Cleavers and the Andersons where children were children free of adult responsibilities, the girls dated and the boys had crushes. At the end of each episode, the growing pains of childhood were ameliorated through the wise counsel of both parents. These elegant TV homes with their white picket fences, beckoned with open arms. Not a hint of danger was visible anywhere. In my mind, the setting could have easily been Parkway Village. My mother's incipient fear that I would become an object of depredation of unknown provenance rattled me. Too young to comprehend the source of her trepidation, I was determined to have some fun even if it meant I had to sneak around. I was drawn to American popular culture be it reading comic books on the sly at a friend's house or dancing to rock n' roll music in the laundry room. By immersing myself in all things American, I freed myself of my mother's protective hold which felt like a noose slowly tightening around my neck.

My mother's dire warnings of "strange boys" as would-be predators backfired as far as I was concerned. I daydreamed about being romanced by them and was smitten with a desire to look beautiful and began to take stock. I recalled the ungainly sight of myself at age seven when I had to wear braces on my teeth and the excruciating pain I had to endure while trying to fall asleep with a night brace.

The dentist had cautioned my mother that without braces, there was a good chance I would develop buckteeth. "No one will marry you," she said when I cringed with fear on learning that two of my back teeth were about to be extracted. As I recuperated, my mother lavished me with the kind of attention I had never known. I was nourished with home-made soups and my favorite green-lime jello. During the day, the sofa was converted into a bed where I could rest in close proximity to my mother. My brothers were warned to be extra nice to me and for the first time I was given a reprieve from my usual chores. At the time, my teeth being straight mattered more to my mother than to me, but four years later as I checked out my smile in front of the bathroom mirror, I found it in my heart to forgive her.

This process of self-reckoning brought on an unwelcome melancholy. A stream of thoughts poured out: Amma had never called me beautiful nor commented on my looks even when I dressed up for special occasions. My brothers teased me about my "cauliflower ears," and my "parrot-beak nose." Appa's pet term for me, "the apple of my eye," was more metaphor than substance. The swim coach praised the sturdiness of my long legs that made me a good swimmer. My long black braid with a natural sheen was the envy of my girlfriends. My big, dark brown eyes with their long lashes, which to me were my best features, were hidden under a pair of glasses to correct my myopia. I concluded that I was simply not beautiful. This realization triggered an unpleasant memory that more than confirmed what I believed all along to be true.

During one of our summer vacations to India, we visited my maternal grandparents in the city of Bangalore. They were living with my mother's brother, his wife and two children, a son and a daughter. The daughter, Urmila, was around eleven years old, about three years older than I. Her very fair complexion, almost white, and pussy cat brown eyes, made her stand out among the darker-skinned relatives (I, being one of them), earning her the sobriquet, "Cleopatra Beauty." I took an instant dislike to her telling myself her forehead was lopsided, one side broader than the other, that her nose was bent out of shape and her teeth crooked. Of course, I was the only one who noticed these deformities, everyone else being blind, which infuriated me even more. Another maternal uncle, sensitive to my feelings, thought I was equally deserving of my own moniker and dubbed me "Roman Beauty" because of what he referred to as my aquiline nose which sounded a whole lot better than "parrot-beaked." One evening, Amma trotted out two identical dresses, one pink, the other blue, she had purchased at Macy's as gifts for Urmila and me. Urmila was given first choice to select the color she liked; she chose pink, the one I really wanted, so I was forced to take the blue. Urmila and I paraded around the house now swarming with friends and relatives who had stopped by to see Amma. Our new dresses garnered much attention among some of the women who ran their hands over the polka dots marveling at the stitchery and lacy texture of the material. I couldn't be bothered about Urmila when amidst all that chatter, I heard someone say, "Urmila looks so beautiful in her pink dress. Vasu looks nice but it's a pity she is dark."

Now, looking into the mirror, I could not help but feel sorry for myself. My self-image refracted through the eyes of others did not paint a pretty picture. Still, I was unwilling to let go of the idea that even if I was not born beautiful, I could still work on my appearance and somehow become beautiful. A recent commercial for Camay Soap gave me hope. Its slogan—the soap for beautiful women—struck a responsive chord. I salivated as I watched the whipped-cream like lather float on the woman's face in soft mounds and was in awe of the silky smooth skin it revealed once it was rinsed off. The notion that "beauty is skin deep," came across as a bunch of hogwash. I was determined to make my face as radiant as the one on TV.

I desperately wanted to buy a bar of Camay but was wary of approaching my mother who was bound to ask why. I would take on my "make myself beautiful" as a solo project. I squirreled away my weekly allowance of 25 cents until I had saved enough money to buy my first bar of Camay; it was a lovely shade of pastel pink. In the privacy of my bathroom which had a good size mirror over the sink, I gingerly unwrapped the soap so I could re-use the packaging, held it to my nose, and breathed in every ounce of its heady perfume. I followed all the steps I had seen in the commercial from working up a creamy lather to the final rinse. I patted my face dry and let my fingers run across my forehead, over my cheeks, and down to my chin. I could have sworn that my skin felt even softer to the touch. I gazed at my reflection and it was beautiful, at least to me. I was about to caress my face one last time when without warning my mother barged in. "Why are you looking at yourself in the mirror?" she barked. Caught unawares, I stammered,

"It's nothing, Amma. I was just trying out a new soap." Her eyes darted to the soap and back to me. "Put this stuff away, and come downstairs. It's time to set the table for dinner," she said brusquely and turned towards the stairs. I gently slid the Camay back into the wrapper and hid it deep under my clothes in the chest of drawers. Next time, I told myself, I'll make sure to lock the bathroom door.

An uneasy silence hung in the air as I ate my dinner and I was only too happy to beat a hasty retreat to my room. My father was back in New York at the time and he often set aside a part of his evening to catch up on the latest news of my life at school—the books I was reading, the projects I was working on and who my friends were. Eager to engage in our private tete a tete, I began to make my way downstairs. I froze after barely taking a few steps. I could hear my mother telling my father, " Vasu is beginning to take notice of herself. I caught her staring at her face today in the bathroom mirror and she gave some excuse about trying out a new soap. She'll be a big girl soon and then she'll start looking at boys. Soon she will want to date. Maybe we should think about going back to India before it's too late." This last pronouncement pounded in my ears, so much so that my father's response was hardly audible. I tip-toed up the stairs and retrieved the bar of Camay from its hiding place. It had become an accursed object, the source of my ills, and an odious reminder of my self-indulgence. I threw it out the window muttering, "good riddance to bad rubbish," but I could not rid myself of its haunting fragrance which lingered in my chest of drawers in the days to come. It would be easy enough to purge my clothes of its smell next laundry day but to wash away my mother's growing suspicions was another matter altogether. She became increasingly wary of my exposure to American culture and had convinced herself that it carried an inherent rapaciousness that threatened to devour her daughter.

Much to my relief I saw no signs of an imminent departure to India. My father was back in Geneva and I went about my daily routine as before. I put the Camay incident out of my mind, abandoned all thoughts of self-beautification, and, with fierce determination, made every effort to be a dutiful Indian daughter. It was the only way I knew to exculpate myself in my mother's eyes. Whatever excursions I took into America culture were safely consigned outside the home and I contrived a life for myself with a distinctly dual personality. My kitchen chores had since multiplied now that my mother had enrolled in evening classes at Queens College. She had decided to pursue a Masters degree in Guidance Counseling with a focus on adolescents from divorced homes. Many an evening found us both at the dining table, I poring over a homework assignment while my mother pecked with two fingers at the keyboard of her Smith-Corona typewriter writing up observation reports of her counseling sessions. "How sad," she exclaimed from time to time, "to see these young people suffer from a broken home. They are so lost without having both parents around." I nodded in agreement but a part of me secretly envied these children, total strangers at that, who had my mother's ear and heart. I wanted to cry out,

"What about our own broken home? Appa is always away. All we have is you." Yes, my mother was physically present, but emotionally absent, especially when it came to me. She was more of a doer than a talker. How could I fault her for the meals she cooked, or for the clothes and toys she bought or for taking the time and effort to teach me how to ride a bike? I was very grateful but once, just once, I wanted to hear her say, " I love you, Vasu."

It was a hot Sunday in June of 1956, I rose early, my mood somewhat foul, as I trudged downstairs to grind the coffee beans, a chore

that had become as routine as brushing my teeth. Just last night, Appa, his arm around me, had pleaded with Amma, "Let Vasu sleep late for once. Tomorrow's a Sunday, the last day of her weekend. The coffee can wait until later." Amma responded with a noncommittal shrug but I could tell from the look in her eyes that tomorrow morning would be no different from all the other mornings. As the water dripped through the filter, I was deeply touched by Appa's concern for me and exceedingly grateful to have him as an ally but it was of cold comfort when I realized that his regard for me was as short-lived as his presence in my life.

Amma fixed the coffee South Indian style, pouring the brew, she called "decoction," into the stainless steel tumbler placed inside a dabara, a wide saucer with lipped walls. Lightened with hot milk, it was the perfect way to start her day and the only proper way to drink coffee, she said. Porcelain cups, in her view, marred the flavor. Appa, preferred to have his coffee in bed while poring over the international and national news in the Sunday New York Times. Amma, who loved bargains, saved the advertising sections for later reading. My older brother, Ramu, was tinkering with his Erector set, while my younger brother, Ranga, read in his room. With everyone suitably occupied, Amma was free to focus her attention on me and started the preparations for my oil bath. As she warmed the Gingili oil in a cast iron skillet, I smelled the nutty aroma of the sesame seeds. Seated on the kitchen floor with an old towel wrapped around my pajama top, I unbraided my hair, normally in a tight plait, and felt weighted down by its length and thickness. Amma, clad in an old sari that bore the stains of previous oil baths, took a palmful of the warm Gingili oil and gently began to massage my scalp. Her breathing was labored as she mustered as much strength as she could in her bony fingers. I savored Amma's sensuous presence: the touch of her hands, the smell of her body and the taste of her breath redolent of morning coffee. I had an irrepressible urge to bury my head in the folds of her sari but I stopped myself. Amma did not like to display or receive affection in a physical manner.

She had an aversion to being kissed and reeled in disgust claiming kisses carried saliva full of germs. She even rebuffed Appa who had a habit of kissing her hello when he returned from work. Without fail, Amma would turn her cheek as Appa's lips brushed her hair. Although hugs and cuddles were germ-free, Amma saved these for Ramu, her favorite, and had none for Ranga and me. She felt Ramu had been deprived of affection since he had been sent off to boarding school at a young age, and therefore deserved to be compensated.

Amma gathered my hair into a knot and tucked it under a few strands to keep it in place and, with the little oil that remained, she coated my face and arms. I had an hour to kill before my bath and wished I could play a board game with Ranga. But Amma would hear nothing of it. She was afraid I would accidentally ruin the furniture with grease stains and steered me towards the bottom step of the staircase where I would be out of harm's way. I could feel the droplets of oil seep into my follicles, and was intoxicated by the aroma of the Gingili oil. The tension and tautness in my muscles started to abate and I nodded off.

I was roused by the whisper of Amma's sari as it brushed against my arm and followed her upstairs. Now, nine years old and more self-conscious of my body, I persuaded Amma to let me bathe in my underwear. The steam arising from the two plastic buckets of hot water did little to ward off the chill of the cold ceramic tile as I lowered myself into the bathtub. Goose pimples rose on my arms and I began to shiver. I looked up at Amma who drowned my stare with mugs of water. She cautioned me to keep my eyes closed as she applied the Shikakai paste.

"Your hair is thick and long and will use up a lot of Shikakai which I can't get here for love or money. I'll have to use a little shampoo at the end to get rid of the oil," she said.

I loved the smell of Johnson's Baby Shampoo in my hair and that it was the Baby No Tears brand was an added plus. Amma concentrated all her efforts on cleaning my hair as if she were ridding a cloth of deeply-set stains. She seemed to have forgotten that it was attached to a human being. Once my hair was cleansed, she swept it up into a pile and stuffed it under a shower cap. She abruptly left having done her bit and instructed me to wash the rest of my body. Amma's cold efficient attitude made me shiver again and I sought warmth in the bath water that had now risen to my waist since the grains of Shikakai had clogged the small drain. I sat chest-deep in a stagnant pool of murky brown water, a ludicrous cloud of white shampoo bubbles floating across its surface. I finished bathing as quickly as I could before the tub could overflow. The only part of me that was squeaky clean was my hair.

I inspected the strands for any tell-tale signs of the Shikakai of which there were many. It looked like I had a bad case of dandruff. I bent my head over the sink and using a terry towel like a threshing machine, I tried to shake loose as many of the tiny particles as possible. My efforts were in vain. My wet hair was a magnet for those pesky granules. I had no choice but to wait until my hair was dry to comb out the remnants of the powder. My stomach began to growl and suddenly I felt famished.

I knew this Sunday lunch would be special because Appa was home. Amma breathed her love into his favorite dishes: fenugreek sambar, tomato rasam, small eggplants stuffed with spices and a carrot and cucumber salad. Forsaking our usual habit of sitting around the dining table, we reverted to the custom of eating Indian style. Unwanted sections of the day's New York Times were strewn across our kitchen floor. Although we were cramped for space, we managed to sit cross-legged in a circle, each of us with our own stainless steel thali, the traditional plate for eating food, that Amma had shipped from Madras. Using only our right hand, we scooped the food into our mouths smacking our lips in appreciation. There was a look of pride on Amma's face, and in every morsel of food, I tasted the love she found hard to express in a hug or a kiss. It was the kind of nourishment that came natural to Amma and it was all I could come to expect. This miniature tableau of family togetherness was a rarity and it satiated a hunger in me that far exceeded the satisfaction of a good meal.

I was in dire need of a post-prandial nap but Amma insisted I either get the tangles out of my hair myself or let her do it. With no hesitation I opted for the former. Amma was rough with the comb and yanked at every knot and snarl with such vengeance I often feared my hair would be pulled from its roots. The heat in the apartment was unbearable and with no air conditioning, the only source of relief was the standing General Electric fan in my parents' bedroom. Amma, more than Appa, relished her afternoon nap and, as a rule, my brothers and I were not to disturb them. Amma made an exception that day and said as long as I remained quiet, I could use the fan to dry my hair.

I pirouetted softly on my toes in front of the only full-length mirror in our apartment. I took my time with the knots in my hair and gathered it up to catch the fan breeze around the nape of my neck. I fluffed my hair and gave it a gentle shake to dislodge the granules of Shikakai. I glanced in the mirror and the fan appeared to have receded in the distance. I stepped back and in an instant I felt the steely grip of the blades as they grabbed at my hair and sucked the strands into its greedy vortex. I pulled with all my might as if in a game of tug-of-war and screamed as the full force of the fan landed with a thud on the back of my head. The last thing I remembered was Amma switching off the fan and cradling me in her arms.

The accident bored a hole in my memory. I was frozen in time. A cacophonous stream of voices flooded my ears that I could barely identify the speaker. I thought I heard my mother telling me that Appa had a heart attack the night of my accident brought on by his fear that I might have suffered brain damage. Someone, maybe a kindly neighbor, or a friend of the family, said I could not visit Appa at Queens General Hospital because children were not allowed in the intensive care unit. I was shocked by the news and even more shocked to discover that up to now I was not even aware that Appa was no longer home. Perhaps I had become immune to his habitual absences which ran like a scar across my childhood.

Another scene was etched in my mind. Amma was seated at the dining room table, her hands cradling the soft folds of flesh below her navel. She pointed to her stomach and told me there's a ball growing inside. The doctor told her it was a tumor which had to be removed as soon as possible. She had to go to Mount Sinai Hospital for surgery while Appa remained hospitalized. A friend of my parents, Miss Olive Reddick, moved in to care for my brothers and me. An emotional vacuum stretched across the absence of both my parents.

My mind raced ahead to an image of my father combing my hair. It appeared anomalous since Amma was the only one who did my braid. She must have still been in the hospital. Appa and I were seated cross-legged on our maroon-colored Bokhara carpet, my back to him. His hand gently glided the teeth of the comb through the strands of my hair as if it were brittle. I could hear and feel Appa's exasperation with every breath he took. He repeatedly tried and failed to braid my hair. I wound up with a pony tail but the tenderness of his touch wrapped around me like a second skin.

These mental photographs were the only ones I could recall. The faces of my father, mother and younger brother stared at me in all their prominence in sharp contrast to my own which remained a blur. I simply could not remember what I looked like after the accident. All that remained were shards of memory floating in a dark pool.

The normal rhythm of my daily activities both at home and at school returned but there was no mention of the accident. The incident was nothing more than a dramatic pause in the passage of time. However, that oil bath Sunday with its allure of restorative calm and peace of mind stoked a burning disquiet that was palpable. Appa resumed his trips to Geneva but now as he got ready to depart, I heard Amma lecture him as if he were a child. She compiled a list of what and what not to do: No salt in your diet; Cut down on eating rice, have fish or chicken instead; Do not stay at the office late; Try to get eight hours of sleep; and please, please, cut down on your smoking. Appa's heart attack made Amma cruelly aware of his mortality and she was nervous to be far from his side. He comforted her with his promise to do as she requested, and in his signature fashion, he urged my brothers and me to be on our best behavior. I hugged Appa tightly, so tightly, I could feel his heart throb against mine. But the usual sadness that came over me suddenly seemed a lot heavier.

The year 1958 was drawing to a close and my father returned as promised to spend the Christmas holidays with us. It wound up being our best and last Christmas together as a family. My mother, who had for the past ten years resisted the idea of purchasing a fresh tree, citing it was too Christian to have one in a Hindu household, finally relented. She had gone so far as to buy an assortment of ornaments, colored tinsel, little red stockings for my brothers and me, candy canes and to top the tree, a gold-colored star that lit up. We were too overjoyed to figure out why Amma had had a change of heart and welcomed with open arms this rare opportunity to celebrate the holiday like every other American. Our living room was suffused with the sweet scent of pine adulterated occasionally by the acrid smell of Indian spices. The Hindu gods scattered among the niches looked out of place amidst the Christmas paraphernalia but no one seemed to notice. Fir needles embedded themselves in our Bhokara carpet adding a dark green patina to the maroon fibers. This little piece of Americana ushered in by my mother had found its way into our home and I wanted it to stay on permanently.

More surprises followed. Instead of her usual gift of a dress, Amma presented me with two life-size dolls, one brunette, the other blonde. They came to my waist and when you lifted their arms, one at a time, they took little baby steps in cute little plastic white shoes. Their red and blue polka-dot dresses set off by a small black bow around the neck rustled at the touch. A pair of white panties modestly covered the private parts. Whatever reservations I had about my mother vanished that instant and in the joy of giving and receiving we hugged for the first time. As befit his nature, Appa gave me glossy editions of Robert Louis Stevenson's Treasure Island, Kidnapped and The Black Arrow to add to my growing collection. It wasn't much of a surprise but I feigned excitement so as not to hurt his feelings.

I named the dolls immediately. The brunette with the brown eyes would be Patty. It came closest to the Tamil word, Patti, as I called my grandmothers, both of whom I loved deeply.

I chose to name the blonde with the blue eyes Jane, a good solid American name I knew well from the Dick and Jane readers of elementary school. I propped them up in the corner of the bedroom I shared with my younger brother, Ranga, their eyes wide open, as if watching my every move. On weekends, I gave them bubble baths, combed their hair and adorned it with barrettes, and accessorized their clothes with discarded pieces of cloth from Amma's sewing to make a scarf or a chic bandana. On Sunday afternoons, I converted my small work desk into a dining table, neatly laying out the plates, cups and saucers, and cutlery from my blue tea set. It was too bad the dolls couldn't sit down and I had to make do by feeding them in an upright position. I showered them with love and attention and they, in turn, breathed new life into me. I retreated in their company building an inner world for myself free of intruders. I nurtured them, an act that came naturally, cultivated as it was through the years spent in caring for my baby brother.

The dolls provided a much needed outlet at this juncture in my life. My repeated efforts to prove I was the daughter my mother wanted me to be forced me to be extra vigilant. However, the consequences of doing otherwise, frightened me. I did not want to give her a reason to move back to India. My younger brother, Ranga, now eight years old, declared it was too sissy-like to join me in my doll play and made demands on my leisure time. Not having the heart to refuse him, we concocted a fantasy game where each of us in our role as a travel agent booked trips for make-believe clientele. We took on fictitious names; Ranga was Kanakula and I was Jani, though I have no idea why or how we came to choose these names. The only cities we knew as likely destinations were the ones my father visited when on assignment—London, Geneva, Paris, Berlin and Moscow. With the Hammond World Atlas as our handy reference we charted the distances between multiple cities and calculated the appropriate fares. Our neatly sharpened No. 2 pencils were stacked in a Player's Navy Cut cigarette tin, the brand my father smoked. Given his habit, we were never in short supply and used them for storing our paper clips and rubber bands. We collected my father's used tickets, and with the fake money from our game of Monopoly, used them as currency for all our transactions. A toy rotary phone linked us to the outside world. In turn we played agent and client, imagining ourselves on an Air-India plane to London or on a Swiss Air flight to Geneva. The sojourns were short, nothing more than tourist stops for sightseeing. The journeys ended in Idlewild Airport until the wanderlust took hold again. Ranga and I made a pact to keep our game a secret from everyone else in the family. As Jani and Kanakula, we kept our father in our midst by hoarding his cigarette tins and used tickets to fill the onerous gap he left in our lives.

However brief an interlude, that Christmas came to represent a tableau of family life that had existed only in my imagination or on TV. Apart from the dolls, my mother had given me so much more—for a few precious moments she had treated me as the child I was meant to be. There was nothing new about the new year as we returned to our all too familiar existence as a splintered family. I indulged in my fantasy games more often to palliate the inner emptiness that had come to infect me whenever my thoughts returned to the idyllic times we had recently shared as a family. It became second nature to please my mother and I looked forward to the awakening of spring when I could blissfully return to the outdoors and once again feel untrammeled and in full command of myself.

I wanted to spend time alone with my girlfriends and hated lugging my younger brother, Ranga, around wherever I went. We had to speak in hushed tones while he hovered around us. We dissected the love lives of Archie, Veronica and Betty and moved on to name the boys on whom we had crushes hoping Ranga wouldn't hear and most of all praying he wouldn't tell our parents if he had. Ranga had turned nine and it seemed unfair that I still had to babysit him. I was nervous and anxious that he might let slip to my mother that my girlfriends and I were preoccupied with boys though our banter was quite harmless. In the wake of the Camay soap incident, this harmless banter would have assumed epic proportions and given my mother more ammunition to exile me to India for good. How I wanted to savor the joy of coming of age with sheer abandon but alas there was too much at stake.

At long last I had a Saturday afternoon all to myself. My mother was taking her usual afternoon nap, Ranga had decided to stay indoors and Ramu was out somewhere riding his bike.

The gilded rays of an April sun made for a refulgent day, a perfect time to go to the neighborhood playground where my girlfriends usually hung out. This time we could all chat freely about anything or anyone, especially boys. I was ready to confess that I had a crush on Sergio Quimper, a tall, dark, handsome Peruvian boy in the senior class, whose sister, Illya, was the heart-throb of all the boys at UNIS. Shikha and I constantly vied for his attention which sadly never came our way. Maybe this time, we would get to peek at Ann Wald's training bra which she never ceased to boast about knowing full well that the rest of us were still not ready to wear one. I entered the playground which was strangely desolate for a Saturday afternoon. The only person I saw was Gauri, the daughter of my parents' best friends, looking rather forlorn.

The same age as Ranga, I looked upon her as a younger sister and reached out to her with the same habit of guardianship I showed towards him. Raised in a South Indian home under strict circumstances that mirrored my own, I could well imagine her plight. She had a melancholic look and her shoulders sagged, as if a weight too heavy to bear, had been placed on them. I felt compelled to rescue her in some way. She probably wanted to have some fun like I did so I coaxed her into climbing the monkey bars on the jungle gym, and later we pushed each other on the swings. My girlfriends were no where in sight and the afternoon which had held so much promise was beginning its descent towards twilight. It was time to head home.

I waved good-bye to Gauri as I turned towards the path that led to our apartment and instinctively looked back to make sure she was heading home. I saw her enter through the backyard door which abutted the playground and continued on my way. I was halfway along the path when suddenly a tall white boy, who appeared to be the same age as my older brother, leapt out of nowhere and shoved me into the bushes that lined the sidewalk. I hit the ground hard winding up prone on my back, my long braid entangled in the nettles. A searing pain ripped across my scalp as I tried to get free. His long body towered over mine and I could only see his face from the nose down. I could smell his breath; it was stale. Long fingers began to claw at my panties pulling them half-way down my thighs just as I yanked my braid free. Trembling with fear, my eyes filled with shock and terror, I thought I had screamed. Had I screamed? There was not a soul in sight. Where was everybody? Apartments close by, yet no one was home? Wasn't it a weekend? With the fury of an animal intent on survival, I grasped a handful of dirt and flung it at my assailant's eyes. Temporarily blinded, he stumbled and let go of me. I scrambled to my feet, pulling up my panties with one hand while I pummeled his stomach with the other. Still trying to get the grit out of his eyes, he turned away while I fled home. I banged on the door while repeatedly ringing the bell, and collapsed in my mother's arms.

The first thing she noticed was my panties, one leg hanging below my dress. I made a feeble attempt to pull it up blurting out, "A boy pushed me in the bushes Amma and tried to take them off. See, my dress is all dirty." Without a word, she led me by the hand and marched me upstairs to the bathroom. She began to run water in the tub turning the hot faucet as far as it would go steaming up the bathroom. She sat on the toilet seat and began to undress me in a methodical manner—first my shoes, then my socks, followed by my dress and finally my underwear. I noticed the nylon had a tear as she inspected it under the light. She lowered me into the tub, her hands weighing me down as I screamed, "The water is boiling hot, Amma!" "Stay there until you're clean," she snapped and shut the door behind her. I unplugged the drain, and refilled the tub to a comfortable temperature. I began to scrub myself vigorously, soaping my private parts again and again until it burned.

I was to tell no one of the incident, especially not my brothers. A few weeks later, I did tell Shikha. She was after all my best friend and I thought it my duty to warn her. She felt sorry for me and even sorrier when she heard what my mother had done. We made a pact never to wander around Parkway alone. In my case, it was a foregone conclusion. There were no more bike rides to Alley

Pond Park or solo trips to the playground. I now had to drag Ranga along even to the laundry room. There would be no more dancing with Shikha. My cherished records gathered dust in Ramu's closet. He was interested in real guns now, having outgrown the toy ones, and spent a lot of time with Timothy, his friend across the street, who had quite a vast collection. More and more, confined indoors, I became a voracious reader finding escape in the exploits of Nancy Drew and thrusting myself into the lives of Meg, Jo, Beth and Amy in "Little Women." I lost interest in my dolls and stuffed them into my closet. Homework had more demanding now that I was in sixth grade with research projects that required numerous hours poring over the encyclopedia. Summer holidays would start soon, my father was due to return from Geneva, and I was hoping a family vacation would chase away the blues.

The announcement came during the last week of school. "We're moving back to India," my parents said as my brothers and I stood before them. " We'll be living with your grandfather in Madras, in your Appa's house on Mahalakshmi Street. Your father will join us later once he finishes his work in Geneva," added my mother. We stood speechless, bewildered by this turn of events. There was no show of concern for our feelings nor any attempt to elicit our opinions. Our habit of obedience kept us tongue-tied. We would soon be asked to compile a personal check-list of what to take and what to leave behind with the proviso that Amma would have the final say.

There was a flurry of activity as the packing began. The steamer trunks that had carried Amma's spices and stone grinders and assorted Indian paraphernalia would be part of the old cargo along with the newer acquisitions of an Osterizer Blender, a Roller-Iron and a Singer Sewing Machine. Ramu and I listened to our favorite songs one last time before he sold his record collection at five cents a piece and gave away the record player to a friend of his. Too engrossed in what I would salvage among my belongings, I did not care what my brothers saved or discarded. I managed to see my favorite show, American Bandstand, before the TV disappeared and the image of a young Dick Clark remained frozen in time. My bookshelf had been cleared and the only books to endure the voyage were the classics. Nancy Drew and The Hardy Boys were relocated to the local library. Scrabble and Monopoly, the only two board games we had, survived the move. My dolls, Patti and Jane, who had suffered a brief time of benign neglect, were to accompany me on the plane—a surprising concession from my mother.

On the last day of school, in June 1959, we each bid our classmates good bye. News of our departure was received in a matter-of-fact way with an occasional hug from a close friend. The UN families in Parkway Village were used to a peripatetic existence and our departure to India raised no eyebrows. There were more intimate farewells at the numerous dinner parties thrown by our Indian neighbors. They lauded my parents for maintaining their traditions despite living in America. This would make the transition easier on the children and everyone appeared confident that our assimilation to Indian culture would come naturally and whatever Americanisms we had acquired would be shed over time. The South Indian families, particularly those with daughters, began to doubt the wisdom of staying on in America. The Madras Brahmin mothers gathered in our home for a final coffee klatsch. Hovering around, dressed as usual in my pavadai, I heard them applaud my mother's decision to send me back to India before it was too late. Fears of their daughters dating an American boy filled them with anguish especially when it came to arranging their marriages. Even a hint that they had been seen with a boy would be scandalous enough to kill any proposal. It was better to nip these tendencies in the bud. I was just the right age to forestall these consequences. At my mother's behest, I ground the coffee beans in the Lovelock grinder for what I hoped would be the last time. There was a glint of pride in my mother's eyes as she watched me serve the coffee in our Indian tumblers. In that moment, I had finally become the daughter she had always imagined me to be, a twelve-year old girl embedded in Indian tradition, unsullied and untainted by American culture.

Chapter 4

Foreign-Returned

My first twelve years of childhood in Parkway Village had come to an abrupt end. My father, soon to be relocated to the Palais De Nations in Geneva, would accompany us to Madras but only for a short while. It would be his first visit home since his mother, my dear grandmother whom I called Patti, had died. I had fond remembrances of her during the previous trips we took during our summer vacations. I felt an overwhelming sense of loss as I crossed the threshold into a world which would soon become my permanent home. I had returned to my motherland but my heart and soul remained rooted in America.

It was a tearful return to No. 3, Mahalakshmi Street, home of my paternal grandparents. The entrance hall looked shabbier than before, the ineluctable void in the wake of Patti's demise lent an air of gloom. I immediately looked towards the bench on which she had lain; it was now strewn with old newspapers waiting to be bundled and re-sold to the paper vendor. The lime-washed walls cried out for a new coat of paint and those pesky lizards, that had frightened me on one of my earlier visits, continued to scale the walls, their sticky tongues darting out to catch the swarm of insects buzzing around the tube light. The ceiling fan, its blades covered with dirt, circulated the hot air flecked with motes of dust. My grandfather, still his curmudgeonly self, sat glued to his easy-chair, and gave us a begrudging welcome. He would always see my family, including his own son, my father, as dirty foreigners and sinners, who according to the Laws of Manu, an authoritative Hindu text, had polluted their pristine lineage by crossing the ocean to take up residence in a land other than their own. I couldn't bear to look at him and sauntered over to the back of the house. The pile of dung cakes teeming with flies were stacked neatly in the cow shed and was as repulsive a sight now as it was when I first laid eyes on them. A familiar past pervaded the present. Time stood still so it seemed, yet as Heraclitus said, one never stepped twice in the same river. Flux was inevitable. At a younger age, I had roamed around this house and nicknamed it the "house of dung" as cow dung was used for everything — the dried patties spread over wood logs provided fuel for cooking; moistened dung shaped like a cylinder was rolled around the areas where we ate on the floor to absorb any remnants of food and to supposedly purify the place said to be contaminated by the very act of bringing food into one's mouth; and on certain ceremonial occasions, a small amount of cow dung was mixed into a concoction of milk, curds and ghee butter. I held on to the more pleasant memories, the ones spent in my Patti's company where I pranced around in my pavadai and sat on her lap while she tucked a bundle of jasmine into my braid. I would never forget her but things were different now. I saw myself as a twelve-year old bubble gum chewing American girl, a rock n' roll aficionado, who enjoyed wearing pedal pushers and eating pizza and Carvel ice cream. How would I ever fit in here, in this house of dung?

Short shrift was given to the process of acclimating us to our new surroundings. Events unfolded quickly. The school year had begun and I was quickly enrolled in the all-girls Good Shepherd Convent while my brothers attended the all-boys Don Bosco Matriculation High School. These arrangements had been orchestrated by my father before we left New York. The Franciscan Sisters of Mary and the Jesuit Fathers who headed the schools were noted for their adherence to discipline and offering of a solid education which required mastery of knowledge of all things British be it history or literature. In an effort to proselytize the "pagan Hindus," a daily reading of the catechism was enforced. The local public schools where most subjects were taught in Tamil, were not an option given our lack of proficiency in the language. French, the only second language my brothers and I knew from our education at the UN School, was accepted by both schools as part of the language component of the matriculation exam, the passing of which earned a high school diploma.

Much happened within weeks of our arrival. My father, suffering from chest pains, most likely due to the grief at his mother's passing, was admitted to St. Isabel Hospital and shortly after his recovery, left for Geneva. Amma, the memory of his first heart attack still fresh in her mind, panicked at the thought of his living alone. She beseeched my Chittappa, Appa's younger brother, and my Chitti, his wife, hitherto childless, to act as our guardians. Amma, whose presence had been constant in our lives, quickly became a peripatetic figure shuttling between Madras and Geneva. My brothers and I were subjected once again to the standard farewell speech we had often received from my father, replete with the usual admonitions to be obedient, to do well in school, and, most important of all, to not cause any trouble for my Chittappa and Chitti. The rapid tempo of change over the past couple of months forced us to start our new life in Madras in media res obviating any of our efforts to make sense of what was happening. We acquiesced without kicking up a fuss knowing it would be futile to do so. I, in particular, being a girl, would find myself caught in the undertow of a tradition, its current strong enough to wash away every footprint of my American identity.

New rules were in effect. Though no stranger to the pavadai, my mother now insisted it be worn every day and at night. My pajamas and dresses were stored in mothballs and would eventually be traded for a couple of stainless steel vessels to the street-vendor who frequented our neighborhood. Even my dolls wound up in storage, wrapped in old towels to protect them from dust and stuffed into a cabinet, or almirah, as it was called. My Chitti, noticing my budding breasts, strongly advised my mother that the time had come for me to wear a half-sari called a davani, that would drape over my bosom. "She's getting to be a big girl and will mature soon," she said with a sly glint in her eyes. "Yes, yes," Amma agreed while eyeing my breasts. In a matter of days, different colored davanis had been purchased, and cholis, short blouses that came to the waist, were hurriedly stitched by a local tailor. Excited at the prospect of wearing my first training bra and wishing I was back in Parkway to share the news with my girlfriends, I was disappointed to learn that Amma had not thought to buy me one. I had to settle for a light, cotton undergarment shaped like the choli with hook enclosures in the front that were uncomfortably tight and flattened my breasts. It seemed ridiculous to wear the davani if there was nothing much to hide. Three-yards in total, exactly half the length of a sari, one end was tucked into my pavadai and pleated half way around my waist with the rest of the material draped across my breasts leaving about a yard of cloth dangling off my left shoulder. The cardinal rule was to make sure my breasts were covered at all times and, if by accident, the davani slipped off my shoulder, my Chitti was quick to admonish me. I discovered multiple uses for the davani. It turned out to be a light protective cover to ward off the mosquitos on a sultry night. It was taboo to eat or bring street food into a house as orthodox as my grandfather's but the folds of my davani turned out to be a good hiding place for the peanuts I bought on the sly from the roadside seller. The light cotton davanis were useful in the sweltering heat to dab at the beads of perspiration and doubled as a towel to dry my wet hands. It soon became an indispensable accessory and its original purpose to sheathe me in modesty appeared inconsequential, but not for long.

With my mother's departure to Geneva a few months after our arrival, my Chitti took charge of my rearing. Orthodox to the hilt, she was determined to groom me in the ways befitting a young Brahmin girl. Ever vigilant, she made sure I wore the davani properly at all times whether it was sitting down to eat on the floor or people-watching on the stoop outside. For good measure, she threw a light coverlet over me at night so there would be no possibility of my breasts being exposed. Every movement I made came under scrutiny and I began to incessantly tug at my davani, adjusting and readjusting it as if I had a nervous tic. It took a year, and by then, I began to wear the davani like a second skin. With a spreading sense of pride, I checked my appearance in the mirror, my davani draped to perfection in a manner becoming a modest Brahmin girl. The candy-striped pedal pushers, the Scottish kilt skirts held together by a huge safety pin on the side, the frilly polka-dot dresses, the sailor dresses with the big red bows—all these belonged to another era and to another girl.

Wearing the davani in the correct way was only the first of many hurdles I would be forced to tackle. My day to day activities were closely monitored. My Chittappa without fail escorted me to the bus stand on school days, despite my pleas that I was old enough to walk the short distance on my own. A barrage of warnings ensued: "There are ruffians on the road who will try to steal from you; strange boys will bump into you on purpose" ending with the most ominous of all, "Someone might kidnap you and if that happens, how will I ever answer to your parents?" Suffice it to say, I had no choice but to be chaperoned. He cautioned me further as I got into the bus: "Always sit in the ladies' section and never walk to the front near the men's section. Get down in the back of the bus. Do not let the conductor touch your hand while issuing the ticket. He might lick his finger while tearing off the ticket and his saliva will pollute you. Where will you get water to cleanse yourself?" I did my level best to do what I was told but once in a while, a mishap occurred, and a saliva coated ticket would land in my palm. It sent me running to the first water tap I could find in school in a desperate attempt to rid myself of the impurity. I remembered an outing with my friends in Parkway to the local Carvel and how we licked each other's ice cream cones. All that saliva commingled with mine made me wince now. Being dirty in India meant something more than I had ever imagined.

The rituals surrounding the purity-pollution divide were not completely unknown to me. Prior visits had served as enough of an introduction to some of its more quotidian aspects. I put up with it as it was only temporary and, once I returned to Parkway, I had a good laugh at what struck me as nonsensical and downright yucky, especially when I thought of the cow dung smeared all over the place. I couldn't afford to laugh anymore, not in my grandfather's house, where the customs were more rigid and demanded strict adherence. There was no use in asking for an explanation; none was forthcoming. I had to live by the rules whether I liked it or not.

That first year back in India, I had cultivated friendships with the girls whose homes abutted ours on each side. A barbed-wire fence demarcated our property from theirs and being low in height, the goings-on in each of our homes could hardly be kept secret. Living in such close proximity invited a lively exchange of gossip, particularly among the women-folk. The drudgery of housework was lightened in small degree with snippets of conversation such as giving tips on where to buy the freshest vegetables at a low price, or the best store to buy the latest fashions in saris, to good marriage prospects for their sons and daughters. The conviviality that prevailed was limited to these over-the-fence chit-chats and I found it odd that there was never a follow-up invitation to extend the camaraderie indoors. On questioning my Chitti, she responded almost in a whisper, "Their husbands might be home or some other male for that matter. It's not proper for me to enter their homes with your Chittappa away at work." I could only surmise that the other wives were of a similar mind-set. What I did not know was being in the presence of a male other than one's kin, was taboo in my case as well. I was never allowed to visit Kalyani and Padma, the Brahmin girls who lived to the right of us, since they had an older brother. It didn't matter if he wasn't home for there was always the possibility that he might return and it would have been the height of impropriety were I to be found in his company. I could never let on to my Chitti and Chittappa that on many an evening, under the pretext of doing homework, I spied on my girlfriends' brother watching his every move through the bars of my bedroom window. Tall, fair, and handsome, he cut a fine figure on the days he wore his all-white cricket uniform. Our rooms were in such close proximity, I could see him steal a glance at me. Under any other circumstance, I might have been tempted to stretch out my arm to him in the hope he would do the same. Alas! It was mere wishful thinking on my part and who knew, perhaps on his as well.

As luck would have it, Jaya, a girl my age, who lived to the left of us, was an only child, so there were no sanctions when it came to my visiting her. My budding friendship with her brought to the fore further idiosyncrasies related to the purity-pollution divide which forced me to confront the more insidious aspects of the caste system. I knew I came from a Brahmin family but to me it was just a label devoid of any significance. I was aware of the orthodoxy it spawned clearly evident in some of the practices in my grandfather's house but until now, I had been a mere observer not a practitioner.

Without warning, my Chitti added more restrictions when it came to playing with Kalyani and Padma. I had reluctantly accepted the fact that I could not go to their house since they had a brother, but it came as a shock to hear they could not enter my grandfather's home because they belonged to a different sect of Brahmins. As if that was not enough, I was forbidden from consuming any food prepared in their home. "They are Smartas," my Chitti said derisively, "followers of Lord Shiva. We are Iyengars, followers of Lord Vishnu and superior to them. They will pollute your grandfather's house with their presence and you will be polluted too if you eat there. However, you can eat at Jaya's house. Her family are Iyengars like us."

The indignation I had felt years earlier when treated as a pariah in public school resurfaced, and I dreaded the thought of having to perpetrate a similar injustice towards two girls who were fast becoming my close friends. Fortunately, I was never in a position where I had to turn Kalyani and Padma away since they knew not to ask for an invitation. I guessed their parents must have taught them the rules for they behaved the same way with Jaya's family, also Iyengars like us. We all made the best of the situation and confined our play to the outdoors. Both Jaya's home and mine had large frontal courtyards, ideal for hopscotch, jump rope and playing tag. I made it a point not to enter Jaya's home whenever Kalyani and Padma were about, although I could, being an Iyengar. It was a privilege I could do without and the very idea of excluding them was something my conscience would not permit. On Sunday afternoons, we congregated at Jaya's home to have our tiffin, a kind of Indian high tea, with hot savory snacks. Her mother was famous for her bhajis (vegetable fritters) and potato bondas (croquettes). We sat in solidarity on the outside stoop stuffing ourselves and paid little heed to the differences others saw in us.

My growing friendship with the girls next door became a vital part of my assimilation at this juncture in time when I felt adrift and orphaned with both my parents away in Geneva. I sacrificed my moral outrage at the denigration of people due to caste for the company of these girls which allowed me to be a child again — not just any child but an Indian child. Life inside my grandfather's home was too rule-laden and at barely thirteen years of age, I felt compelled to act as a young adult. The scenario before me replicated in many ways the tableau of my earlier years in Parkway Village. Still, I did have an outlet in American pop culture. But living here on Mahalakshmi Street, a dominant Brahmin enclave, I was trapped in a net of orthodoxy that enveloped practically every household with little or no connection to the world outside. Television did not exist, radio reception for those who had one, was haphazard at best and the telephone was a luxury item most could ill-afford. We were one of the few families on the street who were fortunate enough to have a telephone. Using whatever ins she had among her friends, many of whom wielded a lot of influence, Amma, before she left, was able to have a phone installed rather expeditiously. It often took months just to procure the instrument and even longer to get a connection. My Chittappa, frugal by nature, padlocked the rotary dial and often denied us permission to make any calls. Chit-chatting with friends, according to him, was a frivolous activity not worth the expense. The only exceptions made were when my parents called us from Geneva but even on these occasions, my Chittappa made sure we kept our talk brief and to the point as possible. My parents notified my Chittappa by mail to the date and time of the call so as to insure my brothers and I would be home. To save time and money, he had my brothers and I write out what we wanted to say to our parents taking great pains to proof-read our comments and correct our grammar, an ingrained habit he acquired in his job as a sub-editor at The Hindu, one of India's national newspapers. By the time the call came in, we successively took a minute each to reel off what we wrote: a laundry list of mundane activities that included doing well in school, eating properly and behaving like obedient children. I can't remember what Appa or Amma said but if they had said "I miss you and love you, Vasu," I would surely have remembered.

The constant vigilance and dictates of customs nearly sapped the joy out of me. I was desperate to hear the sound of my own laughter and rejuvenate my spirits from its moribund state. I grabbed every chance I could to saunter over to Jaya's house where the simple pleasures of childhood games could be relished out in the open with no one looking over my shoulder. I spent Sunday afternoons mastering pallanguzhi, a game played with cowrie shells and puliyankottai, a game that tested prowess in the juggling and catching of tamarind seeds. I discovered how to thread flowers without a needle by looping and knotting natural tree twine over and under the stems. I learned to adorn my hands with henna and how to make a paste by grinding the leaves with a small lump of tamarind whose acid content turned the normal orange hue into a fiery red. I looked at my friends so accepting of the norms I found stifling and marveled at their ability to find delight in play. They made it possible to be a child amidst adults only too eager to rush them into womanhood.

My first menstrual period arrived a year later. I felt betrayed by my own body which seemed to announce that I was a young woman now and no longer a child. The first drops of blood in my underwear sent me into a panic. I was convinced I had contracted some dire food ailment like dysentery. I called out to my Chitti and in the privacy of my room, I nervously showed her the stain that was beginning to spread.

"Am I sick?" I asked, my heart in my mouth "Maybe I have tape worms or something. It could be from the hot mango pickle I ate," I added fretfully.

"Do you have a stomach ache? Are you vomiting?" Chitti asked.

" No, no, I feel fine," I replied.

She looked at me intently and began to smile. "You have become a grown-up girl. You must mark this date on the calendar and in about twenty-eight days time, this will happen again."

"But what is it?" I asked anxiously. "Where is all this blood coming from? Won't I die if it happens again?"

"Silly girl, all this is natural. You need not know anything else. Just do as I say. I'll write to your mother and tell her you have become an adult," she said with an air of finality.

Nothing she said mollified me and I was more bewildered than before. At the time, I just wanted to get clean and change my underwear. Chitti went to a closet and pulled out an old white dhoti. She tore the cloth into strips and neatly folded them into pads. She gave me two safety pins and told me to secure the pad in the crotch of my panties.

I was ill-prepared for what came next.

"You have to stay in this room for three days. Here is a bar of soap to wash the cloth. You cannot touch anyone as you are "theetu" (polluted) now. I, myself, must go bathe again to become "madi" (pure). I'll put a plate and a tumbler outside your room for your meals. You will have to wash your own utensils and keep them inside the room. Make sure no one else touches them."

"But what about school? I can't miss three days," I whined.

" Yes, yes you can go to school but you have to leave and enter the house through the side alley. You cannot come into the main hall," she replied and then added in English, "You are now out of doors."

This last phrase managed to make me smile in an otherwise grim situation. It was a clever use of the English language to describe a context that was so very Indian. I later came to learn that in olden times it served as a euphemism for menstruating women who were forced into isolation in straw-thatched sheds at the outer most edges of the backyards, a good distance away from the main house. I thanked my lucky stars to be spared such an indignity.

I'm not sure what explanation my Chitti gave to my brothers who were surprised to hear that I was "theetu" for three days. Ramu, my older brother, who was aloof by nature, could not have cared less; my younger brother Ranga, made sport of my condition. He would threaten to touch me and shriek with laughter as I backed away to the safety of my room. His pesky behavior injected a bit of light-heartedness in the tedium of being sequestered.

Ironically, there was a very public and embarrassing side to the menstruation process. When Chitti's sisters came calling and were told I was "out of doors," they would chuckle amongst themselves, look in my direction, and remark, "Now, there's a grown-up girl in the house." Over time, I understood this to mean that I was of marriageable age. Jaya's mother, very much the nosy neighbor, saw me entering and exiting through the side entrance, and took it upon herself to keep track of the dates of my period. Like clockwork, she never hesitated to let me know when the next one was due. There was no need to bother with a calendar. Everyone at school found out about my period. I could not prevent the blood from seeping through the cloth pads and by the end of the day, my white uniform sari was stained with brownish blotches. Ridiculed by my classmates, I became the butt of their jokes along with their snide remarks on how uncouth I appeared especially for a girl who came from America.

The purification ritual, meant to be a reprieve, was harsher than the three-day solitary confinement. Roused by my Chitti at 4:00 am on the fourth day, I was taken to the well in the backyard. The pre-dawn hour was deliberately chosen to insure a modicum of privacy under the assumption that none of our neighbors would be up and about at that time. Chitti handed me a thin transparent cotton towel which I draped around me as I stripped myself bare. Cold and shivering in the semi-darkness, I crouched on the mossy bricks as she poured buckets of icy well water over me. The ablution complete, I stood up and was shocked to see the young men who rented rooms in the back of Kalyani and Padma's house, rivet their eyes firmly on my body. I covered my breasts with one arm, while shielding my crotch with the other and fled inside. To be half-naked in front of all those men after all the interminable lessons in modesty, was too much to fathom. The violation I had suffered in Parkway Village at the hands of a stranger had made me dirty in my mother's eyes. This time, however, it was my own eyes that looked upon my body as an object of shame. No amount of water could make me feel pure again.

An air parcel from Geneva arrived shortly after my first period. I was hoping it was a box of Swiss chocolates, maybe Toblerones, my favorite. No such luck. Embedded in a box of Kotex sanitary napkins was a letter from my mother. "Dear Vasu," it began, "Your father and I are so proud to learn that you have become a big girl. Please read the directions on the box carefully. It tells you how to use the belt and attach the napkins. You don't have to use cloth anymore. I will be mailing more to you soon. Tell Chitti to give you these from now onwards. Love, your Amma." No thanks to my mother but many thanks to Kotex, I discovered I had ova or eggs, and according to the pamphlet, they lived in something called an uterus and it was normal to discharge them in a bloody stream every month. All these terms for parts of my body and its inner workings made for a boring read. I saved the insert with its pictorial directions on how to use the belt and napkins and threw the pamphlet away. I could not fathom why my period was a source of pride to my parents. I was not feeling very grown-up and, despite the terseness of her letter, I yearned to have my mother by my side and rescue me from the humiliation of these barbaric practices. Surely, she must have known that Chitti would follow the rituals of menstruation without compromise. How could she have abandoned me at a time like this? Turning to my girlfriends next door for a show of empathy was in vain for shortly after I started menstruating, so did Jaya, Kalyani and Padma. What I perceived as unnatural and cruel, they took to be normal. I was left to voice my protest in silence. The box of Kotex stopped the leakage and stilled the wagging tongues at school, but it did little to stanch the monthly cycle of dread and humiliation.

Chapter 5

Good Shepherd Days

Mother John, venerable headmistress of Good Shepherd Convent, had me stand beside her as she announced my arrival to the entire school at morning assembly. " We have a new student in our school, all the way from America. Her name is Vasundara and she will be entering the third form." Beads of sweat trickled down my back and my brand new white poplin blouse, crisply starched, was close to turning into a wet rag. A sea of faces, in motley shades of brown, trained their eyes in my direction. The very short one minute assembly ended and before the official start of classes thirty minutes later, I was surrounded by my future classmates. An anomalous presence in their midst, everything about me struck them as odd. The minute I opened my mouth, laughter erupted among the quizzical faces as they tried to make sense of my American accent. "You are the first foreign-returned girl we ever met," they chimed in unison. One by one, they took turns to touch my hand or run their fingers up and down my arm, shrieking with delight, " I've touched the hand that has come all the way from America!" It was as if the pores in my epidermis oozed of everything American which they hoped by some miraculous means would literally rub off on them. I wished the kids at P.S. 117 could see me now. The very skin they had found odious enough to spit on, was now the envy of all these Indian girls. They found it incredulous that I would return to a poor country like India after living in a rich country like America. Like a Greek chorus, they chimed a well-known 16th century British folk tale, "Dick Whittington and his

Cat," a rags to riches tale of a poor orphan, who with his cat, finds his fortune in London — a city where the streets were supposedly paved in gold—and ultimately becomes its Lord Mayor. That I came from New York and not London didn't matter to them. Without question, they saw the western hemisphere oozing with wealth and refused to believe that any of its inhabitants were not well-off, including myself. Descriptions of my day to day life growing up in Parkway Village rang hollow, almost as if I had made it all up just to prove how ordinary I was.

My appearance seemed to add to their discomfiture. "You look and dress like all the other conservative Brahmin girls in the school," they commented none too politely. " Even your blouse has the same smelly coconut stain on the back because of your oily long plait." They pointed towards some other girls referring to them as Anglo-Indians, Muslims or just plain rich who, according to them, wore frocks and bobbed their hair in a deliberate attempt to look sophisticated though none had ever ventured outside the city limits. "You don't dress like someone from America," they concluded ruefully.

Firm of the opinion that I was rich, my classmates were flabbergasted that I commuted to school by bus on a daily basis unlike the well-to-do girls who arrived in their chauffeur-driven cars. Trying not to sound overly sanctimonious, I explained how my father eschewed pompous displays of wealth and wanted his children to ride public transportation like millions of others. They still thought it weird but were appeased for the time being. When we recessed for lunch, I could clearly see how caste differences came into play. As was customary in orthodox Brahmin households, I ate the main meal of the day early in the morning, usually around 8 o'clock. A lighter fare to be consumed at school consisted of curd (yoghurt) rice with a slice of hot curried pickle which I carried in a small metal tiffin box. Eating food that had not been prepared at home was an act of pollution, a transgression against the dietary laws that had been laid down centuries ago. The round metal tiffin box was a sure-fire means to identify the Brahmin girls at Good Shepherd. Come lunch time, we congregated under a tree, forcing ourselves to down the curd rice which had invariably turned sour from the heat. The pickled relish, meant to enhance the flavor of an otherwise insipid meal, had — due to the jostling of the tiffin boxes in our school bags — leached out a reddish-orange oil that seeped through the gooey mixture. There was no such things like napkins or tissues in our homes and should some of that pickle oil drip on our pristine white saris, we were doomed to spend the rest of the day reeking of its pungent odor.

A stone's throw away, in sharp contrast, another kind of lunch scene unfolded. Girls who were either Tamil Christians, Anglo-Indians, Muslims or Non-Brahmins gathered under a shed which housed several long cement tables. Their maid-servants or ayahs, carefully laid out colored tablecloths with matching cloth napkins and place settings with real china and stainless steel cutlery. One by one, each girl stretched out her hands to a steady stream of water dutifully poured by their ayahs-in-waiting. Napkins, large enough to cover the front of their uniforms, were tucked under their chins. Five to six dishes stacked in a large tiffin carrier were methodically removed by the ayahs and portions were ladled on to the plates. The aroma of food, freshly prepared at home and piping hot, wafted down to our lunch spot, tickling our taste buds as we stared down at our soggy curd rice with disgust. As soon as they had their fill, their ayahs stood at the ready, jug of water in hand, as they proceeded to gargle their mouths. Unused to this kind of servant culture with all the obsequiousness it demanded, I could not help but look upon these girls as spoiled snobs. Much as I disliked the curd rice which was my lunch staple throughout my years at Good Shepherd, I had no regrets. It would have been more of an ordeal to digest the food with all those ayahs fawning around you, their stomachs growling from hunger.

It was a jarring experience to be labeled a Brahmin or a rich foreign-returned girl at school. The sense of privilege that accrued in being labeled in such a way made me uncomfortable and more alienated than I had expected. Growing up in a place like Parkway Village whose logo could have easily been "unity in diversity," the notion of class or caste distinctions never arose. There was never talk of anyone being rich or poor. The ethnic gatherings that took place were mainly to celebrate regional holidays, but it did not exclude the larger sense of community. That I was born into a Brahmin family had little significance except for the vegetarianism we practiced and for a few religious rituals. As for our lifestyle, it was neither meager nor opulent but comfortable enough to have what most families had—a well-furnished apartment, a car, bicycles and a sufficient number of toys. An education allowance, a perk for UN personnel, helped pay for school. Life in the community continued on an even keel with no evidence of a sudden rise in wealth or a rapid descent into poverty.

Living in Madras was antithetical to anything I had known. The poverty was too egregious to escape notice. Beggars swarmed places that were the most frequented—retail stores, temples, fruit and vegetable markets, railway stations and bus stops. Lepers with puss oozing out of their knobby stumps that once were limbs, children deliberately blinded to invoke pity, mothers cradling starving infants and men with either an amputated arm or leg — all of them wailing with tales of woe as they thrust a tin cup in your face. I had been forewarned by my uncle to ignore their pleas and avoid any physical contact as I passed by them. In any case, I had no extra coins to offer. My uncle gave me a pittance of an allowance sufficient to cover my return bus fare and nothing else. I dodged the beggars the best I could and tried not to stare. Though, at times, my curiosity got the better of me. I was startled to see the menacing looks they returned and hurried off. These daily encounters laid bare the divide between the haves and have-nots which was both stark and cruel. It made me flinch to be thought of as rich by my classmates.

The day to day life in my grandfather's home stood in harsh juxtaposition to the kind of life the girls at Good Shepherd assumed I led. Apart from their jabs at the way I dressed or my riding the bus, to my carrying my own lunch, they somehow got it into their heads that I lived in a spacious bungalow with a retinue of servants. I loved the attention they showered on me and saw it as an opening to assimilate in my new surroundings. I was afraid to disrupt the fantasy they had spun and never gave them my exact street address in case one of the girls chanced to pass by my neighborhood. I gave only a vague reference to the vicinity in which I lived, Mambalam, a local hub, that housed both the rich and not so rich. With no compunction, I lied about having a phone — in case they wanted to call — explaining how we were waiting on a connection which ought to arrive soon. How could I tell them about the penurious conduct of my uncle who kept the phone under lock and key? His frugality extended to the purchase of any item he thought frivolous, like toys and games, though he did not mind purchasing books sold second-hand at the stalls in Moor Market, a huge flea market, situated in a densely crowded part of the city called Park Town. It was not above my uncle to invent ways to get things done in the cheapest manner possible. It was a school requirement to purchase a notebook for each subject and cover it in brown paper with a bright red label on the front that indicated your name, subject and the form (class) you were in. The nuns at Good Shepherd would notoriously conduct on the spot inspections and anyone caught with an uncovered notebook received ten whacks with the ruler, an accessory that was as permanent as the white wimples and black habits of the Franciscan Sisters of Mary. A small bottle of glue was all one needed, but my uncle saw it as an extravagance and was too miserly to purchase it. A good substitute, one that was equally effective according to him, was a paste of left-over rice and water. My notebooks smelled sour once I was done and I laid them out in the sun to dry. I returned a few hours later only to see an army of ants feasting on the desiccated kernels of rice. All this penny-pinching got on my nerves. I could picture the girls in school, baffled expressions on their faces, as I pulled out my notebooks with their tell-tale signs of sticky rice pressed into the corners. How was I to tell them that the girl from America, who in their eyes, had to be rich lived with an uncle who was too cheap to buy a bottle of glue? It was nothing short of a miracle that I managed to escape detection and pass inspection to boot.

I had concluded early on that the path of least resistance would lead to equanimity at home. I did not want to give my aunt and uncle just cause for complaint and it did not take long to adopt and adapt to measures that had once been irksome. I developed a "if you can't beat them, join them," attitude as a coping mechanism. I had an ally in my younger brother, Ranga, and much as we did on earlier visits to my grandfather's home, we sought refuge in each other's company, treating with humor the practices of the household which still seemed bizarre and making fun of my uncle's parsimonious behavior. My older brother, Ramu, who had always remained aloof, escaped into activities away from home. He became an avid tennis and cricket player and spent most of his time after school participating in matches. His studies fell by the wayside and he bore the brunt of my uncle's anger with little effect and was pronounced incorrigible.

Ramu cared little for the orthodoxy demanded of him and he took whatever opportunity he could to flout the rules. He defiantly partook of eating at restaurants, though it was expressly forbidden, and with a vengeance smacked his lips in front of Ranga and me as he described the taste of the little triangle-shaped samosas filled with mutton, a speciality of a Muslim eatery called Buharis. At times, his shirts reeked of cigarette smoke, a smell we knew only too well due to my father's habit. To be in Ramu's company was inimical to the well-being of my brother and me. Unlike him, we suppressed whatever qualms we had and entered into a servile obedience that over time repeatedly hammered home the rules of conduct that governed a Brahmin household. We re-enacted the drama of tradition as it played out each and every day, absorbing its tenets without question. Ranga and I began to perceive Ramu as a renegade who dared to defy a belief system we had come to accept if not fully understood. Our brother, whom we were late to embrace after his return from boarding school, had once again become an outcast. As far as Ranga and I were concerned, he was a Brahmin in name only.

My identity as an Indian girl, no longer a vague and inchoate entity, began to take hold. I was consumed by an urge to belong, to fit in, and not be seen as an outsider. In large measure, my assimilation on the home front was nearly complete. The process had been a trying one, stripping me of all agency. I turned towards the virgin grounds of Good Shepherd Convent to carve a place for myself where the moniker, "foreign-returned," would become a thing of the past. The promise of a good solid education accompanied by a strict disciplinary code, was the mantra of the handful of parochial schools in Madras. The high cost of tuition attracted the well-to-do with a small minority accepted on scholarship. The daily dose of Catholic instruction with its not so hidden agenda of gaining converts was seen as a small price to pay among the majority of Hindu families who enrolled their children. Rock solid in their assumption that Hinduism was a far superior and resilient religion to Christianity, they did not fear conversion. My twelve years in Parkway Village had taught me nothing about religion. All I knew was that Christians celebrated Christmas and Easter, Hindus had their Deepavali festival, and Muslims observed Eid. The term Catholic was shrouded in the same ambiguity as the term Brahmin and it was only after seeing a statue of Christ surrounded by sheep near the chapel grounds that I realized he was the good shepherd, the eponymous savior of my school. The only prior image of Christ that stuck in my mind was the one on the cover of Life Magazine's Christmas issue depicting his crucifixion, the blood trickling in cruel streaks from his nailed limbs. It came as a relief to see him portrayed in a more pacific light, his glance serene as he tended his flock. Such tenderness was in sharp contrast to the grim steely look of our headmistress, Mother John, whose very presence evoked terror in all of the students. Morning assembly was nothing short of an ordeal. Students lined up in neat rows according to their grades better known as forms in the Indian school system and began each day by chanting the Hail Mary prayer. I tried to follow along to no avail. I bowed my head along with others and heard voices ring out with the opening lines, "Hail Mary, full of grace. Our Lord is with thee," quickly rising to a crescendo followed by a sotto voce muttering of words that sounded garbled and unintelligible. A resounding amen brought the gratefully short prayer to an end. I never learned the entire prayer beyond the first line and never bothered to look it up.

"Hail Mary," was followed by uniform inspection, a task Mother John performed in person and with a great deal of perverse pleasure. Ruler in hand, her Irish eyes, almost an unnatural blue, held an icy stare as she walked up and down the rows of students, examining the white uniforms and white sneakers for the slightest trace of dirt or discoloration. Prodding at the hems of our pavadais and saris with the tip of her ruler, she inched them above our ankles to check the whiteness of our shoes. Anyone who failed inspection was pulled out of line and subjected to harsh ridicule. I incurred her wrath on a very wet day during Monsoon season when my sneakers got soaked with the mud and grime from the puddles on the floor of the bus. The white chalk I normally carried to cover the imperfections on my sneakers was of no use when it came to the caked on dirt. " Vasundara," she bellowed, "have you come all the way from America to give me trouble?" Palm outstretched, I received my ten whacks in front of the entire assembly who were once again reminded that I was still a foreigner.

It was also the first time that I had been addressed by my full name, Vasundara, instead of Vasu, the only name to which I had habitually responded. Henceforward, I came to be known by my official name throughout my school days at Good Shepherd Convent. Answering to a new name was akin to becoming a new person. I began to cultivate a personality uniquely my own. I was keen to compensate for the often humorless and austere existence in my grandfather's home with a joie de vivre that had long been suppressed. Ironically, it was another austere environment, a convent no less, that gave me an outlet for all those pent up emotions.

With much aplomb, I threw myself into school activities. At five feet four inches, I was perceived as tall for an Indian girl, and Mother Peter, who directed the Drama Club, and saw my height as an asset, was quick to cast me in male roles. I was surprised by my own shyness as I unravelled my half-sari and slipped into the pants of my costume. I swaggered across the stage, confident and proud, finding an unhampered freedom in my gait that I had not known since the days I wore pedal-pushers. My rapidly fading American accent had now taken on the peculiar lilt of Indian-English along with what was known as the Indian head bobble where 'yes' could mean 'no' or vice versa. There were no more quizzical looks when I spoke; everyone could understand me now. My rich vocabulary, honed over the years under my father's tutelage, made me the per-

fect candidate to lead the Debate Club. I was praised for my delivery
and became a fierce competitor. At home, the only outdoor games I
was permitted to play was an occasional game of tag or hopscotch
with my friends next door. My aunt and uncle thought it was more
ladylike to indulge in sedentary activities like board games. I missed
riding my bike and climbing the jungle gym and looked to school to
revive my desire for something more athletic. My tall stature again
proved to be an advantage and I was recruited to become a member
of the netball team, the Indian version of basketball. My years as
a swimmer had added muscle and strength in my legs making me
adept at jumping hurdles and running in relay races. I discovered a
new game in tennis quoits, aptly named since its scoring system was
the same as in tennis, but instead of a ball, one hurled a quoit or
hard rubber ring with as much force and speed across the court. If
your opponent couldn't catch the quoit, you scored a point. Emu-
lating the other players, I hoisted my pavadai, tucked the folds of
my half-sari into my waist, and hardly cared if my breasts showed.
The only thing that mattered was that I win. The doggedness with
which I pursued these games led me to excel and at the end of my
first year I was recruited to join the Kingfisher House, one of the
four sports divisions, the others being the Swallows, the Canaries
and the Woodpeckers. Our mettle would be tested on Sports Day,
an annual event, that pitted the Houses against one another as they
competed in various games. The ultimate prize was a silver-plated
trophy cup engraved with the name of the winning House and its
Captain. I rose to the rank of Captain of the Kingfishers in two
years but sadly, during my tenure, we came in second to the Swallows on Sports Day.

There was a marked divide between my personality at home and
at school, a trait I had cultivated and found sustaining during the
earlier part of my childhood at Parkway Village. My aunt and uncle,
in keeping with their disposition, were only interested in my academic progress and the very idea that I may be having fun in school
would have rattled their sensibilities. My athleticism had paid off
and I was chosen to compete on behalf of my House, the Kingfishers, at our annual Sports Day. It was an honor I gladly accepted

with much pride and a sense of hard-won triumph. I received the sports uniform that was required attire for the event and rushed home barely able to contain the news from my aunt and uncle. I proudly displayed the white culottes, cleverly stitched to masquerade as a skirt over knee-length pants underneath, and the bright red collared shirt matched by a red tie, the trademark color of the Kingfisher House which distinguished us from the blue Swallows, the yellow Canaries and green Woodpeckers. My high spirits quickly deflated as I saw the look of dismay on the faces of my aunt and uncle. As if reading each other's thoughts, together, they exclaimed, "You cannot wear this kind of dress. What will our neighbors think when they see your legs exposed and wearing nothing but a shirt on top?" "But, I have been selected to represent my team," I implored, "and the uniform is required." My aunt, who seemed on the verge of softening, saw the look of disapproval on my uncle's face, and quickly deferred to his judgement. I was on tenterhooks waiting for his decision.

Sports Day, scheduled to take place towards the close of the school year, during the hottest period of summer, had finally arrived. By that time my parents had arranged for a car to be purchased, a small blue Fiat, and had hired an elderly-looking driver called Naidu. My father, in a letter to my uncle, left explicit instructions that the car be used sparingly when it came to taking my brothers and I to school; as much as possible, we should continue our regular commute by bus. But on this particular day, my uncle had a plan which depended heavily on my being driven to school. He had me camouflage the sports uniform by wearing my pavadai over the culottes and draping the half-sari over my red shirt and tie. This subterfuge would insure my modesty and attract little to no attention from our neighbors while I exited the house. Once the car neared school, all I had to do was to slip out of my pavadai and unravel my half-sari. What my uncle did not or perhaps could not foresee were the numerous maneuvers it took to accomplish what was very much an acrobatic feat. The back seat of the Fiat car, small and narrow, had very little wiggle room. I struggled to untie the knot on the string of my pa-vadai and once I got it off, I had to tackle the half-sari which I had draped rather tightly, in mummy-like fashion, to make sure my uniform stayed concealed. I squirmed around, tugging at the pleats gathered around my left shoulder while trying to coax the rest of the three yards out from under my bottom. Half-standing, my head hitting the roof of the car, I yanked myself free of all the trap-pings. I looked down at my culottes, the neatly creased pleats now all wrinkled, and, to make matters worse, ugly sweat stains began to form rings around my armpits. This was supposed to be my debut. I had finally earned a place among my peers as one of their own and not as an outsider. Preoccupied by the sorry state of my appearance in addition to being anxious, I had completely ignored the presence of Naidu, our driver. The type of person who spoke only when spo-ken to, he had been a silent witness to my disrobing in the back seat. Well into his sixties with ailing eyesight, his gentlemanly demeanor inspired a trust that far outweighed his qualifications as a driver. My aunt and uncle, confident that a man like Naidu would never make any sexual overtures, thought it was safe to be alone in the car with him. It was with the very same confidence that I reassured myself that my goings-on in the back seat must have been nothing beyond a source of amusement to him. As we drove through the entrance of Good Shepherd Convent, our eyes met in the rear-view mirror. There was no mistaking the lascivious grin on his face. I thought of my uncle and the torture he put me through earlier that morning. If he only knew that I had to turn into a strip-tease artist in the back seat, and as a result, become an object of titillation to a man old enough to be my father.

I could not wait to get out of the car and slam the door behind me. My face, a flush of embarrassment, turned redder as I stood amidst my fellow Kingfishers, who seeing me for the first time with-out my half-sari, ran their eyes up and down my body. "I never noticed you were so big on top," one of them said while another remarked, " You have really strong legs, but they're a bit hairy." I was sick of all the attention given to my body since I left the house that morning and ran over to a group of Brahmin girls, who much like me, must have felt awkward and overexposed in their sports dress. I was accustomed to the half-sari by this time, and without it, I felt naked and vulnerable. The competitive spirit in me took hold. Right now, the only thing that mattered, was to insure the victory of my House, the Kingfishers, on my very first Sports Day. I garnered a win for my team in hurdles and in the relay race but we ultimately lost to the Woodpeckers who outscored every team in other events and were crowned the champions that year.

Classroom etiquette at Good Shepherd, like most other Indian schools, was very different from what I had been used to at my old school, UNIS. The lay teachers, mostly women, were to be addressed as Miss and the nuns as Sister so-and-so. When called upon in class, you had to stand up to respond. Should you give a wrong answer, the teacher kept you standing until permission was given to sit. Every subject be it English, Math, Geography or History required memorization of numerous facts and in some cases, entire texts. At exam time, you were expected to regurgitate the information, often verbatim. No one solicited your critique of the material and you had to accept what was written as the Gospel truth. There were no special projects that required research as in the UN School. Even in art class, where I had hoped to give free reign to my imagination, rigid rules were applied that quashed all efforts at experimentation. Every object, every figure had to be drawn to meet certain specifications that I was reminded of the Paint By the Numbers kit I once received as a birthday present. The painstaking efforts it required made it my lease favorite class. Determined to excel, I committed to memory facts both big and small. I became so adept at retaining and regurgitating information that before long I was known as a "mug pot," a label whose provenance I never quite knew. I turned into a walking encyclopedia and during exam week I attracted a small following, a cluster of girls, who picked my brain and hung on my every word as if I were a soothsayer.

I had come into my own by the end of my first year at Good Shepherd Convent. I eradicated all traces of what had been foreign and greedily consumed what I could of local culture. I discovered the importance of cricket in the nation's psyche and the "match fever" that gripped the school during tournaments. Thanks to my uncle, who was glued to the daily commentary on the radio, I learned how the game was played and joined in the chorus of cheers and groans that rippled across the schoolyard during lunchtime. The latest Tamil movies, including gossip about the stars, were hot topics among my friends both at home and at school. My Chitti, who rarely indulged herself in anything remotely pleasurable, would once in a while, egged on by her many female siblings, cave in and take me to the local cinema house. It was hardly a casual affair. My Chitti and I, usually clad in cotton, adorned ourselves in silk and perfumed our hair with the afternoon buds of jasmine that were miraculously in full bloom by the time the movie ended. Despite the stifling heat and swarm of mosquitos, the song and dance routines, the exaggerated display of emotions, the tragedy of unrequited love, the joy of reunited lovers — kept me in thrall. My years of learning Latin and French at the UN School had given me an ear for language, and though I struggled at first, I was able in subsequent viewings to understand the Tamil spoken on the screen. My increased fluency cemented my Indian identity at home and at school. The girls next door no longer laughed at my pronunciation and, at school, I easily switched between English and Tamil. My American accent, which marked my entry into Good Shepherd, had completely disappeared, a lost foreign tongue.

Over the next four years at Good Shepherd I continued to thrive and distinguished myself as a good student, a good athlete, and a good leader. The lay teachers, a mix of Tamil Christians and Brahmin women, were assigned to teach math, science, history and geography. As for English Literature, it fell under the bailiwick of the Franciscan Sisters who were skeptical of the ability of the native Indian teachers to give the subject the due reverence it richly deserved. Mother Peter, who had coaxed me into joining the Drama Club, intoned the sonnets and plays of Shakespeare in her thick cadenced Irish accent. They were totally incomprehensible. The only requirement was to memorize the material and be able to annotate it with reference to the context. A typical question on the exam began with the opening lines of a Shakespearean work and we had to fill in the rest, word for word, including every punctuation mark, and then explain who said what to whom and where. The "why" part was purposely omitted; no one wanted our opinion. I came to hate Shakespeare and it took decades before I ventured to read him again, and even then, I could hear myself whisper each and every punctuation mark.

I found role models in my Indian teachers who taught us math and science. Young, in their twenties, they exhaled an enthusiasm that was infectious. Their embrace of hard core subjects, normally the purview of men, sowed the seeds of my ambition to become a scientist. Whether by happenstance or by choice, they were unmarried at the time, and stood in sharp contrast to some of the more disturbing goings- on around me. Jaya, the girl next door, had been abruptly pulled out of school once she started to menstruate. She was confined to the home and trained in the domestic arts such as cooking and sewing. Twin sisters in my class, who had but a year left to graduate, were hurriedly married off, much to everyone's surprise. To these families, high school was nothing but a pit stop on the path to marital bliss. I was of the firm belief that my college-educated parents would never subject me to such a fate. The company of these teachers only strengthened my resolve.

The girlish chatter among my classmates graduated to dreams of our future careers as teachers, novelists and scientists. Undeterred by the strictures of tradition and caste, we saw ourselves as daughters of a new India, free of the shackles of the past. We saw no need for men either as husbands or fathers, and betrothed ourselves to one other until death did us part. I had indeed undergone a conversion at Good Shepherd but it was definitely not of the religious kind. By the time I graduated four years later in 1963, the geography and landscape of my life had radically changed. I was no longer a foreigner in a foreign land and felt at home.

Chapter 6

A Father's Gift

I missed my father's company, especially our chats about my school activities. In those all too brief overseas phone conversations, I could share very little of my days at Good Shepherd. I made it a point to keep a mental portfolio of all the happenings at school and when I heard Appa would be coming to Madras for a short visit, I could hardly wait to steal a few quiet moments with him. His visit would be all the more special since it would coincide with a special evening at school, the Saturday Social. Juniors, like myself, would be feting the seniors over a lavish buffet as a pre-graduation send off. We heard through the grapevine that we would be subjected to merciless teasing, and out of deference to our older peers, we should not retort. Most of the ragging would consist of insults to our intelligence and to our lack of diligence and no matter how smart we thought we were, there was no other option but to take it on the chin. It was all part of a long standing tradition and having been forewarned, we knew it was all in jest.

What made that Saturday Social all the more special was the fact that it was one of those rare occasions where we were permitted to come to school without wearing our uniform. "You can come in fancy dress," the nuns announced at assembly. For most of my classmates and me, this meant donning a sari for the first time. A famous folktale says that the sari was born on the loom of a fanciful weaver who also had dreams, dreams of "Woman." The shimmer of her tears, the drape of her tumbling hair, the colors of her many moods, the softness of her touch—all these he wove together. He couldn't stop and wove many yards. And when he was done, he sat back and smiled and smiled and smiled. I so wanted to be that Woman in the folktale.

We were filled with chatter at the start of the week. Did you get a sari? What color? Does your blouse match? What's the border like? Are you going to wear flat sandals or heels? What about your hair? Will it be up or in a braid? Can we wear lipstick? Does anyone even have lipstick? I knew I didn't and had never once tried putting it on. We suddenly took notice of the color of our skin, all of us shades darker in the relentless heat of March. Who among us could pull off wearing a bright colored sari? Sudha was too dark, Viji and Rama were fair by comparison, and I was somewhere in between. Maybe I should wear a more somber color, I thought. I could not imagine myself in bright pink or parrot green. Besides, Amma always preferred dark colors and looked beautiful so why not me?

It was 1962, three years had passed since our arrival in India. My mother, who had been shuttling between Geneva — where my father was stationed at the Palais de Nations —and Madras, decided on one of her trips to build separate living quarters sans kitchen above my grandfather's house. It was a bold move for an Indian daughter-in-law who was expected to live with and do the bidding of her father-in-law. Amma, unused to living with a joint family after all her years abroad, cherished her privacy and independence. She wanted to go and come as she pleased, answerable to no one, and be able to freely converse and entertain her friends without fear of being overheard. None of this was easy in the main house with my aunt and uncle constantly underfoot along with the steady stream of visitors, mostly my aunt's sisters —who were often loud and chatty and had a tendency to stay for a long time. The orthodoxy of my grandfather demanded a lot from her. She was forced to wear a nine-yard sari, draped in a special way with convoluted folds, rather than the customary six-yard sari. The extra cloth greatly restricted her movement. Baths had to be taken very early in the morning to purify oneself for the prayers that followed. Food was to be consumed shortly after, usually around 8:00 am, whether one was hungry or not. All root vegetables like onions and garlic were taboo. According to Ayurveda, they promoted passion and ignorance, traits that were seen as impediments to meditation and devotional prayers. The meals were tolerable for the most part but they were also incredibly insipid — the same old vegetables prepared the same old way, the same type of rasam and sambar, and the same mushy rice — all cooked in well water at the insistence of my grandfather. Everything had an awful brackish taste. I yearned for Amma's cooking, for her baked casseroles topped with garlic bread crumbs and the occasional cheese pizza she bought us when we lived in Parkway Village. Most of all, I missed all the love she poured into every dish she made.

Amma also had our best interests at heart. She could see how difficult it was for my brothers and I to find a quiet spot to study, away from the distractions of the household. She did not subscribe to the mandatory confinement during my menstrual periods and by moving upstairs, I would be spared the embarrassment of neighbors and visitors pointing out loudly that I was "out of doors." The best part of having our quasi-apartment was the intimacy it provided. Now that Appa had arrived, we could finally be all together as a family, just the five of us, a sweet reminder of my childhood in Queens. Although area-wise our living space was small, with two rooms, an outside bathroom, and an airy verandah, the freedom it offered was expansive. Appa, could easily hide his smoking habit from his father. Amma was only too eager to whisk off the drab cotton nine-yard sari and switch into a six-yard one, most often silk. She now felt presentable enough to go out and socialize with her friends. My older brother, Ramu, now 17 years old, was focused more on girls and hanging out with his friends than on his studies. It was his final year of high school and he would soon have to take the Matriculation exams and pass all his subjects if he hoped to go to college. My parents had received an earful from my aunt and uncle regarding his rebellious behavior and lack of respect for authority. "He must have his own room so he can study hard for his exams with no disturbances," my parents declared. Ranga and I, used to sharing a room in our apartment in Queens, were only too happy to keep the same arrangement. We studied in separate corners and kept each other company much like we did in the past. For the first time we had comfortable cots with thick mattresses to sleep on, a welcome change from the hard cement floor down below. Thanks to Amma, I enjoyed a degree of emancipation that I had not thought possible under my grandfather's roof. And so did she.

"Let's get Vasu a traditional sari. It will be her very first one which she can wear for the Saturday Social," my mother said to my father. " We can go to Radha Silk Emporium and Sampurna Sastri. Both have good selections."

Appa, whose preference leaned towards very classical South Indian weaves, insisted they go to Sampurna Sastri first. I could not believe the interest Appa was taking in sari shopping for me and saw a side to him I had never seen before. I knew I was the apple of his eye, as he would often call me, but in many ways I felt as if I were a stranger to him. Ever since I could remember, he had been off traveling and we had to play catch up each time he returned. On this visit, I showed him some of my essays and he instinctually began to correct my grammar —a purist to the hilt when it came to the English language. I introduced him to my friends at Good Shepherd Convent: there was Rama Devi, the math whiz who got 100% on every exam; then came Sudha Nair, the best writer in school, who we all knew would become a famous novelist; and my best friend, Viji Krishnaswami, with whom I shared everything and had lunch with everyday. I launched into my criticism of Mother John, the very mean headmistress, who hit us with her ruler if she thought our sneakers were not white enough and who insisted on calling me Vasundara which I disliked, instead of Vasu. She also thought that Hindus were pagans and should convert to Christianity and dragged us Brahmin girls to the chapel to pray, in what she announced defiantly, was the only proper way to pray. On a proud note, I told Appa that I had just been made the Captain of the Kingfisher House and although we lost to the Woodpeckers the first year I joined, we were definitely going to win this year. I crammed as much of my life as I could in a breathless stream of anecdotes making sure not to omit anything and to include every detail. I wanted Appa to see how grown up I had become before he left again.

Sampurna Sastri was a small store, nothing more than a hole in the wall, nestled in a recess off the main street in an area called Mylapore, a predominantly Brahmin enclave in the city of Madras. Mylapore was also the place of my birth and it seemed like an act of fate that my first sari would be purchased there by both of my parents charting my existence from childhood to adulthood. The store was famous for its elegant, traditional silk saris woven in the Tamil Nadu district named Kanchipuram. One could always be sure that the silk was pure and heavy and many of the designs hearkened back to the era of my grandmothers, lending a continuity with the past. Deep inside I wanted to accompany them but knew I would not be asked. Since I was a child, Amma had always selected my wardrobe with no input from me. I always wore whatever she bought without complaint. Besides, they had planned to shop when I was in school. On the bright side, the sari would be a surprise.

Finally, the day of the Social arrived and, with it, the onset of my period. It put me in a foul mood and I began to fret about the very real possibility of leaking blood onto my brand new sari and how my evening would be ruined. Teary-eyed, I sought out my mother.

"Amma, I got my period and don't know if I even want to go the social. What if I leak into the new sari? Everyone will laugh at me."

"Vasu, don't cry. Nothing will happen. Everything will be okay. You can use two pads and pin them tightly to your panties. No need to tell anyone downstairs that you got your period. They'll say you'll have to be isolated and cannot go out. We can tell them your period started tomorrow," Amma said hugging me close.

It was the first time I felt so comforted by my mother and wished she could always be with me. We sat under the fan, my back to her as she undid my plait.

"Sit straight Vasu, don't hunch," Amma said as she dabbed coconut oil on my scalp and caressed it into the long strands of my black hair lending it a silky sheen.

"Amma, be careful when you take out the tangles. It hurts when you pull," I said.

I turned, facing her, as she carefully parted my hair to form a straight line down the middle. I turned again so she could make three equal strands and weave them into a long single plait. She then tied a bright red ribbon at the end to keep my hair from unraveling. As a final flourish, she gently tucked a string of freshly cut jasmine just above the nape of my neck.

" The buds will open by the time you leave. The flower seller said the jasmine was very good and fragrant," my mother said. "Go wash your face and get ready."

I applied a light coat of Cuticura talcum powder on my face, lined my eyes with kohl and finished with a red bindi on my forehead.

"Amma, Appa, I'm ready," I cried out both nervous and excited.

It was already dusk and the light in the room cast a dim shadow. Nestled among an array of bananas and grapes, I saw my very first sari. It was gorgeous, with red and green threads alternating in a pattern of undulating waves called "Veldari" with a bright green border; the pallu glistened with flecks of gold thread interrupting a sea of green. An auspicious occasion, I prostrated myself, and asked for my parents' blessing.

"May you have a long life!" they said in unison.

"Appa, I have my period," I said softly. "Was it alright to prostrate before you when I'm in this condition?"

Amma jumped in quickly: " It's okay, Vasu. These things do not matter and are not important. Your Appa has come all this distance and it's a special occasion. Accept his blessings. Who knows when you'll get to see him again?"

"Thank you Amma, thank you Appa. It's beautiful. I love the pattern. Amma will you help me put it on?"

We unraveled the sari and I ran my fingers over the silk feeling every thread and held up the pallu admiring the gold shimmer.

"Hurry up! Take your clothes off and just leave your bra and petticoat on," Amma said.

As I peeled off my clothes, I suddenly felt shy. Since I reached puberty three years ago, I had never undressed in front of my mother and instinctually crossed my arms over my breasts as she handed me the choli.

"Put your hands down. It's not like I haven't seen breasts before. Make sure the blouse fits. See if you can raise your arms easily without it being too tight," she said in a business-like manner.

It fit perfectly. I looked down at my bare midriff and I felt sexy. I remembered the Tamil actresses in the movies, dancing around the rose bushes in their see-through saris, draped seductively below their navels, while playing hide and seek with their lovers. A part of me wanted to bare even more, but I didn't dare — not in front of Amma. The sheer weight of the sari took some getting used to. I gingerly paced back and forth and heard the swish of pleats, magic to my ears.

"Amma, what if the pleats fall out? Then what'll I do? I wouldn't know how to re-tie my sari."

"Don't worry. They won't fall out. I have tied your petticoat very tight so there's no chance of that happening. Just make sure you don't walk too fast or make any sudden moves."

"How do I look Amma?"

"Nice, nice. Now go show Appa."

I longed to see myself in a full length mirror but there wasn't one.

"Appa, is the sari nice?" I said as I pirouetted before him. I watched his eyes as he was about to answer.

"Babu," he called out to my mother, his voice choking. "Take a look at our daughter. She is maturing into a beautiful young woman."

There was such happiness in his tears and in mine.

What a refreshing sight it was to see the girls of Good Shepherd Convent out of their white uniforms! It was as if a painter's brush had drizzled every hue and color onto a blank canvas. I walked cautiously, as Amma had instructed, towards my classmates. We hugged and squealed with delight, as we eyed one another. Sudha was wearing a shocking pink sari that contrasted sharply with her dark skin.

Rama was in midnight blue, her choli modestly long to hide her midriff. Viji was in magenta with gold stripes rippling down her sari.

"Let's see what your pallu looks like," we shouted all at once. As if on cue we lifted our pallus and fan them out, the array of colors billowing in the soft evening breeze like rainbows in motion. Where did you buy your sari? The names of the top sari stores of Madras came tumbling out — Radha Silk Emporium, Nalli's, India Silk House and Sampurna Sastri.

"Vasundara, yours is so traditional," they exclaimed. "Lovely, Veldari pattern."

" My Amma and Appa picked it out for me," I proudly replied.

We ran our fingers over each other's sari, feeling the different textures of silk, peering closely at the designs, letting out oohs and aahs, while calling ourselves the Mutual Admiration Society. We looked around furtively to make sure none of the nuns was watching and bare our midriffs to one another. Rama was the most modest and Viji, the most daring we all agreed. Sudha and I were somewhere in between with just a little hint of exposed flesh. We giggled at our newly discovered femininity and headed for the food table.

There was a sumptuous spread—fried samosas, parathas, subzis, biriyanis, dhals and rice pilafs and a separate table of desserts—gulab jaman, assorted petit-fours, and different flavored ice cream. We dug in, careful not to spill anything on our saris. We saw our teachers coming towards us — Miss Rajam (mathematics), Miss Hamsa (Chemistry) and Miss Bennett (History) who told us how beautiful we looked.

"Soon they'll be finding husbands for you," Miss Rajam teased.

"No, Miss," I said in a defiant tone. "I'm planning to study chemistry and go to college. No marriage for me now. My Appa said I could study at the Sorbonne and live with him in Paris."

Sudha and Viji chimed in about their plans to major in English and Rama confidently stated that she was going to study mathematics just like Miss Rajam.

"You are all smart girls," Miss Bennett responded and "will do very well I'm sure."

When they were out of earshot, we gossiped about Miss Rajam and how she was in love with the brother of one of our classmates,

Jayashri, and wondered if it would lead to marriage. Miss Hamsa always looked so forlorn and so mouse-like; we could not imagine her wedded to anyone but chemistry. We made fun of Miss Bennett's accent and the way she pronounced Massachusetts as "Mussachoo-suts." We were giddy with laughter and did a final spin with our pallus held high as the evening drew to a close. We promised to remember this Saturday Night Social at Good Shepherd Convent as a glorious time in our lives where we got to share our hopes and dreams in living color.

My parents waited up for me, as I knew they would. It was nearly 10:00 pm when our driver dropped me back home which was rather late by Madras standards where the city buses no longer ran after 8:00 pm.

"Amma, Appa, I had such a great time." In rapid fire I gave them the highlights of the evening, saving the details for a later time.

"It's getting late," Amma said, "and I am so happy you had a good time. Now take your sari off carefully and get to bed. You didn't spill anything on it did you? Any leaking from your period?"

"No, Amma I was very careful and thank God nothing leaked," I replied.

"Vasu, we'll chat some more tomorrow morning," Appa said as I bade them good night.

With Appa about to leave for Geneva soon, I wanted to rekindle the intimate conversations we shared when I was a child. I caught him alone on the verandah, stubbing out his cigarette, and although I was nearly fifteen, I felt young enough to cuddle up with him and rest my head on his broad shoulder.

"So, Vasu tell me whose the favorite among your friends? Is it Sudha, Rama or Viji?" he asked with a twinkle in his eye.

"Oh, Appa I like all of them but Viji is really my best friend. I feel sad when everyone teases her and calls her 'jingle bells' because she is a bit big on top. She always starts crying and says she can't help being big. I like Sudha and Rama too. Rama is a mug pot, always studying and cramming for exams. She gets first rank every term and as I told you she scores 100% in math. She's too serious and hardly laughs but she's always willing to help me when I get stuck. I'll never beat her and always have to settle for second or third rank. Sudha writes beautifully, Appa. Her English is so good. She only reads good literature and thinks Viji and I are wasting our time reading romance novels. She loves books much like you. You would like her a lot," I replied.

"Listen, Vasu. Rank is not important. What's important is that you try your best and study hard. I want you to be happy with your friends and don't pick fights with them. Remember to turn the other cheek if someone says something nasty."

"But Appa," I protested, "why should I let someone hurt me?"

"Vasu, there's no use in being violent. You must embrace everyone no matter who they are, rich or poor, whatever their caste. You should never show off around those who are less fortunate than you. Remember what I've told you."

I got up slowly and gave Appa a hug, caressing his bald spot with my hand. Suddenly I felt wise beyond my years.

The day of Appa's departure had arrived. There was a flurry of activity as relatives and friends came and went, each making a last ditch effort to request a favor of some kind. His older brother — who had refused to practice birth control despite my father's urging — found himself saddled with too many children and pleaded for money to support his large family. His younger sister complained that her husband could not hold down a job and that she too needed money to tide her over. A friend wanted to know if Appa could use his influence to find a job for his son; another wanted a recommendation for a company position. They had all come at the last possible moment which left little time for my brothers and I to say our goodbyes. We swallowed our disappointment knowing we would be with him soon once school let out and summer holidays began. As soon as we returned from the airport, I went to my room and took out the sari he had so lovingly purchased. I clutched it close to my heart. Somewhere in the distance I heard the sound of a plane as it soared across the sky.

T.G.Narayanan dead. Stop. Heart Attack. Stop.
Sunday, March 25. Stop. Palais De Nations,
Geneva. Stop.

I was in class when Mother John, the headmistress, asked me to step out and follow her. "Your aunt is here to take you home," she said. I kept asking what was wrong but she didn't say a word. Once I got into the car and we started speeding home, my aunt said, " Your Appa has died. A heart attack." Just like that, in such a matter-of-fact tone. I immediately tried to open the car door and jump out but she held on to me as I dissolved into tears. Everything else remained a blur.

I ran into my mother's arms. I still remember the nine-yard sari she had on when she found out that in an instant she had become a widow: Of all things, it was vermillion, the color of wedding saris. There were traces of blood in the pleats, real blood. She had collapsed when she read the telegram and cracked her tooth on the hard floor.

The details came later: Appa had died all alone in his hotel room. No one knew exactly when he died. The maid came to do up the room late Sunday morning and found him asleep in bed and decided to return later. His phone had been ringing. He was late for a luncheon engagement which was highly unusual as he was known for his punctuality. The maid returned in the late afternoon and saw that he was still asleep in the same position. She was a bit alarmed and alerted the desk downstairs that something might be wrong. When the concierge went upstairs to check on my father, he found him dead. The phone rang. His luncheon friends, increasingly anxious by now, were calling again. He gave them the bad news.

By this time it was the pre-dawn hours on Monday, probably around three or four am. Amma had gone out to a dinner party the evening before. She was a vision of beauty in her midnight blue sari with the solid gold border, her hair up in a bun, a string of pearls around her neck. I recall the delightful fragrance of Chanel

No. 5 that lingered long after she left. She would later say how much fun she had that night blissfully unaware that Appa's body was turning cold.

Chapter 7

Chaos

We had to wait four days for my father's body to arrive from Geneva. There were so many protocols and details to attend to, leaving us more bereft and enervated. First, there was the autopsy to rule out foul play since he was top United Nations official in the field of disarmament. Just a year earlier in 1961, his boss, Dag Hammarskjold, the Secretary General of the United Nations, had died in an air crash near present-day Zambia. Many thought the crash was a deliberate act of sabotage by the CIA. It was the Cold War period and the deaths of two prominent UN diplomats following close on the heels of one another, aroused suspicion. It was confirmed that my father died in his sleep of a silent heart attack. And then came all the red tape when his body arrived in Bombay. Airport officials wanted to know who had the authority to claim the body. Who would arrange for a chartered plane to transport the body to Madras? Once this was solved, there was further red tape when the plane landed at Madras Airport. Customs officials, who had received a list of what was in the casket, trained their attention on the Rolex watch that had been placed on my father's wrist. It was an expensive item, and according to the rules, subject to import duty. It was of no consequence, they asserted, that it was worn by a dead person. My uncles, who had come to take Appa's body home, lashed out with such fury, shocked by the visible lack of empathy, until finally the customs officers relented. My dead father was allowed to enter duty free.

The house on Mahalakshmi Street was filled to capacity as I waited with Amma and my brothers to see Appa for the very last time. Relatives, friends, curious onlookers, and Vedic priests formed a circle around the casket as it was opened. There lay my father, clad in one of his Savile Row suits, a neatly folded handkerchief in his breast pocket. He looked so handsome much as I had remembered. I looked for his shoes, the ones I polished as a child. There were none. He was barefooted which made him appear a bit ridiculous given his posh attire. The head priest took charge of his body. It took many hands to gently lift it out of the casket and lay him on the floor. "He cannot be cremated in western clothing," the priest insisted. Off came the suit, the shirt, his tie and the duty free Rolex watch. Appa was now clad in a silk dhoti, his chest completely bare, befitting a Hindu Brahmin. I saw beads of sweat oozing from his pores though the ceiling fan was whirring at full speed. I grabbed a hand fan and waved it as rapidly as I could, back and forth, over his big frame. He continued to sweat. Someone told me later that dead people don't sweat; it was all that embalming fluid seeping out of his pores. Freshly bathed with sacred water, Appa's body was hoisted onto a bier of sandalwood logs and carried to the cremation ground by his three brothers and my older brother Ramu who was only sixteen at the time. As the eldest son, it was his filial duty to light the funeral pyre. He never spoke about that day and for reasons that continue to be a mystery, no one in my family ever thought to ask.

Back at my grandfather's home, another type of ritual was underway. The women, barred by tradition to enter the cremation ground, were beating their chests, slapping their foreheads in shock and disbelief, and pleading with whatever god they worshipped for an explanation. They then turned towards my mother and led her to the backyard, to the cow shed to be precise. I stayed a comfortable distance away and watched while one of my paternal aunts wiped the vermillion colored bindi off my mother's forehead with a swift stroke of her palm. She pulled the gold bangles off both her arms and, lastly, lifted her wedding chain off her neck. All three symbols indicative of her status as a married woman had been removed in one fell swoop. I could not bear to look at my mother. Just a few days ago, she was resplendent in her fine silk. I collapsed in tears.

The days that followed were a blur of activity. There were the Brahmin priests, a slew of them, admonishing my brothers and me to keep our distance while they performed the last rites for our father. They had taken over the main hall of the house and built a small hearth, an Agni, in the center. The smoke was fanned by an endless pouring of ghee which polluted the air with an acrid smell and made us all cough. The Agni had to burn continuously and never die out while they chanted from the Vedas. This of course meant that the ceiling fan could not be switched on. We were told not to go near the priests as they were madi, meaning pure. They had undergone specific rituals so they alone could conduct the death rites for our father. If we were to touch them, even by accident, they would be polluted and would have to undergo the purification process all over again.

It took twelve days of rituals to ready my father's soul on its journey to heaven, the abode of the gods. The thirteenth day was to be one of celebration, for on this day his soul was said to leave the material world and start its ascent towards the ethereal one. There was a chorus of voices pleading, "Do not cry, do not cry. You must not cry. You want your Appa to rest in peace don't you? Your tears will fetter his soul to us; it must be set free." The weight of ritual injunction bore down heavily. I steeled myself and let go of my father without shedding a tear.

Soon, I lost count of the days and tired of the keening as people dropped by to express their condolences. I found refuge upstairs sitting in the verandah staring emptily into space. Amma often joined me, her face blank, her eyes devoid of tears. We hardly spoke. A few of her close friends would drop by to check up on her and all she could do was to repeat the story surrounding my father's death. She stoically looked on as they wept.

My brothers and I could no longer afford to miss school with end-of-the year exams looming ahead. We went about our daily routines numbing our emotions. Amma had some quick and difficult decisions to make. Although Appa had been stationed in Geneva, he often had to travel for work to the UN's main offices in New York. Since we had vacated our old apartment in Parkway Village, he decided to rent another smaller one for his stay. He had also planned to retire early and began construction on a house near Marina Beach in Madras which was as yet unfinished. For a fleeting moment, Amma considered moving us all back to New York but was immediately dissuaded by her siblings. "What will you do by yourself in a foreign country?" they asked. "The children are now accustomed to our Indian way of life. You have to think about Vasu's welfare too. She's your only daughter. What if she forgets our ways and goes with boys? How can you protect her with no husband? She is fourteen now and innocent. She will follow our ways and have an arranged marriage as is our custom. We will all be here to guide you and support you."

Their arguments held sway and with Ramu in tow for male protection, my mother abruptly left for New York. Ranga and I were shipped off to Delhi and entrusted to the care of my uncle, Amma's younger brother, and his wife. In a month's time, she systematically closed up the apartment in Queens, packed up Appa's belongings in Geneva, and returned with a well-stamped passport, a sad relic of happier times.

I was entering my last year of high school and had to pass the public matriculation exams in a variety of subjects in order to apply for a Pre-University program. A failing grade even in one subject meant I'd have to wait another whole year to retake the exam. The fear of failing eclipsed my sadness and grief. My mother, physically and emotionally depleted after closing up our establishments abroad, was in a frenzy as she scrambled to secure admission for Ramu in a prestigious engineering college in Madras. A few palms had to be greased before he was accepted — an apparently normal course of action if you wanted an education in India. Naive, when it came to money matters, Amma, in a blur of efficiency sat down with an accountant and pored over a stack of bank documents as if they were written in a foreign language. If we were in financial straits, she did not let on. We continued to maintain the same lifestyle as before and the lessons in frugality forced on us earlier on by my Chittappa, had not been lost on us. My mother appeared stalwart and if she did happen to cry, it was always in private, never in front of us. We felt safe and secure. None of us talked about my father either to ourselves or to one another. In death, as in life, he was mostly absent.

It was the whispering behind closed doors and the sly yet meaning-ful glances that first caught my attention. My Dad's siblings— his older brother, two younger brothers and two younger sisters — converged in my grandfather's house with a regularity that was rare. It was nearing the first year anniversary of my father's death when all hell broke loose.

My father's older brother, my Periappa, approached my mother and in a self-righteous manner said, " Narayanan was giving me a monthly cheque to help with my children's tuition. I want to know if you'll continue."

Next in line was my aunt, Yasoda Atthai, Dad's youngest sister. "My husband hasn't found a job yet. Narayanan was helping me out. I'm going to need money for our family."

His younger brother, Ranga Chittappa, and his other younger sis-ter, Janaki Atthai were after a bigger catch and demanded to know, "How much pension are you getting? How many rupees to the dollar is the UN giving you? Did Narayanan leave a will? Just so you know, we are entitled to a share as his surviving siblings."

I stood close to my mother as they circled her like vultures over a dead carcass, and I heard her angrily shoot back, " I am alone now. His pension will not kick in immediately. What will I do? I have three children to raise. The house by the beach is not even finished. How will I pay for the rest of the construction?"

Janaki Atthai, her eyes filled with venom, lashed out at my mother, "How bold you are! What audacity! Don't forget you are the daughter-in-law of the house, an outsider. He was our brother first. You have no rights to his money."

The mere mention of the will, in particular, riled my mother. "I'll see you in a court of law," she spat back. " I am his wife, not you. My husband has hardly been dead a year and look at all of you! You just want his money."

At this point, my mother's anger gave way to tears. Her hitherto, brave facade, crumbled. My brothers and I could no longer stand by quietly. We immediately formed a protective shield around our mother and dared anyone to get anywhere near her.

Veera Chittappa, my Dad's youngest brother, and his wife, Saroja Chitti, who had been our guardians when we first arrived, were strangely quiet amidst these outbursts. Unlike the others, they made no demands of my mother. She looked upon them as possible allies, silently imploring them for their moral support. She was totally unprepared for what followed. Veera Chittappa, whom she had trusted more than anyone to look after her children, very calmly turned towards my mother with eyes cast down, as if afraid to face her directly, and stated in no uncertain terms, "I will not perform the first year death rites for Narayanan. You better find a priest to do it."

I was too young to realize the import of his words as my mother stood aghast. Ramu, being the eldest son, would have normally performed the first year death rites for Appa but he had not as yet had his Upanayanam, the thread ceremony. For young Hindu Brahmin males, this was their initiation into manhood, where they learned the teachings of our sacred texts, the Vedas, and are given a sacred thread to wear across their chest by their fathers. This sacred thread made them eligible to participate in and conduct certain religious rites. Both a celebratory and auspicious occasion, it could not take place during the first year of mourning rendering it impossible for Ramu to carry out what was considered his sacred duty. My mother, without giving it a second thought, had depended on Veera Chittappa to take Ramu's place. His blatant refusal to perform the last rites for my father was unconscionable as far as she was concerned.

It came as no surprise that my grandfather sided with his children and not with my mother. In his eyes, we would forever remain "dirty Americans." His stone-cold demeanor on hearing about the death of my father was very much in character. When all my aunts and uncles unanimously decreed that we move out of his house as soon as possible, I yelled "Good riddance to bad rubbish!"

My mother quickly found a priest who was willing to overlook the sacred thread issue and assist Ramu with the appropriate Vedic chants and mantras that accompanied the death rites for our father. Appa's soul could finally rest in peace. Meanwhile, our lives were in turmoil. We hired packers and crammed the last three years of our lives into a big lorry. We had no choice but to move to our half-finished beach house.

There was yet another nasty encounter on the day we left. Ranga Chittappa, another younger brother of my father's, known for his nasty temper, nearly slapped Ramu because he dared to talk back. My mother came between them in the nick of time, accosted my uncle and screamed, "Don't you ever try to lay a finger on my child again! If he hits you, you won't be able to get up and I will not be responsible for his actions. I will come after you with everything I've got!" Just looking at my mother rally to my brother's defense reminded me of a popular image of the goddess, Kali, dark and violent, each of her four arms carrying a sword, a trident, a severed head and a skull-cup catching the dripping blood.

It was an unceremonious exit. My aunts and uncles slammed shut the main door of the house and peeked through the window bars to make sure we were leaving. The packed lorry had attracted the attention of residents on our street who whispered among themselves in an attempt to find out what had happened. I took a quick glimpse at my neighbors' homes hoping to catch sight of my friends so I could at least wave good-bye. By this time, they had become my best friends. I would miss their company and never forget the role they played in helping me to assimilate when I landed in Madras. I wondered what the neighbors thought about this ignominious display of behavior by my father's siblings. They had often told me how proud the whole street was of my Appa. He was the native son who made good and went far in his career. He rose to the top from humble beginnings and brought pride and prestige to all the Brahmin families here on Mahalakshmi Street. Yet, he never forgot his roots and showed compassion and humility to those less fortunate. Their words would have made for such a fitting obituary.

I thought back to one summer evening, Appa and I sitting on the front stoop after dinner as darkness set in. The daytime cries of the street hawkers were now replaced by the plaintive wails of beggars. "Amma, saatham podu," they pleaded hoping for some leftover rice and curd. The gate creaked open and a young girl, not more than seven or eight years old guided her blind father towards us. She held out an aluminum vessel expectantly. I could see the look of awe on Appa's face as his eyes traveled the length of her tightly braided plait that came down to her ankles. Unlike most of our neighbors, who saw the night beggars as nuisances that needed to be sent away as quickly as possible, Appa was most eager to find out about their lives. This little girl with the long hair intrigued him. Her name was Sivakamasundari, the beloved beauty and consort of Lord Shiva. He was visibly shaken by her plight at losing her mother and the sickness that had left her father blind. After I filled her pot with the evening's leftovers, Appa made her promise to come back the next day. She struck a chord in him. In the years to come, well into my adulthood, that encounter would continue to resonate inside me.

We trailed the lorry, its big tires kicking up the dust and odors of Mahalakshmi Street, spewing them into the air as if they too had had enough of this place. No longer would I have to smell the stink of garbage piled high outside the gate. No more black ugly pigs, rabid stray dogs or scrawny looking cows tussling with one another, as they vied for scraps in the dumpster across the street. I would miss the mango tree and the coconut palms but maybe we could plant new ones, I thought. Our car, a new blue Fiat, twisted and turned through the narrow streets dodging cows, rickshaws, and pedestrians chatting in the middle of the road. Before I knew it the vast expanse of Marina Beach lay bare in the scorching heat of the midday sun. A few scattered fishermen huts dotted the pristine shoreline. The cool waters of the Bay of Bengal beckoned invitingly, masking its treacherous undertow. By evening, caste and class would mingle as everyone sought respite during the hottest time of year when temperatures soared above 100 degrees Fahrenheit. Brightly colored kites waved their tails in the sky while young boys played cricket below. Vendors hawked cotton candy, salted peanuts, ribbons and bangles. No one dared swim. Rumor had it there were sharks in the water. A few gingerly dips, toes only, was as safe as it got. Maybe now, we could have a family outing at the beach since we would be living nearby. But, then again, it dawned on me that family outings were a rarity. Appa was always away. Amma was always left to manage things and my brothers and I had to find ways to amuse ourselves. On a few occasions, my aunt Sasi, the youngest of Amma's siblings, would cajole her into letting me go to the Marina. She relented but not without issuing a string of precautions:

"Make sure Vasu does not wander off. There are all kinds of rowdies on the beach. Do not buy her any food there. It's unclean and she'll wind up with a stomach ache."

Once we turned on to South Beach Road it was hard to imagine we were still in Madras. The normal bustle of the city turned eerily quiet and there was an air of seclusion surrounding the stately homes that lined the street. There were hardly any people around save for the Nepalese Gurkhas, the watchmen, who stood at attention in their crisply starched khaki uniforms outside the tall wrought iron gates. Towering well-trimmed hedges flanked the entrance to the driveway. Shiny brass name plates identified the occupants and the "Beware of Dog" signs deterred any would-be trespassers. Our neighbors were rich and famous and included the Rajah of Chettinad, a well-known philanthropist and educator, and Mr. R. Venkatraman, a Gandhian activist, now Minister of Industries who would later become President of India.

In stark contrast, our plot of land was dry and parched despite the verdant surroundings. Nothing could be planted in this blistering heat. We had no driveway to speak of. Stacks of red brick and piles of mosaic stone lay in heaps. I noticed the lovely balcony off what would have been my father's bedroom where one could see the Bay of Bengal in the distance. A shaded portico on the side, led to the front door. Dust and painters cloth greeted us as we stepped inside. It would be a while before this house became a home. This was a posh area with a fancy address, but we were neither fancy nor posh. If only Appa were alive. His name, T.G.Narayanan, would have been etched in brass, like the others. We might have had a watchman too, someone to open and close the gate. There might have been tables set up on the lush green lawn where local intellectuals would be invited to dine and converse on the political events of the day. As things stood now, we were anonymous. Nothing set us apart, not even a compound wall.

An early riser, I often stood on the balcony, squinting hard to see the bay my father so loved. I had seen him poring over the blueprints exclaiming with joy that he would now see the sun set and rise on the waters. The sea breeze felt cool in the stillness of the morning. In a few hours, the harsh rays of the sun would beat down upon us mercilessly. I, at long last, had my own room having shared one with Ranga all these years. It was on the first landing to the right at the top of the stairs. My brothers' rooms were adjacent to mine while my mother's room was downstairs. The house was not in too bad a shape, better than I had expected. We still had no running water but fortunately, there was a bore well in the backyard. Brightly colored tesserae paved the floors and the mosaic felt cool in the heat of day. The living room was spacious, airy, with lots of light filtering through the glass paned windows. My mother's bedroom had almirahs, built-in closets, made of teak, as did ours. They were a great storage place for all our clothes and knick-knacks. There were attached bathrooms for each bedroom, a real convenience, compared to the single bathroom we shared upstairs in my grandfather's house. There was a large inner courtyard also paved in mosaic with a lovely skylight. We had two dining rooms, one for eating Indian style seated on the floor, and the other for eating Western style seated around a dining table. Our more traditional-minded friends and relatives loved to sit and have their meals on banana leaves. Using their right hand — the left hand was taboo — they would slurp the liquid rasam and sambar with much gusto, something that was hard to do with flatware. According to them, this was the best and only way to relish a good South Indian meal. There was in all likelihood much truth to what they said but my brothers and I, who had never mastered the technique of sitting cross-legged on the floor, were thrilled to eat at the table. I was reminded of our dining room in Queens and how we loved being a family whenever my father was with us. In fact, most of the furnishings of our New York apartment had been shipped to Madras and held in storage. Amma had packed up her past and given it a new life on South Beach Road.

And she, too, seemed to have undergone some kind of a transformation. Always a stay at home mother, she now informed us that she was planning to attend Madras University to pursue a degree in Library Science. She expected us to be responsible when she was in school.

"But, Amma, you already have a degree in Psychology. The one you got in New York at Queens College," I said.

" Vasu, that's of no use here. I counseled children from broken homes there but here in Madras we don't have such problems. I need a degree that can land me a job," she explained.

" But Amma, going to school at your age, won't you be out of place?" I asked, fearing she'd be ridiculed.

"Maybe. I know it's not like America where anyone can go to school at any age but I'm going to do it," she said, her voice filled with conviction.

Her determination should not have taken me by surprise. After all, here was a woman who in 1947 had been suddenly uprooted from humble beginnings in India and forced to make a life in America by way of marriage. With an absentee husband, she had no choice but to acquire the skills required of suburban living. She rode the subways amidst the glares of fellow passengers who had never seen an Indian woman in a sari with a dot on her forehead and a diamond nose ring; she took driving lessons and would hitch up her sari as she pressed the clutch of our Austin stick shift; she drove us to Jones Beach for a picnic with friends and to Connecticut for an outdoor barbecue; she formed a bridge club with other UN wives; she played poker late into the night after hosting a traditional South Indian dinner for fellow diplomats. Whereas my mother might have appeared as two disparate selves to the outside world, I saw her as a unique blend of both worlds. She possessed an innate instinct to survive. Why would it be any different now?

Yet, in one key respect, it was different. After the sudden move to India and the — at times — difficult process of assimilation, along with the onset of puberty, I had my mother all to myself. After all the drama and chaos of the past few months, she was now free of her obligations as a daughter-in-law and with Appa's passing, sadly free of her obligations as a wife. The intimacy of a mother-daughter relationship that had long been denied me and for which I craved, could at long last begin to take root.

I often plopped, belly down, on her bed as she emerged from her bath, almost naked, but for the thin cotton towel she swore was more absorbent than any of those foreign terry towels and less itchy too. I took a strange delight in watching her dress wondering if the budding contours of my body turn out like hers. She struggled with her heavy breasts, coaxing and kneading them into the pointy cups of her Naidu Hall bra, and let out a huge sigh once she was hooked up. An ugly scar from a long ago hysterectomy marred the milkiness of her skin. Amma never wore panties and I lacked the courage to ask her why. Once she had tied the petticoat around her waist, and put on her choli, she unraveled a deep maroon sari with gold swans on its border. I counted eight pleats as she pirouetted in front of the mirror, making sure her pallu was the right length. Her beautiful, long, silky hair, jet black, with no signs of gray was swept up into a chignon. A dab of Cuticura powder to her face, followed by a light trace of kajal applied to the lower rims of her pussy cat brown eyes and a small black bindi, completed her make up. Her big diamond earrings, too big for her thin ear lobes and her small diamond nose ring glinted in the morning sun. The favorite fragrance, Chanel No. 5 wafted through the air as she spritzed herself and as if an after thought, turned around and spritzed me too. She looked just as beautiful as the evening before Appa died.

As if seeking my approval, she said, "I'm not supposed to wear a bindi after your father's gone. Widows are not allowed."

"Oh, Amma," I said, "there's nothing wrong in wearing one. It's so small anyway and you can hardly see it. Besides who cares what people say?"

"You know, Vasu," she replied, "your father's brothers and sisters think I'm too forward, too bold. One of them apparently saw me driving with my sunglasses on and spread a rumor that I'm behaving like a modern woman and have no shame. If they think I should only wear white and shave my head, they are sorely mistaken. I think it's such a barbaric custom. Why should a widow be made to look ugly? Isn't it enough punishment to lose one's husband?"

"Amma, why do they shave the woman's head?" I asked.

"If she's ugly, she won't attract a man. In our custom, widows cannot get married again though the law says they can. It's all utter nonsense to me," she replied angrily.

I absorbed what she said in silence. Her air of defiance and progressive thinking fostered a sense of hope that I, too, would one day, sooner rather than later, become an independent modern young woman. I soon discovered that what I had hoped for myself was not what my mother had hoped for me.

The vigilance she exercised in my early childhood, continued unabated. The desolate surroundings and lack of means to hire a watchman put her on edge. She feared I would be easy prey for the young men who often loitered by the roadside. Her fear was further compounded when she had taken on a young male to be our live-in cook. In this regard, she had given in to tradition. Female cooks of menstruating age were rarely hired as they were thought to be unclean and polluted during that time of the month and hence barred from entering the kitchen. These periodic absences (literally and temporally), made running a kitchen difficult. Orthodoxy and necessity gave added value to male cooks in one arena, but for families with young daughters, the sheer fact that they were men implied a sexual threat. My mother's solution was to make sure I was never alone in the house; my brothers became my chaperones.

She had little to fear. Our cook reeked of body odor a mile away that I often gagged in his proximity. I kept my distance out of choice. However, an incident occurred, though amusing to me on its recounting, that seriously distressed my mother. While I was in college, she had come home unexpectedly and caught the cook and the maidservant locked in embrace on her Castro-Convertible couch. "What's going on here? What are you two up to?" she demanded to know. They hurriedly adjusted their clothing and cowered in shame. Amma issued a stern warning to the cook, "Better be careful. She belongs to the fisherman's family close by. If they catch you with her, they'll come after you with a machete!" "And you," she said turning to the maid,

"What if he gets you pregnant? What will you tell your family? He's a Brahmin, you are a Sudra, do you think these two castes can ever join together in marriage? Haven't they already picked a boy for you." Her ire up, she delivered a final salvo, " You have some cheek lying on my sofa. It's from America, I'll have you know. Is this the only place you could find to do your nonsense? I may not be able to control your urges, but don't ever lie on my sofa again!" Unsparing and harsh, she fired them on the spot.

At times like these, my mother baffled me. The very idea of hiring a menstruating cook chafed at her sensibilities and evoked, I suspected, a certain repulsion in her. Yet, she sported a cavalier attitude in her refusal to wear the mantle of Hindu widowhood. Once our cook revealed himself in flagrante delicto as a sexualized being, she was hell-bent on protecting my chastity within the four walls of our home. The world outside, however, presented a different story.

A long and lonely stretch of road lay between my home and the bus stand. There was only one bus, 21B, that traveled the route to my college. I was attending Stella Maris College and had enrolled in the Pre-University Science and Math program, commonly referred to as PU 1, and dreamed to become the next Marie Curie. This was fueled in part by our all-women's institution, where the nuns never hesitated to tell us that we could all become "stars of the sea," if we put our minds to it. I was also encouraged to pursue my dream by a trio of female teachers in Math, Physics and Chemistry, who through their own brilliance, exemplified the best of their profession. Saturday was lab day where we empirically tested the various physics and chemistry laws taught to us during the weekly lecture periods. Not quite my forte, I was grateful that these lab sessions ended by noon. The timing synchronized perfectly with my catching the 21B bus to get back home. If I missed this bus, it would be a long and rather unpleasant wait for the next one given the scorching heat.

It was one such Saturday afternoon that I alighted from the bus and started my walk towards home when an army jeep with four men dressed in khakis and red berets careened towards me and came to an abrupt stop. Before I could catch my breath, one of the men jumped out, his eyes all bloodshot, slurring his words as he approached me saying, "Hey sweetheart, how about we give you a lift." I reeled at the smell of his breath. It reminded me of the detestable odor of hospital antiseptic and I began to panic. I looked around hoping to catch a glimpse of someone, anyone, a passer-by, maybe even one of the watchmen up the road, but there was no one. The usual hustle-bustle of the morning crowds near the bus stand did not last long. At this hour in the afternoon, it was completely deserted. The heat was its peak. It was the perfect time for an afternoon siesta. No one in their right mind would be out at this hour and these men were definitely not in their right minds. As the others egged him on, the foul smelling army guy grabbed my arm and tried to drag me into the jeep. My screams rented the air as I pried loose of his grasp and started running towards some huts a short distance away. I did not look back. Drenched in fear, I crouched under a thatched roof and looked furtively in the direction of the jeep. The rapid beating in my heart began to slow down when I saw the jeep had left. I had decided to wait a while just to be sure, when out of nowhere, an old man stood before me. "What's wrong Amma?" he asked using a polite form of address reserved for the upper class. His age and air of kindness imbued a sense of trust and I mumbled, "Men in a jeep, tried to grab me. I live up the road across Minister Venkataraman's house." If there was ever a time to cash in on the renown of my neighbors, it was now. Just mentioning his name made me feel more secure. "Sit, Amma, sit. Everything will be alright. You can leave in a little while," he said in a comforting tone. Whether out of deference or as someone who was wise to the ways of the world, he asked me no questions.

I hastened towards home. My mind, now in instant replay mode, kept harkening to the old man. I had passed his hut and others like it every day and never gave a thought to the people who lived there. Most likely, they were Sudras, members of a lower caste, stereotypically described as unruly, dirty and deliberately belligerent from what I had been told by my aunt and uncle when I first arrived. They had gone to great lengths to shield me from any contact with them by acting as constant chaperones. I was aware of their existence but was far removed from their world. I never imagined their lives, only my own. Until now, I had blithely dismissed the perniciousness of the caste system and felt deeply ashamed.

I was relieved that my Amma wasn't home yet. It gave me time to scrub down my arms, particularly the spot where the man had grabbed me and to vigorously brush my teeth to expurgate any vestiges of his foul smelling breath. I heard the familiar sound of the Fiat as it pulled up under the portico. I slowly descended the stairs, my heart in my mouth. What, if anything, should I say to Amma?

"How did your lab class go?" she asked. The brave front I had managed to put on up to now collapsed, as the events of the afternoon unfolded, punctuated by my sobs. Amma stood stiffly, hands by her side, silently staring at me. "Was it just your arm he grabbed? Did he do anything else?" she asked with a sense of urgency. "No, Amma, just my arm. He smelled bad too," I replied. "From now onwards, I'll pick you up on Saturdays. No more taking the bus," she said matter-of-factly. We kept the jeep incident a secret. On my part, I had no wish to relive what had happened. Amma, however, had her own reasons. Though I didn't know what they were at the time, I came to understand much later that Amma was afraid that if word got out that I had been accosted by a group of men, rumor and innuendo would eventually follow and my virginity would undoubtedly be called into question. This would effectively dash any hopes of finding a suitable boy for marriage. I would be labelled spoiled goods.

I lay in bed that night, staring at the ceiling, unable to sleep, a prisoner of my own thoughts. I wanted to go downstairs and cuddle up next to Amma but couldn't push myself to make it to the door. My mind flashed back to the brazen young boy in Parkway who had pulled me into the bushes and had tried to rip off my panties. I remembered the aftermath — the sting of the hot bath water, the aloofness of my mother, and her stern admonition to get clean. There was little difference in her stance then and now. The male predation she had fought hard to shelter me from, had twice insinuated itself into my life and hers. Her response, the only one she could muster, was to keep silent and continue living. Compassion and empathy did not come easily to Amma. It was a realization that hit me with a greater force than I had anticipated. To yearn for a more intimate mother-daughter relationship was self-defeating. The face of the old man in the hut loomed large before me. He became my father. His words, a balm for my troubled soul, lulled me to sleep

Chapter 8

The Bride-Viewing

The jeep incident had many repercussions for me, none of them good. The Saturday bus rides came to a halt. Amma had now made it her mission to pick me up after lab class. One time, however, she said she would be late and at the urging of my classmates, I decided to join them for a quick afternoon snack at a lovely drive-in restaurant, Woodlands, a stone's throw from the college. Famous for their tiffin—an Indianized term for British tea and muffin—it was a popular hangout for college students. It was not uncommon to see the Loyola College boys eye the Stella Maris girls, leering at them lasciviously as they drooled over their hot dosas and puffed puris stuffed with spicy potatoes. They often revved their motorcycles to a deafening roar and circled the girls, their shirts as large as their egos billowing in the breeze. There was never any chit chat; that would have been too cheeky. My friends and I often huddled together giggling at this display of bravado. The more daring among us — there were very few — would taunt the boys by fidgeting with their saris to show off their curves and bare their midriffs. I lacked the temerity to follow suit even as I envied them. With the jeep incident fresh in my mind, I could not afford to tarnish my reputation no matter how much I wanted to be noticed by a boy, any boy.

Amma was increasingly on the phone with her brother, my Uncle Raghu, and I couldn't help but overhear snippets of their conversation, mostly in Tamil, with the occasional English thrown in. "Thank God, she is OK. Vasu is very naive. She knows nothing. She is very sheltered. This place is too deserted. Maybe I'll move closer to her college in the city," I heard her say. I bristled when she referred to me in Tamil as ashadu, a person who was foolishly or stupidly naive. Why couldn't she have told my uncle how savvy I was in escaping the clutches of those military men? What about my presence of mind in running towards the huts for protection? Surely, these were not the acts of an ashadu. The very idea that we might move again after barely three months in our new home dampened my spirits.

Under Amma's ever expanding watchful eye, I sought sanctuary in the privacy of my bedroom. I delved into my school books determined to ace my exams and escaped vicariously into the romance novels of Denise Robins and Georgette Heyer. The plots followed a similar trajectory, the outcomes unfailingly predictable. Nevertheless, the exploits of the heroines on their tortuous path to true love and their devil-may-care attitude appealed to me. An air of triumph pervaded these novels which to some extent assuaged my sense of defeat. My favorite radio program, Listener's Choice, aired every Saturday night. It brought back memories of Dick Clark's American Bandstand when I heard Bobby Darin's "Splish Splash I Was Taking a Bath." His recent hit, "Multiplication," from the about to be released movie, "Come September," starring Rock Hudson and Gina Lollobrigida was number one on the charts. I was dying to see the movie. Madras was plastered with billboards showing a scantily clad Gina Lollobrigida in a tight embrace with Rock Hudson. It was a raunchy image, too raunchy to gain Amma's consent.

My life, choreographed and circumscribed by my mother, was in a word, monotonous. There was an occasional respite when Amma's siblings dropped by on Sunday afternoons, usually unannounced. Few people had phones and even if they did, it was customary to drop in without notice. It was a safe bet to assume that on most Sundays one could find families at home. Amma's younger sister, Sasi Chitti, usually came by with my Uncle Raghu who was visiting Madras from Delhi. They ogled the house, its airy rooms, mosaic floors, the fancy grill work framing the windows and its proximity to the beach. They eschewed our Castro- Convertible preferring to sit on the floor as they drank their afternoon coffee. They looked at me and chuckled, "Vasu, you have come of marriageable age. It is good to be settled when you are young. It's so beautiful to be married at a young age." I laughed away their remarks and told them how much I loved chemistry and how I was going to be the next Marie Curie. "If you study too much, it will go to your head and it's bad for your health too," my aunt replied. She had been married off right after finishing high school and I wondered if her remarks merely echoed what she had been told by her own parents. All this badinage left me uneasy as if something portentous was brewing in their coffee tumblers.

Sure enough, as July approached with the threat of the monsoon close on its heels, my mother uttered a simple declarative sentence, "It's time to get you married." Just like that. No fanfare, no easing me into a conversation, no explanation except to say, "Your dad died suddenly. God knows how long I'll live. If something happens to me, you'll be at the mercy of our relatives. There is no guarantee they will find a suitable boy for you. Better to arrange your marriage while I am alive." I couldn't believe what I had just heard. Had I not done what I was told? The anger that had been simmering within me erupted. I lashed out, "I'll study and get a job. I'll be independent. If Appa were alive he would have never agreed to this. He wanted me to study at the Sorbonne. What about my school? My education?" My mother's pragmatic nature kicked in and in an attempt to comfort me she replied, "I'll make sure the boy allows you to get a college degree. I'll make it a condition of the marriage proposal." The assurance in her voice did little to hearten me. I took a good, hard look at my mother, the plight she was in, and felt torn between my concern for her welfare as well as my own; I did not want to see her suffer more than she already had and I told her softly, my voice filled with resignation, "Do what you have to do."

Later that evening in the quiet of my room, I cried for my father, feeling cheated by the promises he had made to me and by the ones I had made to myself. Edgy and restless, I scanned my bookshelf and pried out Georgette Heyer's, "The Convenient Marriage." How apropos I said to myself as I turned to a dog-eared page and read on. There was poor Horatia pinned in a tight embrace by the cad, Lethbridge, struggling to free herself. The lace of her corsage rips and she kicks hard at his foot. "Gad, you little spitfire!" he laughs, "Damme, I believe I shan't let you go back to that dull husband of yours after all." Despite her protestations, he had locked the door, the key tucked away in his pocket. I quickly glanced at the last line on the page, "I wish," said Horatia forcefully, "you would stop talking about l-love. It makes me feel sick."

I decided to live in silence as much as possible, speaking only when spoken to. This was my only defense. My life did not seem to be my own. I had no idea if proposals were coming in. Whatever arrangements or machinations my mother hatched were solely her own. I saw no point in seeking comfort in my brothers. Ranga was too young to understand what I was going through and Ramu was too preoccupied with his friends to give me the time of day. I decided to confide in my best friend, Viji, who had also joined Stella Maris after graduating from Good Shepherd Convent. I told her about my mother's plans to get me married soon.

"Viji, I'm so sad. I want to study. Remember how we talked about changing the world. I wish my Appa were alive. He was going to take me to Geneva with him and enroll me at the Sorbonne in Paris. I would be close enough to visit him often. Now, I don't know what's going to happen to me," I said despondently.

Viji put her arm around me and said softly, "Maybe they'll pick a nice boy who will let you continue your education. I'm sure my parents will do the same thing to me. I'm hoping they'll wait till I finish college. You know how it is in our Brahmin tradition. There's nothing we can do about it."

"Do you remember Vishalakshi and Meyammai from our Good Shepherd Days?" I replied. " They were married when we were all in fifth form together, hardly fourteen years old. Look what happened to them. They never even went to college."

"That's the Chettiar way. In that community the elders want to make sure the girls marry young so they won't stray. They are very rich and want to make sure the money stays in the family so they often choose a boy who is a relative. This keeps them close-knit. Be grateful that our Brahmin community is not as strict, " Viji said, as if my only choice lay with the lesser of these two evils. I had wanted her as an ally, one who would egg me into rebellion or at least give me a way out. Her conciliatory tone and sense of complacency both irked and baffled me. Had she forgotten those lunchtime conversations not that long ago when we spoke about being independent career women? Did we not proclaim ourselves to be daughters of a new India? Did Viji now believe that a college education was nothing more than a pit stop en route to marriage? Was it wrong of me to think I wanted something more to my life?

My sixteenth birthday was coming up when Amma announced, "I have a proposal from the family of a boy. His uncle actually asked about you right after your father died but at the time I told him I had no intention of marrying you off. It's been a year now and he approached me again. I told him I would consider it. The boy's an only child, studying mathematics in Calcutta. Fortunately, your Uncle Gidi, (one of Amma's younger brothers), living as he does in Calcutta, was able to make some inquiries about him. Apparently, he is a very good boy. No bad habits. He does not smoke or drink and has never had any girl in his life. They say he is very brilliant and will go far. In fact, his father is my mother's cousin though I have not seen his family in many years. The only thing is they are a bit orthodox but I'm sure you can manage."

She sounded convinced that this was the right boy for me. Except for these traits, which had been reeled off as if from a checklist, there was no mention of his looks or even his name. I mentally reiterated his good characteristics and strained to no avail to picture this man who might very well wind up being my husband. I was drowning in a maelstrom of emotions. A part of me was flattered to have been chosen as a prospective bride, yet, there was something daunting about becoming someone's wife at such a young age, especially when I knew next to nothing about this someone. I asked myself what, if anything, did the boy's family know about me. Did they have their own checklist of my traits?

I couldn't wait to see Viji at college and tell her my big news.

"He's coming to see me in a few weeks. I wonder what he looks like. Hope he's not fat or bald or anything. He's in mathematics, an only child. His parents are orthodox but Amma says we might go to America after marriage and I won't have to bother about them. I wonder what he'll think of me. I'm so nervous. I'll have to figure out what to wear. Maybe a new sari?"

Viji began to tease me, "Now, you have a boyfriend. You sound like you're in love already. Maybe he'll sweep you off your feet like those chaps in the romance novels."

"It's not at all like that," I protested feebly though I secretly wished for everything she said to come true. I also wanted my own dreams to come true.

The date for the bride-viewing had been fixed. It was a hot Sunday in early August with nearly a hundred percent humidity, typical pre-Monsoon weather for Madras. Amma had asked the boy and his parents to come over at 3:00 pm for what was commonly called SKC. S stood for something sweet, K was for karam, a Tamil term for savory and spicy food and C was short-hand for coffee. It was the standard fare for afternoon tiffin. We had not replaced our recently fired cook so it was left to Amma to take charge of the kitchen. She started on the Rava Kesari, a sweet concoction of cream of wheat with lots of cashew nuts and clarified butter. Next she boiled and mashed the potatoes adding a few spices along with some chopped ginger and finely minced green chiles. She shaped little balls with the mixture and kept them ready. Just before serving, they would be rolled in chickpea flour and deep fried until golden. The bondas, or vegetable fritters, tasted best when eaten hot. Amma possessed a hidden talent when it came to brewing coffee. She used the same roaster for the raw beans as she did in New York and ground them in the same Lovelock machine that had been nailed to the wall in our kitchen. Her coffee came out perfect each and every time and had earned her quite a reputation both here in Madras and in New York. With the SKC out of the way, she turned her attention towards me.

Amma, as usual, had decided beforehand what I should wear. She insisted on the half-sari, a style normally reserved for girls once they had reached puberty and of the type I wore soon after my arrival. I, however, had envisioned myself draped in a lovely silk sari, the entire six yards, to give me a more mature appearance. I knew better than to question Amma's decision and could only speculate on her motive. Did her preference echo an ambivalence within? Was Amma trying to tell the groom that I was still a child who would eventually blossom into a bride? Was she afraid to see her little girl become a woman in one quantum leap? The three o'clock hour was fast approaching and by now, my nerves had got the better of me.

She laid out a beautiful dark magenta colored pavadai , flecked with gold threads woven into a checkered pattern, a matching velvet magenta blouse and a lighter magenta colored half-sari on my bed. "This is what I want you to wear," she said. She opened a jewelry case with a gold necklace, a pair of gold bangles, and gold earrings adding, "These will match perfectly."

I dabbed a lot of talcum powder under my armpits to absorb as much of the sweat as possible. I put on the dark velvet blouse and realized too late that ugly white rings had begun to form. I'll just keep my hands by my side, I said to myself and hope no one would notice. I finished dressing and chafed at the weight of the necklace and the bangles. I was so used to wearing nothing more than a pair of earrings to college. I brushed a little powder over my face, lined my eyes with kohl, and pasted a maroon bindi on my forehead. Satisfied with my appearance, I sought out my mother for her seal of approval. She looked right past me, a vacant stare in her eyes and said, "Make sure you don't get dirty or wrinkle your clothes before they arrive." Crestfallen by her response, I wondered what I had to do to get Amma to say I looked nice.

The living room clock, a memento from Dad's Geneva days, ushered in the three o'clock hour with its melodic Westminster chimes. I looked out the window for any sign of the boy and his parents. I sat on one sofa and then another afraid to cross my legs in case I rumpled my skirt. I fidgeted with the pleats of my half-sari making sure they were well-creased and perfectly aligned. I took a quick look under my armpits and saw that the white rings had increased in circumference. I practiced walking with my arms at my side like a soldier. It was now nearing 4 o'clock and still no sign of the groom's party. I began to nag Amma who assured me with great certainty that they would arrive before 4:30. "It's Rahu Kalam between 4:30-6:00 pm on Sundays," she explained. "It's an inauspicious time and as orthodox Brahmins, they will not arrive during this period for such a momentous occasion. You wait and see, they'll be here any minute." I tried to remain calm. It was 4:15 and I prayed our clock was fast.

I heard the dreadful chimes signaling it was 4:30 and started to panic. What if they came during Rahu Kalam? Would I be doomed from the start? I stared at the clock as it pealed five times, a harbinger of bad tidings. Angry and frustrated, I told Amma I was going to change out of my clothes. It was bloody hot and humid to boot. The white rings had now turned into big white circles. My body freighted with jewelry, my mind heavy with doubt, I ran for the shower. The water, refreshingly cold, cascaded over my thoughts. Maybe I was not good enough for the boy. If so, they could have at least called, but maybe they didn't have a phone. I scrubbed myself clean till every vestige of make-up disappeared down the drain. I slipped into a printed turquoise nylon sari, put a small black bindi on my forehead and breathed easy for the first time that day, glad to be rid of all the trappings. I bounced down the stairs and no sooner did I hear the six o'clock chimes, our doorbell rang. The groom had arrived.

Amma shoved me hastily into her bedroom and snatched my glasses whispering hurriedly that boys don't make passes at girls who wear glasses, an adage she had heard in America, and for some reason believed to be true. Devoid of any jewelry save for the gold earrings and clad in a nylon sari, not even a silk one, proved to be an embarrassment to my mother. She had wanted to show off our status by parading me in all this finery. But it was too late to rectify the situation. I dabbed a little powder on my face at her urging and muttered to her, "Better he sees me as I am. I can't always be dressed up for him. Besides they're late." With a look of hopelessness and helplessness, she scurried to attend to our guests. Ranga, and sometime confidant, decided to be my eyes and ears. "I'll take a close look at him since you're blind without your glasses and tell you everything," he said officiously. Unlike, Ramu, who was out cavorting with his friends, Ranga had taken a keen interest in the bride-viewing ceremony. I could trust him to tell me the truth.

Everything was a blur as I squinted behind the half-ajar door, of Amma's bedroom. The boy, seated on the sofa, was a disappointing blob of flesh. Ranga, who was flitting in and out of the room, told me he had come with his aunt and uncle and not his parents. No one knew why. I pleaded with Ranga, "Get close and tell me what he looks like. Look at his eyes. See if he smiles. See if his teeth are straight. See if he smells or has B.O." It was all I could think to ask at that moment. Ranga returned a few minutes later, only to announce rather tersely that the groom looked nice and seemed kind. I wanted to pester him further but there was no time.

Amma came up to me and said it was time to serve them the SKC. She had kept the batter ready to fry up the bondas, the Kesari was warming over a double-boiler, and the coffee had been brewed. I rushed past the boy, keeping my head down all the way to the kitchen, where everything had been laid out on a gleaming silver tray. The Rava Kesari oozed with ghee in the silver katoris; the potato bondas, crispy and warm with a side of coconut chutney were neatly arranged on the stainless steel tiffin plates and the aroma of Amma's coffee filled the silver tumblers. I gave myself a quick once-over and adjusted my sari to make sure it was modestly draped and tucked the pallu into my waist to keep it in place. I steadied my hands as much as possible as I carried the tray to the living room. As I offered the SKC, I quickly glanced upward at the boy and our eyes met for a fleeting moment. Just as quickly, I glanced down and skittered back to Amma's room.

With the SKC out of the way, my role in the bride-viewing ritual was over. I beamed with pride for having followed the proper etiquette, something Amma had never bothered to teach me, but had gleaned from watching countless Tamil movies. Acting demure, modestly attired, with her head down except for that sly peek at the groom, I had emulated the performance to perfection. I could only hope, like in the movies, it would be met with approval.

The groom's party was about to leave when Amma offered them a ride to the train station. They lived in Tambaram, twenty miles away on the outskirts of Madras. When she asked me to come along, I was taken aback. Did Amma think this brief encounter was perhaps too brief even for her? Would buying a little more time really make a difference? Newly widowed, bereft of the counsel of my father, she was taking a huge step and could not afford to falter.

My glasses back on, I could now get a closer look at the groom. He, however, sat in the front seat with Amma as it would have been improper to seat us together in the back seat where we might come into physical contact. All I could do was marvel at the nape of his neck and his healthy shock of hair. I was dying to hear his voice but everyone was strangely quiet in the car so I peered out the window and felt the eyes of his aunt and uncle boring into me. We arrived at the station and Amma bid them a quick good-bye. I merely nodded my head in their direction and said nothing. The event had gone off without a single word being exchanged between the boy and me.

There was an uncomfortable silence between my mother and me as we drove home. I wanted to tell her that the boy wasn't bad looking, though a bit chubby, and that I had sensed in him a kind temperament, but I didn't know how to begin. I had never opened up to Amma in the past; she was simply not the type to sit down for a heart-to heart talk. Emotions were for weak-minded people. Sentimentality was a hindrance when things needed to get done. This was pretty much how she had survived most of her life. Still, I felt a need to say something and settled on an innocuous question as to why the boy's parents did not accompany him. The boy's uncle, his father's brother, had apparently been asked to initiate contact with my mother whom he had known in her youth.

"I'm fond of Gopal Mamma, his uncle," she said. "When I was young, I ran away to his house," she continued. "Your grandfather, my father, you see, did not want me to go to college. He felt I was getting old, though I was barely twenty, and wanted to marry me off. But I wanted a college education so I ran away to Gopal Mamma's house hoping he would protect me. And he did. My father came after me but Gopal Mamma convinced him to let me study and stay with him. Without his help, I would have never gone to college. I have a soft spot for him which is probably why he came along."

These nuggets from Amma's past related at the most unexpected moments made her more human in my eyes. It allowed for a measure of empathy to creep into our relationship, a rare occurrence. She had shown great resolve in fighting for her education and it gave me hope that she would fight with a similar tenacity for my college education.

Ranga was all aflutter when we got home. "You've got a cute guy," he cried out. "He's fair and handsome and has a Rock Hudson hairstyle!" That the boy could be compared to the latest heart-throb of my generation made the prospect of marrying him even more inviting.

Later, in a quieter moment, Amma asked," So, Vasu, what did you think of the boy? Do you like him?"

Her question, its tenor, the first of its kind to be ever asked of me, left me tongue-tied.

Amma, totally out of character, was making a concerted effort to tap into my emotions, to give me a chance to tell her what I really thought. I should have seized the opportunity to pour out my feelings, my fears, my hopes, but I didn't know how. This was a new type of conversation that demanded a new kind of vocabulary that was far beyond my ken. Ill-equipped to say anything of substance, I lamely answered, "He's a bit fat Amma."

" Oh, is that all? He can diet and all will be fine," she answered flippantly, brushing aside my concern.

"Let's see what his side says. He's a good catch, very smart," she added, hoping to dispel any reluctance on my part.

I retreated by habit into a world of fantasy. I dreamt about the boy, a mere stranger, with eyes that seemed kind in that fleeting glance. I dressed him in a nice suit, instead of the rumpled shirt and baggy pants he wore. I traded in his plain looking glasses for classy Ray-bans. I sculpted him into an Adonis without a trace of flab and, as I drifted off, I made a mental note to ask Amma tomorrow what his name was.

The next day I gave Viji a blow by blow account of the bride-viewing.

"His name's Raghu and he's a bit chubby but has such kind eyes and nice eyebrows. Amma doesn't know I've told you about all this bride-viewing stuff so keep it a secret. She says that if the arrangement doesn't go through, people will talk and think it's my fault and that perhaps there's something wrong with me," I told her in hushed tones.

"It's his loss, if he says no," she replied. "Where will he get a girl like you, foreign-returned and all? You know our customs and put up with all those orthodox traditions when you lived with your grandfather. How many girls who lived in America will be like that? Girls here who have never stepped outside India act hoity-toity and put on airs and phony accents. You are not at all like them," Viji exclaimed.

The idea that I was a good catch had never occurred to me. It was always the boy's credentials that were on display. The bride was to be merely viewed, a tabula rasa, empty of content. Why couldn't Amma see me through Viji's eyes? Why did we have to wait for approval from the boy's side?

Gratefully, the wait was a short one. Within a few weeks, the boy's side agreed to the match, leaving matters such as the actual date of the wedding and my dowry — which I knew nothing about — to be negotiated later on. The arrangement was semi-formal, a tacit agreement between his family and mine that the wedding would take place the next year, sometime in

June, 1964, as the boy would be leaving for the United States in September. I learned much later that his father, fearful that he might succumb to the wiles of an American girl, wanted his son anchored to India. Our engagement would seal his fate and my own.

Chapter 9

Courtship

Now that a year of mourning was over, arrangements were made for Ramu's sacred thread ceremony, his Upanayanam. Amma felt that such an auspicious and festive event would usher in an aura of well-being and good fortune into our new home and to some degree palliate our sorrow over losing Appa. It was also an opportune time to invite the groom and his parents partly as a polite gesture, but mostly, to give Amma's siblings and good friends a chance to scrutinize the groom. Still tentative as to whether she had made the right choice, she was looking for assurance. None of this mattered to me. I was excited to see the groom again and couldn't wait to wear the mauve sari with a contrasting grey and gold border, a gift from my Uncle Raghu. I would be honoring my uncle with this gesture and no longer clad in a half-sari, I could finally present myself in the way I wished to be seen, a young mature woman.

I went up and down our staircase on some pretext or another hoping Raghu would catch sight of me and I of him amidst the throng of people. He was in deep conversation with a friend of the family who happened to have been a classmate of his. I stared at him directly for the first time which made him uncomfortable. He quickly lowered his face out of embarrassment. I suppressed a smile and scooted off to attend to our guests until the festivities came to a close. Except for acknowledging their presence with a quick namaste, no words passed between me and his parents nor between me and Raghu. Having met his parents for the first time, I wondered what they thought of me. Was I pretty? Pretty enough for their son? Had I acted modestly or had they noticed how I had flitted around hoping to catch the eye of their son? Would they have frowned upon my behavior? Had I followed the right protocols as a hostess? All I had were questions and no answers. Apart from physical appearances, there was little to no information to judge the content of one's character. His parents appeared old, almost too old, to have a twenty-two year old son. I would find out later that his mother, married at the age of twelve, had had a series of miscarriages after reaching puberty and miraculously, at the age of thirty-five, had managed carried the baby to full term. His father, a good deal older than his mother, was well into his forties at the time. The birth of what would be their only child, my future husband, had been heralded as a boon from the gods, and combined with his extraordinary intelligence, he was hailed as a child prodigy.

His mother's eyes, naturally small and slanted, bulged through her thick-lensed glasses, derisively called "soda bottle" lenses due to their opacity and density. I noticed a white wire dangling over her chest and traced it to a hearing aid in one ear. Her hair, though plentiful, had yellowed with wisps of grey framing her face. She might have been tall in her youth but her body now stooped with age. I noticed that her sari, a deep purple bordered in rich gold, was nine yards long as opposed to the traditional six yards. It was common practice in very orthodox Brahmin households to require all women to wear only nine-yard saris. I recalled Amma adhering to the rule at the behest of my grandfather and wondered if my future in-laws would insist I do the same. As a novice sari wearer, it was complicated enough to master the technique of draping all that material to achieve a modicum of elegance. To handle an additional three yards and also learn an intricate method that involved numerous tucks and pleats would have been a formidable task. Maybe they would make an exception in my case.

The groom's father, whom my mother addressed as Ranga Mamma, appeared hale and hearty compared to the frailty of his mother who shared the same name — Janaki—with my mother. His bespectacled countenance gave him an air of seriousness and it was hard to imagine him smile. Yet, there was a tenderness in the attention he showed his wife. Poor in sight and hard of hearing despite the hearing aid, he clutched her hand tightly as he guided her through the house. He was solicitous about her every need and the closeness between them seemed poignant. It was this very tenderness I had sensed in the groom at the bride-viewing, a demeanor he obviously inherited from his parents and perhaps one I could rely upon to help me negotiate my entry into a new home with a different and — rigid — set of rules.

The night before the groom was due to leave for New York, Gopal Mamma, who had escorted him to the bride-viewing, decided to hold an informal engagement dinner. A meeting of the two families would indicate a tacit agreement that the marriage had been fixed. The more formal engagement ceremony would take place only later, a month or two before the actual wedding, and I was surprised to learn from Amma that the groom did not need to be present. His parents would serve as his representative, my mother as mine. The most important part of their coming together would be the handing over of my dowry which that I, as the bride, would officially become part of the groom's household. When Amma mentioned the dowry part of the ceremony I could not help but bristle at the thought that I was somehow being sold; I pressed her on the matter. However, she dismissed me curtly saying it was a matter between adults and there was no need for me to worry about these things. Months later the question of my dowry would come to the fore but for now I was too giddy with excitement to pursue it further.

As we drove towards Tambaram, about fifteen miles outside the city of Madras, the once urban landscape turned more rural. Thatched huts dotted the roadside and evening fires had been lit for the night's dinner. Children romped in muddy waters where the cows and buffalos quenched their thirst. On the other side, the electric train that connected the city to the outlying areas rattled on the tracks. Overcrowded during the evening rush hour, I saw many of the passengers hanging precariously outside clutching on for dear life.

Tambaram bustled with activity. Rows of fruit and vegetable vendors lined the streets trying to sell the remnants of the day in the glow of kerosene lamps. Raw sewage seeped from the gutters spilling on to the pavement. The eyesores reminded me of Mahalakshmi Street and it depressed me to know that my future in-laws lived in this neighborhood and, that after marriage, I would have to live here too. Fortunately, it wouldn't be for long since we would be moving to New York a few months after the wedding. I had never considered the groom's economic status until now and for the first time I realized his family was of lesser means than we. For some reason it bothered me. I had not forgotten the childhood sermons drummed into me by my father about the vainglories of the wealthy and in recalling them, I felt I had betrayed him by my reaction. Our new home on South Beach Road assumed a palatial grandeur compared to what stood before me — a series of slum dwellings. I had adjusted before and begrudgingly would have to adjust again.

His uncle's house, just one street away from that of my future in-laws, took me by surprise. On the corner of a well-maintained street, it looked recently white-washed and stood out among the other houses whose frontal walls were streaked with water stains the color of mud. A trellis supporting verdant climbing plants framed the entrance. The inner central hall was cool and airy. A long wooden swing, propped up by heavy black chains hooked to the ceiling swayed gently in the breeze. The olive-green tiled floor had been swept clean and felt cool to the touch. Things looked tidy. His aunt and uncle quickly ushered us up a flight of stairs to the roof where we would dine al fresco under the stars. The groom and his parents had arrived early and were waiting. The adults exchanged a few pleasantries while my brothers and I, not knowing where to turn our attention, gathered near the balcony and took in the view under the splendor of a starry summer sky.

We were seated on the cement floor, the two families facing each other, as we ate off the green plantain leaves customary for such occasions. Somewhere from a loudspeaker, probably a corner cafe, a Tamil love song from a current hit movie blared. In a plaintive tone, the woman beseeched her lover, " My dearest, full of benevolence, why are you like a shadow flitting in the moonlight hiding from my eyes? I ache to see you, be with you. You, filled with benevolence, cannot deny my love for you."

As we ate in silence, those lyrics, which I knew by heart, gave voice to my own nascent thoughts about love. I flash-backed to my American Bandstand days and my pre-pubescent fantasies of love which involved nothing more than a desire to dance close with a boy. After moving to India, I had devoured the ever popular British romances—published by Mills and Boon and later acquired by Harlequin— hoping to be whisked away by a knight in shining armor. Then there were the not so happy endings in the many Tamil films I had seen where unrequited love often ended in the death of the hero and heroine. This was countered in the imported Hollywood movies, particularly the Rock Hudson/Doris Day romances, a favorite staple among the audiences, with their discreet allusions to sex which registered in my adolescent-mind as nothing more than a passionate kiss on the lips. All these fantasies collided head-on with some of the stricter aspects of my upbringing and left me straddling two worlds. A part of me wanted to love this man with the Rock Hudson hairstyle, sing him Tamil love songs, dance the Lindy with him, and be swept away to America.

My childhood ended abruptly that August of 1963 and I entered adulthood at the age of sixteen, my future mapped out with exceeding care by my mother. For all intents and purposes there was little for me to complain about. After all, my mother had found a good catch for me, a brilliant young mathematician who had the prospects of a stellar career and in whose care she was willing to entrust her daughter. She had fulfilled her duty beyond reproach. Yet, I felt like a voyeur, an outsider, observing the events in my life as they unfolded, helpless to change anything, and equally unsure of what I would change if I could.

The initial euphoria surrounding the engagement dissipated quickly. Now that I was betrothed, my mother worried more than usual that nothing tarnish my reputation. She was quick to point out that the mere whiff of impropriety could poison the air and derail the arrangement and any blame to be had would be squarely placed at my feet. I did not doubt her. I had seen enough Tamil films to know that women were often seen as the bane of men's existence. Should a woman lose her child or husband to a pre-mature death, it was considered to be her fault. According to the Hindu theory of reincarnation, she must have committed sins in her past life and divine retribution demanded she reap the punishment for those acts in her current life. Amma, herself, would often wail that she was cursed to become a young widow for some grave misdeed in her previous life. The fact that Appa continued to chain smoke after two heart attacks was lost on her. She often said she had suffered enough and wanted to make sure that my life be free of sorrow. It was of paramount importance that my marriage take place without a hitch and with my virtue intact. The risk of another "jeep incident" was too real as long as we lived in this isolated part of town. In October, after barely six months of living in our beach home, Amma of her own accord, rented a house in the city, in a safe neighborhood, where everyone on the street kept an eye out for one another. Once again, we uprooted ourselves just as were settling in and waved a permanent farewell to my father's dream house.

The new house at 23/12 Luz Avenue exuded a charm of its own. A stately mango tree arced the entrance, its bright green leaves brushing lightly against the dark red exterior. Huge sturdy pillars, reminiscent of an older architectural style, propped up the house giving it a palatial air. There was a well in the backyard along with various flora in bright verdant hues. Fairly large, but not overly so, it was able to accommodate private rooms for each of us, and yet maintain a cozy feel. A sit-out balcony off my room upstairs reminded me of our beach house but instead of the vista of the Bay of Bengal, I looked out on the intimate apparel of my neighbors hung out to dry on plastic clotheslines. Bras, petticoats, boxer shorts, jockeys, dhotis, and saris fluttered shamelessly in the breeze.

It was a noisy street with early morning vendors shouting out the prices per kilo of okra, brinjal, beans, tomatoes, and other assorted vegetables. The quietude of the afternoon hours offered some respite before the evening hawkers made their rounds. Around the corner was Nageswara Rao Park with a manicured garden surrounded by hedges sculpted in precise geometric designs. Come evening, weary commuters would stretch out on the park benches and pay a little extra to savor a Rita ice cream bar — a real treat since most people at the time could ill afford a refrigerator. The bus stop was a few minutes walk from our house and Amma no longer felt the need to chaperone me to and fro from college.

My brothers and I quickly adapted to our surroundings that were not entirely new to us. Threads of Amma's history found their way into the fabric of mine. Her parents lived in a small house on nearby Mandavalli Lane, the place where my older brother and I were born. The store where she and Appa bought me my first sari was around the corner. Amma took great delight in taking me shopping at the stores she frequented in her youth. I had my blouses stitched by the tailor she still used, a Muslim gentleman named Zynul, who despite being old, had eyes as sharp as his needle. The best tailors in Madras happened to be Muslims and the majority of their clientele happened to be Hindus, and, despite their political differences, it seemed to be a natural fit. National Leather Works, Amma's favorite shoe store, custom made sandals for both of us. For her maiden trip to America, they had hand-crafted her very first pair of shoes which she forced herself to wear when she encountered snow for the first time. We prayed to Hanuman, the monkey-god, at the temple built in his name. It was here, twenty years ago, soon after her bride-viewing, that Amma had broken one hundred coconuts — an exceedingly high number considering one coconut was the norm — beseeching the god to convince my father to take her as his wife. Her exaggerated behavior had become the stuff of legend in the family lore and, according to her siblings, it was clearly evident that Amma had been swept off her feet after laying eyes on my father. And then there were the sari shops. Sampurna Sastri, home of my first sari, would soon be asked to design my wedding sari. Radha Silk Emporium, with its more upscale contemporary styles, would offer the best selection for the evening reception. Mysore Silk House, famed for its crush-resistant silk crepes would come in handy for travel. All these sari stores had at one time or another clothed my mother, her mother, and now me. Here we were, three generations of women, swaddled together in lustrous silk spun from the same loom.

The travails of the past year were behind us. We came to think of our new home on Luz Avenue as one filled with rasi, good fortune. Amma, who had never had a career, decided to enroll in the Masters program for Library Science hoping to become a professional librarian. Ramu had started engineering college and found a new coterie of friends. Ranga, though at times melancholic at the thought of losing me to marriage, remained my playmate and confidant. He often joined me on Sunday afternoons when we idled the time away with two friends of mine from college who happened to live down the street. Amma had a renewed sense of energy and purpose in her life and began to relax, though not utterly relinquish, her hold on me. I wanted to come into my own and this was possibly a good first step in that direction.

The groom's first letter, dated October 9, 1963, took ten days to arrive from New York. Amma and the boy's father had agreed there would be no harm in getting acquainted through a mutual exchange of letters. An arranged marriage at my tender age of sixteen, with a twenty-two year old groom, was considered early, even by the standards of the time. He and I were virtual strangers. We had never spoken to one another on the few occasions we met and when I went to the airport to see him off, not so much as a smile passed between us. These letters were my only hope of finding out what kind of man he really was.

Amma handed me the letter hoping I would read it in front of her. I stalled; she got the hint and left me alone. With sweaty palms, I fingered the envelope, paying particular attention to his handwriting and was taken aback when I noticed he got my name wrong,. The envelope had been addressed to Miss Vasumati Narayanan instead of Miss Vasundara Narayanan. The error continued in the body of the letter. He had mistakenly assumed Vasumati to be a natural extension of Vasu. How was it he didn't even know my proper name? Had he not thought to ask his parents? I was extremely annoyed — a poor start, I thought to myself, like a racehorse that died at the gate. But then I began to read.

I detected a soft-heartedness between the thin sheets of paper. His thoughts of me kept him company in the aloneness of a big city like New York, he wrote. This was both strange and surprising as he hardly knew me. Then came a flurry of questions: What books did I read? What movies did I like? What hobbies did I have? When was my birthday? Where did I go to school? What subjects did I like? The letter ended with "affectionately, Raghu," a nice closing, nice enough that I mentally forgave him for getting my name wrong.

Amma was curious yet respectful, which prompted me to share his letter with her. I was eager to reply right away and reel out the answers to all his questions but felt stymied as how to address him. I asked Amma if I could write, "Dear Raghu," or maybe just "Dear," omitting the name. Would a "My" before the "dear," be too forward? Too possessive? What might have appeared simple and straightforward under ordinary circumstances became a tad more complicated when it came to the proper forms of address in Tamilian culture.

A wife was never to call her husband by name (though not vice versa) in public particularly within earshot of any elders who might be present. It would be considered disrespectful and also indicate that both sexes were on an equal footing. This was unacceptable in a culture where women were expected to be subservient to men. I never knew this as a rule per se, but had witnessed enough encounters between my parents to realize that I had never heard Amma directly address Appa as Narayanan. She often inquired about his well-being by saying in Tamil, "Yenna Na, ippidi irakal?"; the Na, having no definition as such but serving more as a referent for the husband's name. Here in Madras, Amma was careful, particularly in the company of elders, to refer to Appa either as my children's father or as athakar, the generic term for husband. However, I had no idea what the rule was for husbands-to-be?

Perhaps it was okay to write out his name; at least I wouldn't be accused of saying it aloud. Amma and I finally settled on opening my reply with "Dear Raghu." She advised me to exercise restraint in my language. "You never know what will happen in the next few months," she said. "If, for any reason, the marriage doesn't come through, your letters can be held as proof that you had relations with a man. Even if you are innocent, people will talk and say you have been loose and immoral. No one will want to marry you after that. The boy will be let off easily and he can always find another girl. Just be careful in what you write." Little did I know that in a matter of months after numerous letters had been exchanged, I would throw caution to the winds and call him: "My dearest darling Raghu."

I was duly wary in the beginning, however, censoring thoughts that could be construed as flirtatious or, god forbid, amorous. I corrected him gently on the misuse of my name only to find that I was guilty of the same mistake. I had assumed Raghunathan to be the natural extension of Raghu and had no idea his full name was Srinivasavaradhan; Raghu, it turned out, was his pet name. His name underwent a further change after arriving in America. The United States Immigration and Naturalization Service required an official first and last name so he split his name in two: Srinivasa became his first name and Varadhan, his last. He retained the name of his ancestral village, Sathamangalam, along with his father's name, Ranga Iyengar, and was officially known as S.R. Srinivasa Varadhan. His close friends knew him as Raghu; at the office he was known as Varadhan.

We were pen pals at first, jotting down our answers to the questions we asked of one another. We both bemoaned the vagaries of the postal system: the interminable delays of letters traversing the 10,000 miles between us; no postal deliveries for him on Saturdays (unlike India) because the University where he received his mail was closed; on my end, were all the postal holidays to mark the religious observances of Hindus, Muslims and Christians alike — too many as far as I was concerned. At times, my miscalculations on the right amount of postage would find my envelope lying forlornly in the mailbox with the "Return to Sender," stamped in angry red letters across the address. Though it didn't happen too often, there were times when my anticipation was richly rewarded with two letters from Raghu arriving at once. Over the nine months of our correspondence, he calculated that the ratio of his letters to mine was 2:1 and chided me for not keeping up. I argued back that my letters were longer, therefore, quality far outweighed quantity. A feistiness in my tone that I rarely exhibited in public had found its way into my writing. It was both cathartic and amusing to feel I had one-upped him.

We both liked the mysteries of Agatha Christie favoring the ones with Hercule Poirot as lead detective over Miss Marple. I confessed my addiction to the romances of Georgette Heyer and Denise Robins which felt childish compared to his penchant for political biographies of famous people like Nehru and Churchill. He saw life in binary terms: serious and light. Mathematical research was a serious part of his life while comedy films, particularly those starring Rock Hudson and Doris Day, along with the books by P.G. Wodehouse, made for lighter fare. An intense film like "A Farewell to Arms," had made him lose sleep for two days. Movies should entertain and not be didactic, he claimed in one letter, and then contradicted himself in another when remarking how lucky he was to be in New York, a mecca for foreign films, which he found educational and insightful. I suppressed the urge to quibble over the inconsistency of his argument unsure of how he would respond.

My own tastes in popular culture were more of a pastiche of American and Indian media. I watched American films with my classmates on the few occasions Amma permitted, but it was to the more weighty and often, tragic-ending Tamil films that Amma and I gravitated on our outings together. The pathos of unrequited love, the injustices of caste, and the fatuousness of tradition spoke to me in a loud and forceful way and, at times, sadly echoed some of my own circumstances. The songs were melodious, rife with double-entendres, many of them sexual in nature. Many of the nuances were lost on me due to my naiveté and poor comprehension of the Tamil language. Still, I managed to memorize the most popular lyrics with the help of song booklets released at the same time as the movie. It was a practice I continued well into adulthood and which, over time, increased my proficiency in the language. I owed much to the Tamil Film Industry which would decades later come to be called Tollywood, a neologism that inferred that our local language movies were as worthy as those produced in Hollywood.

Raghu enjoyed listening to the classical Carnatic music of South India, especially instrumental songs on the flute and violin. I was a die-hard rock and roll fan, the vestiges of my American Bandstand days in New York. He mentioned his failed attempts at learning vocal music until he was finally told by a not so well-meaning teacher that his voice was awful. He then wrote, "You know, I have never heard your voice. When I last saw you at the airport, you only nodded your head. Can I have your phone number? I may call you one day and listen to your sweet voice." Once again, I was reminded of the fact that I had been a silent presence in his life. I gave him my phone number but the call never came. Perhaps, it was mere wishful thinking on his part for it would only be in mid-May when he returned that we would speak to each other for the first time.

His first letter, he admitted, was actually the third letter he had written me. Diffident and unsure, he got cold feet and never mailed them. He had not reckoned on having his marriage arranged at such a young age anymore than I had. Arguments with his father got him nowhere. He begrudgingly consented to the bride-viewing but once he saw me, he was swayed, so he said. Flattered as I was, it was difficult to gauge if he was being truthful and when he asked me to describe myself, I was at a loss for words. Not wanting to appear immodest, I took the safe route and began by writing about myself in self-deprecating terms. I told him about being teased incessantly by various aunts and uncles for my cauliflower ears, money-purse mouth, and parrot-like nose. I shifted my tone slightly and described my eyes — a deep dark brown with long black lashes —as my only redeeming features. I was considered tall for an Indian girl at five feet four inches and of medium color, not too fair, not too dark. I wore little to no make-up save for the bindi on my forehead and kohl in my eyes.

"My tastes are very simple in nature," I wrote him. "They say if you have been abroad you're tendency is to act superior and stylish but these two words are not in my dictionary. I hate to dress up and act sophisticated. I like, of course, to be well dressed and decent and yet modest," I added. I told him about a fashion show at my college, Stella Maris, and how shocked I was on seeing the models bare so much flesh. I did not tell him that Amma had put her foot down when it came to my wearing sleeveless blouses, the current fad, which she found risqué and vulgar. "What is so sexy about showing off one's armpits?" she exhorted. Put it that way, it was hard not to disagree.

He responded in good humor to the description I gave of myself. I would certainly lose a beauty contest, he wrote, if Venus and Cleopatra competed and then quickly softened the blow in his next sentence which read, "An ideal wife is one who spreads sweetness and happiness around and besides you are a charming girl. I like you, I adore you and I am looking forward to our future of eternal bliss and happiness." I read the lines over and over again, and by the time I was done, I invested his last few words with new meaning. "I like you, and I adore you" was really his way of saying "I love you."

What did I think of his looks he asked. "You have nice eyebrows, a lovely smile, a casual way of dressing, and I sense a kindness in you," I began and stopped, pen poised on the writing pad, wondering if and how I should tell him he was overweight. Eschewing the word, "fat," I settled on "chubby," and added "cuddly like a teddy bear," to cushion the impact. Just to be safe, I parenthetically remarked that weight did not matter and that, "Character was the crowning glory of man," a line I had lifted from one of my novels. Surprisingly, he was not offended and candidly admitted that he had always had a weight problem. His goal was to lose thirty pounds and be a trim 135 pounds before the wedding. He mentioned the onslaught of television ads promoting thinness, America's obsession with fad diets and the push to label the caloric content of every food item. Having grown up in India where being thin often meant you were poor and malnourished, he was amused and mildly shocked that people would actually pay money for a popular soft drink called NOCAL.

By December, we were well beyond the "getting to know you" phase and ready to broach the topic of how and why our marriage proposal came about. My version comprised nothing more than a series of anecdotes about meeting him for the first time at the bride-viewing ceremony, followed later by his presence at my brother's thread ceremony, and culminated in the engagement dinner at his uncle's house. I purposely omitted any mention of the jeep incident and its cataclysmic effect on my mother. That she had been unable to protect me made her confront her own vulnerability as a single woman, a widow at that, and in large measure pushed her in the direction of arranging my marriage. It was too early in our relationship to relay the doubts and fears I had about marrying so young and the possibility that I might not be able to pursue my studies in chemistry. Instead, I focused on the excitement of seeing him at the bride-viewing and my first impressions of him. I threw in a few lines about not wanting to be a burden to my mother and how she had suffered with the loss of my father. I wanted to give Raghu the impression that I was more than willing to marry him although the concept of marriage and what it entailed was alien to me.

Raghu was more forthcoming in his response. He thought he might have met me years earlier at the wedding between my uncle, my mother's youngest brother, and his first cousin, the daughter of his father's younger brother, but was not sure. He knew I had two brothers and that my maternal grandmother and his father were cousins which was news to me. Like me, he too had been kept in the dark about earlier conversations between our families where the possibility of a match had been discussed. He wrote about the formal relationship with his father and how it little it surprised him that the topic of a marriage proposal had never come up. The forty or more age difference between them deeply influenced their respective outlooks on life and he could never imagine them as confidants. It was to Gopal Mamma, his uncle, younger in years to his father, that he turned when the idea of marriage arose. Despite their four hour conversation in which he was told that I would make a perfect wife and keep him happy, and he'd be a damn fool in his uncle's words not to marry me, his initial reaction was one of resentment.

Initially stung by his candor, his ensuing explanation made me more empathetic. He wrote about the difficulty of being an only child and how well-meaning friends and family dished out all kinds of advice in their eagerness to map out his future. He didn't mind their counsel but the decision-making, he felt, should be in his hands alone. In subsequent conversations, Gopal Mamma realizing his proclivity for independence, would preface his marriage pitch by saying, " Well, in my opinion, though it's your decision." This tactic was partially successful; he would give the proposal some consideration but not necessarily accept it. Twenty-two to him seemed too young an age to be married. At twenty-five, he would be willing.

Despite his resistance, he seemed to have given some thought to what constituted a good marriage. He formulated a numerical list of statements that read like the axioms in my geometry text — self-evident and true and not subject to proof. He began: (1) Marriage was not just sex and sex was not just physical charm; (2) Intellectual companionship was an absolute must; (3) A wife must participate fully in the life of the man; and (4) Love before marriage or love at first sight was not important. Provided there was cooperation and compromise, two people could grow to love one another.

He then added another subset of qualifications listed alphabetically this time, on the expectations he had of his future mate. He began: "(a) He should like her at least mildly at the start; (b) She should be reasonably intelligent, preferably with an interest in the sciences, so they could be mentally compatible; (c) She should be tolerant and willing to give him a chance to love her and be prepared to love him back; and (d) She should have varied interests and be full of life and decidedly not moody."

He must have had second thoughts about what he just wrote for his next paragraph held a tinge of remorse. He apologized for making love and marriage appear unromantic but quickly added that it was best he be frank. He then plugged me into his schema and was satisfied that I met his expectations as stated in (a) and (b) but then admitted that he had no way of judging me with regard to (c) and (d). If we had dated, he would have had more to go on, but as he wrote, "We don't go in for that stuff in our society. I'll be taking a risk regarding (c) and (d)." As if talking to himself, he then exclaimed, "What the hell! Why should I be a pessimist?" In one fell swoop, all doubts allayed, his words screamed from the page, "I have fallen in love with you."

A torrent of thoughts poured out. He wrote he had loved me the first time he saw me but needed assurance on my end. He had found this in my letters and that was all the proof he needed. According to him, I was superb and surpassed his imagination. Life for him had taken on a new meaning; there was beauty everywhere he turned even in the dingiest streets of New York. With each passing letter, his love for me grew "second after second, minute after minute, and day after day." His voice filled with urgency begged me to come visit him over the Christmas holidays instead of going to Delhi as planned. I could fly to New York and be there in twenty-four hours; the train to Delhi would take two days, so according to his calculations, New York was actually closer! He reveled ever so briefly in this bubble of fantasy and promptly punctured it when he realized this would never come to pass. He had no choice but to wait until June. Thoughts of me invaded his mathematics and drove him to distraction, so much so, that he amusingly noted that interspersed among symbols like x, y, and z, he found himself jotting down, "vasu=love." For the first time, he signed off, "Your loving love, Raghu," abandoning hereafter his usual "affectionately yours."

Unlike his other letters — which were safely tucked among my clothes in the dresser drawer, away from prying eyes — I kept this letter under my pillow. Every night I carefully unfolded the ten pages hoping the crinkling sound of the tracing paper would not awaken Ranga, fast asleep in the bed next to mine. His words like a bedtime story lulled me to sleep and as the day dawned it brought the promise of a marriage filled with bliss. I wrested his thoughts and possessed them as if I were physically holding on to him. The depth of his emotion revealed in the intensity of his expressions was something I had never encountered. To share them with anyone else, would be adulterous, diluting them of their essence. I brushed aside all the criteria he had painstakingly formulated and chalked it up to his mathematical bent of mind. It was this pulsating, passionate Raghu I wanted and had dreamt of. The swashbuckling hero of my fictional romances had leapt off the pages and swept me off of my feet. I was going to have that fairy-tale ending after all.

Emboldened by the frankness in his letter, I forsook my usual opening of "My dear Raghu," and summoned up as much emotion as I could by addressing him for the first time as "My beloved." I stopped not knowing how to proceed. We had crossed the two-month mark and this would be my first love letter. The earlier ones, though not completely devoid of emotion, were easier to write, seeing how they were filled with the mundane facts of my life. I began with a show of support and empathized with his initial feelings of resentment and concurred that at twenty-two years of age, he was quite young to be married. I expressed my admiration for his independent spirit and lack of nervousness about going abroad for the first time. I referred to myself as a "dependent character," looking for security in a person more mature than I and that I was certain to find this in him. I was a great believer in first impressions with no misgivings about being that way. I, like him, detested moody people, and was drawn to people who were sociable and chatty. I thought of myself as a person of candor and detested flattery. By page three, still struggling to find the right words to say that I loved him, I wrote, " I would like to be by your side and confide my love to you but cannot bring myself to write what I feel on paper." I lauded his ability to express his love for me so openly. I would have never guessed by just looking at him that he had it in him. I suppose I could have filched a few choice sentences with their declarations of love from the many romance novels dotting my bookshelf, but it seemed a corny thing to do. When I needed it most, the English language had failed me.

I propped his letter in front of me and re-read for the umpteenth time the characteristics he had laid out for a good marriage. I honed in on my views of marriage agreeing with him that any union based solely on sexual attraction, was bound to be short-lived. I told him that in the early years of marriage, "the couple is madly in love, but later the man (maybe I'm mistaken), tires of the woman's physical beauty and even abhors her." What really mattered and sustained the relationship was intellectual communion. A wife, I felt, should stand by her husband undaunted by the obstacles they faced. Each was part of the other.

Eager to show him that I, too, could be as methodical as he, I listed my criteria for an ideal husband: "(i) He should be capable of supporting his wife and be responsible; (ii) He should be independent; (iii) He should ease his wife's difficulties and understand her feelings; and (iv) He should be able to talk intelligently and hold his own in a conversation." In triumphant tones I declared: " You are the ideal husband for me!"

Despite what I thought was an equally matched response, a sense of unease persisted. I wrote about feeling stupid and said that my letters were babyish compared to his. Though I was only sixteen, I would strive to be worthy of being his wife. A cascade of doubts tumbled onto the page: I was immature; I would never be able to run a household; and I was too young to be married. I could get through it all provided he took care of me.

I reverted to the schoolgirl in me and bemoaned my upcoming French exam and it only seemed appropriate to sign off with, "Je vous aime beaucoup. Au revoir my dearest Raghu darling." There was a P.S. "I did very well in my English exams. Thanks for wishing me luck. I would have flunked otherwise."

So in the mail it went, my first ever love letter, seven pages of musings on marriage culled from nothing more than my own limited exposure to the outside world. I had bandied around words like "sex," and "love," ignorant of their connotations. Sex, as far as I knew, involved only kissing and hugging. Love, I had written Raghu, was just another way of saying "I like you very much," and "true love," I added, was "the foundational basis constructed by two people and in no way was it spontaneous."

There was no singular source I could point to that shaped my views on marriage. Growing up in Parkway, I gravitated toward shows like Father Knows Best, Ozzie and Harriet, and Leave it to Beaver. At the time, their idealized versions of a happy united family provided a much needed escape from the reality of my own circumstance. My father was essentially absent while my mother held down the fort. Their marriage was built on sacrifice. It was in his best interest to encourage her to be independent and he did what he could to see that she was. He pushed her to take driving lessons and bought her a car and supported her desire to pursue a graduate degree in psychology at Queens College. He was also the more visibly demonstrative of the two. He never failed to give Amma a peck on the cheek when he left for work and on returning home, or look at her adoringly when she fixed his favorite food. Married for eighteen years, much of that time spent apart, there was nevertheless a deep and abiding commitment between them. Although I admired my parents for their fortitude, it was not the kind of marriage I wanted for myself. I bore witness to the toll that kind of sacrifice and prolonged separation had taken on my mother and the sense of abandonment that afflicted my childhood.

My craving for intellectual stimulation was due in large part to my father. His love for literature, our poetry sessions, the spelling bees with my brothers — had left an indelible impact. I clung to those memories after his death and yearned to resurrect them with Raghu. I wanted a husband with a literary bent, an avid reader like myself.

Unsure and anxious as to what is response might be to my views of love and marriage, imagine my surprise, as I tore open his letter — which took ten days to arrive — and found its entire content to be a three-page poem he had composed professing his love for me. Its exultant tone tinged with the despair of being so far away and the concomitant longing to see me in person touched me deeply. He had written:

> *The streets of New York are very bright*
> *But my eyes see none of the light.*
> *My love is not within my sight,*
> *I wish she were, day and night.*
> *That I reciprocated his love was clearly evident in one verse:*
> *The winds of December cold are blowing.*
> *Protected I am for my heart is glowing.*
> *With tender thoughts of someone very loving,*
> *Yes, my darling, from you warmth is flowing.*

Although his poetry paled in comparison to those of Byron and Shelley my father had so lovingly read to me, the very fact that he had spent his Thanksgiving break composing this paean of love more than made up for the simplicity of his lyrics. It was flattering to think of myself as his Erato, the Greek Muse of lyric poetry.

His subsequent letters, written in quick succession, took on a decidedly pragmatic tone. He honed in on my sense of dependency claiming I was wrong to think of the man as being solely responsible in a marriage. Rather, he viewed marriage as a partnership based on equality. Who knows? He might need my help one day. He now wished we had spoken to each other when we first met. He chastised himself for being confused and such a fool but quickly rationalized that this only added to the mystery of love. He worried about our six-year age difference but then quipped about a colleague who told him men never get old — they just go from being a child to old young men.

He discussed his career choice to be a theoretical mathematician and how he would never accept a statistician position in the industrial sector; this would be pure anathema to him. He wanted to continue at NYU for at least another year and then perhaps find a research position in Calcutta. He refused to discuss the assassination of John F. Kennedy and tersely stated "It was a brutal attack on humanity." His thoughts hopped to the movies he had seen at a recent Charlie Chaplin Film Festival and concluded with his current reading of Henry Miller's Tropic of Capricorn, "a notorious book," he wrote, and one he thought I might have read.

Acting as if he were bored by what he wrote, and for all I knew, the manner in which he wrote, he broke loose and gave free reign to his imagination. He shared his dream of a honeymoon on Dal Lake in Kashmir, both of us snuggled together in a house boat. His words overladen with sensuosity revealed his inner desires: "his eyes longed to behold me; his ears wanted to hear my sweet, silvery voice; his hands were eager to stroke my angelic face; and his lips could not wait to kiss his beautiful bride." He wanted to end his letter adopting the vocabulary of Henry Miller but dared not do so. His language, as Raghu put it was "unmentionable," in the presence of a young girl as myself. He closed with a sigh and begged me to send a photograph of myself as his only consolation for the time being. It was December and, with six months to go before our wedding, the wait seemed all the more interminable with his mounting desire to consummate our union.

His wave of letters left much to digest on my end. Pricked by his comment that I was wrong to think that the husband should shoulder all the responsibility, I was determined to exonerate myself. I glossed over his romantic ruminations; I'd attend to that later. It was more immediate to prove — perhaps more to myself than to him — that I was capable of standing on my own two feet. I searched for an incident to bolster my point.

In great detail I narrated an afternoon outing to a local cinema with my college friends. I asserted in a defiant tone, how unlike my classmates, I was not intimidated by standing in the all-male queue to purchase the movie tickets seeing that the ladies' queue was too long. A clearly marked sign prohibited men from entering the ladies' queue, however, women could cross over to the men's side though very few did. Modesty, the fear of being ogled at, or worse, a deliberate or even accidental touch by a male stranger — these were sufficient reasons to keep women away. I, on the other hand, had literally crossed the line amidst the stares of men and women alike. In a conservative place like Madras, it was a bold move.

Since the jeep incident, Amma had taken strident measures to protect me from what she saw as the unwanted gaze of the opposite sex. If I found myself alone at home after returning from college, I was to lock myself in my room upstairs if our male cook was downstairs in the kitchen. When my older brother's friends came calling, she quickly shooed me out of the way to prevent any form of flirtatiousness. All men were sexual predators in her eyes. The only way to challenge her view was to test the waters for myself outside her purview. I needed more than anything else to prove to myself that I could ward off the advances of male strangers — jumping into the men's queue showed I had guts.

I kept these thoughts to myself not knowing how Raghu would react. The conflict between defining myself and being shackled by a tradition endorsed in full by my mother had been brewing since childhood. With no resolution in sight, it left me in a quandary as I had a tendency to second guess everything I did or said. I began to rue what I wrote. Would Raghu see me as shameless and not independent as I had hoped? Was this incipient rebellion brewing inside me misguided? To assuage my doubts as well as any Raghu might have, I hastily added that I was an obedient daughter and never did anything without my mother's permission. It was a truth to which I had been conditioned and only half-believed.

I could now turn my attention to the more amorous aspects of his letters. I embraced his idea of a honeymoon in Kashmir writing, "anywhere is paradise with you." I dismissed his concerns about our age difference citing the nine year age difference between my parents which in the long run happened to be inconsequential. Besides, I told him, women aged more quickly than men and I might look like a hag at thirty-five while he still looked young. As I re-read his more explicitly written thoughts on wanting to hold me and kiss me, I hesitated to reciprocate his sentiments. Not wanting to appear cold and distant, I feebly responded with, "I wish to thread my fingers through your silky hair." His allusions to physical intimacy made me blush while his reticence to use the "unmentionable language" of Henry Miller left me baffled. I had never heard of this writer nor knew what constituted a "notorious book." My wildest fantasies went no further than the romantic escapades of my bodice-ripping novels where a passionate kiss on the lips sealed the destiny of the lovers thereafter. All the novels shared a similar ending with no intimation that something more was in store. My imagination was effectively shuttered until now.

Raghu's recent letters were suggestive of something more intimate as if he was privy to a secret that he was dying to reveal yet hesitant to actually get the words out. He must have intuited through my letters that I was too young to hear of such matters in a straightforward way, hence his allusions to Henry Miller — allusions totally lost on me but nevertheless piqued my curiosity. I tried to piece together his teen-age years from the casual snippets interspersed in his earlier letters. He lived a carefree existence while residing in the dormitory at Presidency College in Madras. Unchallenged and quite bored by the academic curriculum, he resorted to late night cavorting with friends be it at the movies or walking along Marina Beach. At the Indian Statistical Institute in Calcutta, with a new set of cohorts, he discussed deep mathematical problems late into the night again finding respite at the local cinema house. This pattern of socializing continued in New York with a few of his Indian friends, but for the most part he spent his time alone, doing math, reading and writing letters to me. Nothing he told me appeared egregious or out of the ordinary. So what was the spark that ignited his fantasies? The question, tantalizing and taunting, dangled elusively in mid-air.

It was becoming increasingly difficult to continue with my response. As I scanned what I had written, my own words sounded tinny and divested of real emotion. They stared back at me in stony silence. In as much as I wanted to express in my own way my love for Raghu, the terrible news I had just received stopped me dead in my tracks. A close childhood friend whose wedding I had attended was being divorced by her husband of barely two months on the grounds of physical repulsiveness and mental incompatibility. This had sent shock waves through the Brahmin community in Madras and hit closer to home as the family had been friends of my parents for over a decade. The devastated bride turned to my mother rather than her own for consolation. She leaned on Amma's background in psychology as a means to shed light on the groom's behavior. For weeks on end, I saw them huddled in Amma's bedroom, conversing in hushed tones. Though not privy to the details, I could see from Amma's reaction that a cloud of doubt had begun to form. Was my impending marriage in peril?

Raghu's declarations of love, his dreams of a happy future together, his assurances to stand by me through thick and thin, churned in my mind. Self-censorship set in as panic and uncertainty took over. Would the letters I had written him be used against me if the marriage did not take place? Would my words betray me and make me a barefaced pariah? I began to lose confidence in myself, in Raghu, and in the very idea of an arranged marriage. I could not keep news of the divorce secret. It had begun to consume me and threatened to corrode the burgeoning love I felt for him.

"Please forgive me," I wrote, "but the devil puts these questions in my head." A litany of self-doubt followed: Would something prevent us from loving each other? Would he tire of me? Was I stupid and babyish? Would I make him a good wife? The divorce had unsettled me to the point of asking inane questions and again I begged his forgiveness. Re-reading his letters, I told him, only confirmed the sincerity of his love for me. I had absolved him of all doubt transferring it instead to my shoulders. By letter's end, the image of the dauntless girl who took pride in crossing the line had dissolved into a maze of trepidation. In its place, a child cowed by fear of the unknown, stumbled beneath the weight of circumstances beyond her control.

Raghu's response which customarily took ten days stretched to two weeks, making the wait agonizing, to say the least. Amma had become strangely quiet as if the very mention of divorce would jinx my engagement. I came to know that the parents of the girl, completely distraught over her divorce, had written a letter to Amma begging her to call off my wedding. Thankfully, it fell on deaf ears. She did not ask me to stop writing to Raghu though every time she saw me rushing towards the mailbox, she became increasingly apprehensive that it was too late to reverse the course of events. She need not have worried. On the first page of Raghu's letter, in big capital letters, screaming for attention, he had written, "DON'T HAVE ANY DOUBTS ABOUT US! WE ARE THE LUCKY ONES!"

In clinical fashion, he dismissed the notion of physical repulsiveness as a ground for divorce as a trivial excuse. He justified his reasoning by pointing to the numerous marriages of Marilyn Monroe, America's blonde bombshell. He elaborated on his interpretation of emotional incompatibility in greater detail. Emotions, according to him, were developed and cultivated and subject to change. A conflict that might arise between husband and wife could be resolved through compromise if both parties were willing and loved each other. True, they could get divorced over irreconcilable differences but he refused to believe that any matter could be that serious to warrant such action. "If the US and USSR can coexist, so can we," he concluded.

He understood the doubts I had as we did not know each other intimately and promised they would vanish once we got married in June. He indulged in the reasons people got married and fell back on his usual pattern of numerically listing them all: (1) People marry to have a healthy sexual relationship; (2) People see marriage as a form of social security; (3) People marry because they are attracted to each other; and (4) People who are unhappy hope marriage will change their lives and promise them Utopia but if it doesn't, they divorce. He created another list outlining matrimonial expectations: (1) They should be within reason; (2) They should be verified as being compatible according to the judgement of each partner; and (3) Each partner should make an honest effort to satisfy their respective expectations and this could be easily achieved through sacrifice and compromise.

As in his earlier letters, he apologized for being prosaic and matter-of-fact and abruptly shifted the subject to himself. He confessed how lonely he was and ached for my companionship where moments, no matter how trivial, of happiness, sorrow and anxiety could be shared. He, in turn, would give of himself completely to make sure my needs were met. He professed his love for me over and over again in an attempt to wash away any trace of doubt I might still harbor. His letter dated December 27, 1963, bookmarked the end of the year and presaged a deepening commitment between us.

I was slowly beginning to see myself as a budding young woman with a mind of her own. I let loose a stream of thoughts about my expectations of marriage — empathy for one another was paramount followed by compassion and sacrifice. "Our life together will be a never ending song of joy for we are its composers," I wrote, waxing poetic. I articulated my reservations of a strictly arranged marriage where the boy and girl knew nothing about each other and how this could possibly lead to disastrous results. He and I, on the other hand, were more fortunate; we had come to love one another through our exchange of letters. With a final flourish, I stated unequivocally that I was prepared to marry him.

Chapter 10

Dowry Matters

Four months had passed since the initial exchange of letters and Raghu and I ended the year firm in our commitment towards each other. By now, we had exhausted the quotidian aspects of our lives and parsed our respective definitions of marriage until the ink ran dry. We entered into a new phase of our courtship in the early days of January, 1964, when our thoughts shifted to an imagined future together. I wrote in great earnest about my desire to cook for him although I knew next to nothing about fixing a dish let alone an entire meal. Since we had a cook, there was no reason to venture into the kitchen. In turn, Raghu's overture to make me coffee in the morning so I could sleep a bit longer, sweetened a bitter memory from my childhood days in New York when I was forced to rise early (weekends not withstanding) and laboriously hand-grind the coffee beans in the Lovelock Machine. We day dreamed of strolling hand in hand through the streets of New York followed by dinner and the movies. It was an idyllic reverie where my thoughts were free to roam without constraint.

Amma, although I never told her explicitly, seemed to know I was in love. My frequent trips to the mailbox made it hard to hide my expectant longing for Raghu's letters; my crestfallen look was a dead give away that nothing had arrived. When luck did shine, I quickly sought the privacy of my room and could hardly wait to tear open Raghu's letter, shunting aside all other demands on my time. This pre-occupation, bordering on obsession, was not lost on my mother. The time had come, she said, for the Nichayathartham, the formal engagement ceremony. Little did she know that Raghu and I had privately betrothed ourselves to each other and that neither of us felt the necessity of a formal pronouncement. Amma, however, insisted that the Nichayathartham was a vital component to make permanent the alliance between the two families; the ritual would seal the deal with no possibility of an escape clause. The lagna patrika, a marriage document printed for the occasion, would herald the date, time and venue for the wedding. The written word represented a guarantee that both parties had entered into a pact that could not be broken.

"But Amma," I pleaded, "Raghu has promised to marry me. He said so in his letters. He's not even here so how can there be an engagement ceremony?"

"All this kadhal-peedhal stuff is fine," she replied, her derisiveness clearly evident by pairing the Tamil word for love, kadhal, with a nonsensical term which essentially trivialized the depth of my feelings for Raghu. "But we must now finalize matters between the two families; Raghu's presence is not required. You have to participate and I'll tell you later what needs to be done. But for now, write Raghu right away and find out when he plans to return. I have to find a wedding hall, print the invitations, notify the relatives, and get the house ready."

Amma's pragmatic attitude rained down on me like a cold shower on a drunkard. How ironical, I thought, given the lengths she had gone to in order to marry my father. The breaking of those one hundred coconuts at the Hanuman Temple came to mind. Only someone in love would have resorted to such an act. Had she forgotten the numerous times she had recounted the story of her own courtship which landed her in trouble. It happened after the bride-viewing, when Appa wrote her a letter addressed to the school where Amma was a teacher. It landed on the desk of the headmistress who, upon seeing the sender's name as one Mr. T.G. Narayanan, immediately called Amma into her office demanding an explanation. In the 1940s, it was not uncommon for the young unmarried Brahmin women of Madras to enter the teaching profession provided it was at an all-girls institution. The school, acting in loco parentis, fiercely guarded the chastity of its charges and female staff. Any breach in behavior was a serious offense. A letter from a man to an unmarried female teacher could not go unheeded. It was a trembling Amma who stood before the headmistress as the latter angrily waved the yet unopened letter in front of her face. "What is all this nonsense Janaki? Who is this Mr. T.G. Narayanan and why is he writing to you?" she bellowed. Amma, her voice barely audible, meekly admitted that she was betrothed to him and that there was no cause for concern as the wedding date had been fixed. This proved to be enough of a guarantee for the headmistress who obligingly turned over the unopened letter to Amma. It contained a declaration written in a passionate hand of the love my Appa had for my Amma. Why belittle the love between Raghu and me? Perhaps time and circumstance had dimmed her memory, or perhaps it was a memory too painful to revisit with the premature death of my father.

My feelings about the Nichayathartham were ambivalent at best. I embraced the fact that it was a public acknowledgement of our union and the surety it provided but was skittish about the questions that would inevitably follow. Friends and relatives on our side would put the groom under a microscope. His background, his character, and his professional prospects, would become topics of discussion with everyone weighing in on the merits and demerits of such an union. Tongues would wag, rumors would fly and most comments would begin with a " I heard someone say…" The Tamil Brahmin community could be quite unforgiving at times and I felt powerless to do anything about it.

I broke the news of the Nichayathartham in my next letter with none of the exuberance usually associated with the occasion. To be part of the ceremony without his presence made it all the more clear that this was an affair more for the families than for us. His parents were not ones to buck tradition and I surmised from Amma's frequent trips to their home, that the plans had already been set in motion. To my question about the date of his arrival, Raghu responded that he planned to return on May 17th. He also mentioned how relieved he was that his presence at the engagement ceremony was not required. The tenor of his letter evoked no curiosity nor a trace of interest in what the ceremony entailed or in the role and rites I would be compelled to perform. His lack of empathy irked me. It was hard to draw any definitive conclusions regarding his views of traditional Hindu practices. Despite his personal reservations about marrying young — which he kept from his parents — he had not balked at their request to a bride-viewing. His compliance, I suspected, arose out of a sense of duty to his parents. To buckle under the weight of tradition was all too familiar to me and by marrying Raghu I had hoped to liberate myself. But if he succumbed so easily, I began to wonder if he expected me to do the same.

I remembered only too well the countless rituals imposed on me when I newly arrived from America, the most awful of them having to do with my entrance into puberty and the most tragic of them having to do with the death rites for my father. In every instance, I was forced to quell my emotions in service to a higher ineffable authority. I had donned so many roles; they hung on me like layer upon layer of skin, clogging every pore in my body that I could scarcely breathe. I had reached a stage in my courtship with Raghu where those layers of skin were beginning to molt. Deep in the recesses of my very being, a sense of who I was and wanted to be, stirred. I was in the process of finding a comfortable niche for myself, a sanctum sanctorum, where I could define myself without fear of reprisal. I was not blind to the fact that part of my identity had been shaped by tradition, but I wanted to control what aspects to embrace or discard. I had faced a similar dilemma during my childhood days in Parkway Village which forced me ultimately to live in two distinct and separate worlds, one American, the other, Indian. It was the lack of choice I found oppressive. I no longer wanted a bifurcated identity nor do what was expected of me. I wanted to set my own expectations and taste the independence I had long been denied. To wed a man who touted the idea of compromise as the key to a successful marriage seemed a promising start. But his cavalier attitude about the engagement ceremony gave me pause. Buried between the lines of the letter I caught a glimpse of a man who appeared more intransigent in matters of tradition than I would have liked.

The lagna patrika was ready to be printed. We were to be married on June 5, 1964 at the A.V.M. Rajeswari Kalyana Mandapam, a brand new wedding hall. It was owned by the family of my former classmate at Good Shepherd Convent and inaugurated at her wedding in 1963. Ours would be the first public wedding. I found it odd that the date of the wedding had been set before finalizing the date of the Nichyathartham. No matter how many times I pestered Amma about it, she kept putting me off mumbling something about negotiations that had to be ironed out. However, this did not stop her from telling a few close friends and family members that my marriage had been fixed. Now and then, they would drop by for a visit and after greeting them, Amma shooed me away and made it clearly evident that the conversation to follow was for adult ears only. It was a common sight to see them gathered in the alcove pumping Amma for information. Seated in the dining area, just off the alcove, I was able to eavesdrop without being seen. The venue for the wedding had a certain cachet and they wondered how an unemployed widow living on her husband's pension could afford the cost. Speculation was rife that the groom's family must be well-off and by choosing such a grand wedding hall, my mother was going all out to impress them. They were prompted to ask, "So Janaki, what does the boy do? Is he making a good salary? In America, they pay well. All those dollars! Must be rich." Amma's usual refrain was, "He is a math teacher doing research. I don't know his salary but they say he is smart. He's an only child. His parents are a bit old-fashioned and live in a modest house in Tambaram." I wished Amma had boosted Raghu's status by mentioning he had earned a PhD at the age of twenty-two instead of referring to him as a "mere math teacher." It sounded banal even to my ears. Disappointed that they could wrestle little else out of my mother, they cut short their visit much to my relief.

It was an unusually quiet Sunday evening in March. Amma had gone to Tambaram to see Raghu's parents about "marriage business," as she put it. Both my brothers were off somewhere, the cook had the day off and it was unlikely anyone would drop by in the oppressive heat. It was the perfect time to hole up in my room and cram for my final exams barely a month away. Competitive by nature, I would settle for nothing less than a score of distinction in all my subjects. I would brook no interference or distractions and cut back my letter-writing to Raghu much to his consternation and, when I did write, it was all about my mastery or lack of in every subject. The lovey-dovey phrases I normally peppered throughout my letters, were clumped together as I signed off. "Lots of love and kisses, and an extra gigantic one," I wrote with the promise of a longer letter to come. Afflicted with a pang of guilt, I hastily added a post-script, "Bye for now my dearest, my sweetie." I was filled with angst which was further exacerbated as I tried repeatedly and failed miserably to find the right solutions for the quadratic equations in my math text. A coffee-break, I decided, would do me good. As I descended the stairs, in stormed Amma looking absolutely livid.

"This marriage will not take place," she shouted. " Who do these people think they are? They want me to buy a first class plane ticket for Raghu. Why, even your father never went first class! I have given you a good dowry, the best I can afford. They want more? My answer is no!"

All this outpouring of rage left me flabbergasted. I had no idea what she was talking about. It was the first time the matter of dowry had surfaced and it hit me in a flash that I had become an object to be sold. The custom of giving a dowry was one I disdained. I was shocked that my mother had literally bought into it. First I needed to quell her anger. Then I would demand an explanation.

"Amma, calm down please. You're making me scared. What's going on? What is all this dowry stuff?" I said as I reached an arm out to steady her body visibly convulsed with rage.

She thrust my arm away as if I were the cause of her plight and threw herself on the sofa. A dose of caffeine usually had a palliative effect on Amma and I scurried into the kitchen in dire need of the same. I stared blankly at the water impatient for it to boil, and managed a weak smile as I remembered the old cliché about a "watched pot never boils." I shuffled the utensils around, banged them on the granite counter and, then, seized by a quick sense of remorse, began to check for any dents. It would take a good twenty minutes for the coffee to drip through the tiny perforations of the filter, enough time for me to collect my thoughts, quiet my racing heart, and prepare for my confrontation with Amma.

"Amma, why did you agree to a dowry?" I asked trying to keep my temper in check. "Am I crippled, blind, deformed in any way that no one will marry me? If Appa were alive, he would have put his foot down. He often told me how he never asked your father for a dowry and that he married you for who you were. He placed a simple yellow thali (marriage thread) around your neck and only later gave you a gold chain. Do you remember how angry he got when you bought me gold earrings when I was a child? He hated any display of wealth. Too ostentatious, he said, and had me look the word up in the dictionary so I would never forget its meaning. Why Amma, did you agree to this?" I sobbed.

The stoic facade, I had been careful to maintain following my father's death, was beginning to crack. I had tried not to think about him and hardly mentioned him in my letters to Raghu except for a perfunctory aside on the breath-stealing view of the East River from his office on the thirty-eighth floor of the United Nations. Of all things, why did this damn dowry have to be the catalyst to churn up memories of him? The moral lessons he taught me on so may occasions came flooding back. His large heart that grew larger to accommodate the pain and misfortune of the poor and marginalized brought tears to his eyes. I could hold back no longer and began to mourn his loss as if for the first time.

Amma sat on the couch impervious to my torrential outpour. "Oh, Vasu, you will never understand these things," she intoned as if addressing a petulant child. " I know you have no physical deformity but your Nachatram, your birth star, is Moolam, not a good one for a girl," she began.

"But Amma I'm a Virgo, according to the astrological calendar," I protested. "What's this Moolam star you're talking about?"

"Virgo is a Zodiac sign in western astrology. In India your birth star is different as it's based on the lunar calendar. The astrologer charts your horoscope noting the position of the planets and the moon at the exact time of your birth. In your case, the star was Moolam, an ill omen for girls. They say demons will rule your life. But boys born under Moolam are very fortunate, and will reach great heights. No man will marry a Moolam girl because it portends an early death for his parents. Now, you see why this match is a god-send," she said, incredulous of our own good fortune.

This was the first time I had learned that my entry into the world had been tainted from the outset by an astrological curse. The shock of discovery barely registered given the very real possibility that my marriage might not take place.

"But Amma, it makes no sense to me. Why would Raghu's family take this risk and accept the proposal?" I asked, bewildered by her response.

"I shared your horoscope with them from the very beginning; I didn't hide anything. Gopal Mamma said he would match your horoscope against Raghu's and maybe the combination would offset the bad predictions. According to their family astrologer, you were born on the cusp of the star which negates all the bad effects. There was some talk at the time about how much jewelry I planned to give you and, since you are my only daughter, I told them I would do what I could. Look, Vasu, Raghu is an only child so when his parents pass away, everything will come back to you. In the end what difference does it make?" she replied with indisputable logic.

Convincing as Amma's argument was, it failed to appease me. I was convinced that nothing but avarice had motivated Raghu's family to demand such a large dowry. It appalled me to the point of disgust. Trying as hard as I could to digest Amma's explanation, I detected a more sinister motive: Maybe our horoscopes had been nudged into compatibility so as not to forsake the promise of a handsome dowry. That we were people of means was not lost on Raghu's family. They had seen the opulence of our South Beach home where the bride-viewing was held and again at my older brother's thread ceremony. Even Amma's wealthier friends had been dazzled by the splendor of the architecture and the rich teak furnishings. What no one knew at the time, including myself, were the debts Amma had to incur to meet the demands of Raghu's parents.

"All right Amma, I know eventually whatever you give me will be mine. So what's all this about a first class ticket for Raghu?" I asked, trying to get to the heart of the matter.

"His parents drew up a list of items for your dowry. His mother wants the sliver lamps to be extra tall and heavy and then there are other silver vessels like basins, tumblers, thalis for you and Raghu to eat on, and other assorted utensils of stainless steel. We are required to give some brass vessels for their use on religious occasions. I promised to adorn you with diamond earrings and a diamond necklace on your wedding day and I have to buy a suit, watch and ring for Raghu as part of the bride's gift to the groom. However, they want a diamond ring, not the usual gold one. They will buy the gold wedding chain and wedding sari as is the custom. To all this I agreed. But now suddenly they want me to purchase a first-class ticket for Raghu and when I refused, they threatened to stop the wedding. As it is I am spending so much and still they are not satisfied. I have Ramu and Ranga's education to think of. Where will I go for the money?" she replied, her voice erupting with anger.

I was stunned by the enormity of the dowry and by the audacity of Raghu's parents to actually make a list as if shopping for a bride. I could find no way to reconcile the disparity between the admirable traits I saw in Raghu and the odious behavior of his parents. For a split moment, I wished he were an orphan. Ashamed at such a vile thought, I begged God to forgive me. Now that I knew I had been doomed at birth, why collect more bad karma? The extravagance of the dowry belittled my self-worth to such an extent that I could hardly look my mother in the eye. Her unapologetic acceptance of the dowry system had turned me into a commodity, a bargaining chip, and left me utterly dehumanized.

Vignettes from my childhood days in Parkway Village flashed by in quick succession. In scene after scene, there I was, deferential, doing my mother's bidding, just to prove I could be a good Indian daughter. The tableau shifted to my early adolescent years in India and the shame and humiliation I endured during my first menstrual period without my mother by my side. I had done all I could to assimilate and had made a deliberate effort to efface all traces of my American upbringing. In every instance, I had willed myself to be obedient in order to coax my mother into loving me. I knew no other way. Until now, I had not questioned her motives but the dowry matter was anathema to me.

What could have possessed such an educated and cosmopolitan woman to stoop to such a custom? Did she feel compelled to sweeten the deal to insure the marriage would take place? Where was the woman who staunchly abnegated her status as a Hindu widow in defiance of tradition? I no longer recognized her. To suddenly reveal in a moment of crisis the very existence of a dowry overwhelmed me to the point that I found it hard to sympathize with my mother's plight. Her complicity in perpetuating a pernicious practice confounded me and I felt humiliated. I walked away simmering with anger and desolate about my future.

In the privacy of my room, I dug out Raghu's letters, seeking solace in his unconditional love for me. I wept profusely as I pored over his words, my tears bleeding the ink on the pages. The news of my accursed birth with demons wreaking havoc in my life began to seep in. Up to now, I had but a passing interest in my horoscope, amused more by the uncanny match of my personality to the leading traits ascribed to Virgos — fastidious, fault-finding, and perfectionist. I began to wonder if indeed demons had ruled my life. All of a sudden, the losses in my life loomed before me as proof of their presence: the premature death of my father; the futile yearning for my mother's love; and the missed opportunities to enjoy a childhood unencumbered by responsibility and cultural imperatives. I consciously erased the happy memories with a renewed focus on the sadder ones and tailored my past to fit the truth of my cursed existence.

I stretched out on the bed, tucked Raghu's letters under my pillow, and tried to rid my mind of painful speculations of my past and future. I recalled a recent conversation with my college friends that seemed prescient. We were lauding the progressive stance taken by some Tamil filmmakers in depicting the dowry as an evil practice. We were surprised by the strong showings at the box office given the pervasiveness of the custom that cut across caste and class. The films invariably revolved around the plight of two lovers whose impending union is thwarted by the avarice of dowry. Their only way out is to flee from their families and get married in secret. Once the families learn of their plan, they agree to dispense with the dowry rather than lose the love of their children. The final scenes are filled with contrition, redemption and atonement — the necessary ingredients for a happy ending. I began to fantasize eloping with Raghu.

The films generated interest in the English and Tamil dailies, all of them making pointed references to the Dowry Prohibition Act of 1961 which declared the practice to be a criminal offense. There were numerous reports of police raids at wedding halls where in an attempt to be discreet and escape detection, the dowry was tucked away in a back room. These raids rarely led to any arrests as the bride's party often claimed that the array of objects was nothing more than gifts to the couple. The dowry, primarily an oral agreement between the families, not a written one, would constitute hearsay evidence in a court of law, rendering it inadmissible. Lists that had been drawn up were quickly destroyed before the wedding. My friends and I marveled at the ingenuity of such subterfuge which ultimately allowed the parties involved to circumvent the law. But deep in our hearts we also knew that we would have to reluctantly accept that our families would engage in similar shenanigans. To expect or want something better for ourselves was a celluloid dream.

I became uncharacteristically lethargic. The feverish pace at which I crammed for my exams came to a grinding halt. I simply could not concentrate. My usual chatty conversations with Amma were reduced to a few perfunctory exchanges on matters of little consequence. I left Raghu's letters unanswered and envied him for being far away and out of the fray. I did nothing but stare at the growing pile which groaned under the weight of his plaintive pleas urging me to respond immediately. But I was in a quandary. I saw no delicate way of raising the topic of the dowry without casting asper-sions on his parents which were bound to hurt him deeply. I also did not want to exacerbate my existing fear that our marriage might not take place. As it was, Amma's mounting recalcitrance to the increas-ing demands of Raghu's parents posed enough of a threat.

Our house on Luz Avenue, once a harbinger of good fortune, was now cloaked in a miasma of despair. An eerie silence haunted the place. Nearly three weeks had passed since the dowry matter had come to the fore and an uneasy peace marked by a forced civility prevailed between my mother and me. Neither of us broached the dowry issue again though its insidious effects were hard to dispel. My brothers knew nothing of what had transpired and I preferred to keep them in the dark. Besides, Ramu had never been my confi-dant and although Ranga was more my intimate, a perceptible dis-tance had begun to develop between us. Although I was older to him by a mere three years, my new status as a bride-to-be had thrust me into adulthood without warning or preparation. As a result, it truncated the normal span of my adolescence. The games and light-hearted banter that had once forged a closeness between Ranga and me gradually abated. I felt too grown-up to indulge in behavior that appeared increasingly childish. My concerns were too serious for a sibling whom I had nurtured over the years and often thought of as my child. Like any mother, I felt duty-bound to protect him and spare him of my agony. I opted for silence as far as my close friends were concerned. I was too ashamed to admit that a family like mine with its worldly pedigree had so readily given in to the iniquitous custom of the dowry. Uncertain of my own future, I came up with a back-up plan. I would tackle my studies with a renewed deter-mination and set out on a path to fulfill my long-held ambition of becoming the next Marie Curie.

Raghu's letters, filled with anguish at my long silence, began to arrive with an alarming alacrity, at the rate of two a week. They be-came increasingly hard to ignore and I finally caved in. For the first time, I wrote back using the self-sealing aerogramme instead of the usual loose-leaf paper. I figured the small amount of space would force upon me an economy of thought and save me the bother of providing a long-winded explanation for my prolonged silence. I stuck to a safe and innocuous topic, namely, my upcoming exams. In staccato fashion I made a long list of the subjects I had yet to master and charted my progress in each. I exaggerated the pressure I was under and turned it into a convenient and plausible excuse for my tardiness. Unconvinced by my own words, I ended the letter with a feeble gesture of conciliation and hastily scrawled "I love you and miss you." I sealed the letter and mailed it immediately lest I had a change of heart. Another kind of letter was brewing in my mind, one that would never be written. Those thoughts had been effectively censored, smothered by the weight of the dowry.

The scorching heat of mid-March was relentless. Public transportation stunk of public sweat. The tar-paved streets rippled like molten lava and except for a handful of vendors peddling garishly colored bamboo fans, there was no pedestrian traffic. The heat brought tempers to a boil no matter how slight the infraction. Street cops bellowed at drivers stalled in overheated cars. Tongues lashed out at servants for letting the tap water run. Amidst the hottest month of the year, the only signs of fecundity were the flowers sprouting from the mango trees with their promise of a rich harvest in the months to come. It would have been sheer insanity to venture outside, particularly after midday, when temperatures peaked, unless it was a matter of the utmost urgency. Yet Raghu's uncle, Gopal Mamma, boarded the electric train from Tambaram, and endured the thirty-minute ride in the blistering heat. He arrived at our doorstep on a Saturday afternoon, his crisp white shirt and starched dhoti limp from perspiration.

Amma welcomed him with a warmth and affection that surprised me given the recent acrimony surrounding the dowry negotiations. I could barely summon a smile and after a quick hello went up to my room. I mulled over my own feelings for Gopal Mamma which up to now had always been those of fondness and trust. He had served as an amiable conduit between Raghu's parents and my mother when the possibility of an alliance between Raghu and me was first raised. Held in high esteem by Raghu, it was he and his wife, Rukmani Mammi, who were entrusted to accompany him to the bride-viewing in lieu of his own parents. As a key player, it was nothing short of obvious that he must have had a hand in calculating the amount of the dowry. Doubts about his sincerity crept in. Was it Gopal Mamma who had demanded the first-class ticket and not Raghu's parents as I had originally thought? Had he also convinced Raghu's parents that my ill-fated horoscope actually revealed a star with a proverbial silver lining? Had I all along assigned blame to the wrong party? If only I could eavesdrop on the conversation downstairs.

I stood on the balcony adjoining my room staring at the sun as its rays bent imperceptibly in the western part of the sky. It would soon be sunset; the city would awaken from its siesta. I could feel the stirring of the ocean breeze wafting across the dry city, scattering the clusters of dust motes that clung in the air. It lifted my depressed spirits to see the street come alive. The vendors resumed the singing of their wares; housewives emerged to inspect the vegetables neatly arrayed on the rolling cart and, after the customary haggling over the steep prices, made their final purchases; joggers ran their usual laps speeding by elderly couples on a leisurely stroll. It was a scenario I had witnessed time and again, still, it was its very ordinariness that I found strangely comforting. Amma's voice pierced the tranquility of the moment and I was summoned below to bid Gopal Mamma good-bye.

Amma could hardly wait to escort him to the gate and once he turned the corner, she dashed inside, barely able to contain herself.

"I have good news, Vasu. The negotiations are on. The marriage will take place after all. I need not buy a first-class ticket; economy class will do. Gopal Mamma and I discussed everything. You have nothing to worry about," Amma said triumphantly.

I was elated by this sudden turn of events. I wanted to know what had happened but Amma was tight-lipped and refused to give any details. She insisted it was an adults only matter not meant for my ears. The shift in my mood was so immediate that I hardly cared. My first impulse was to write Raghu a much overdue letter, a long one this time, free of constraint, and filled with assurances of my love for him. There would be no mention of the dowry matter. Our epistolary romance was too pristine and I would not allow it to be sullied under any circumstance.

It was during the quieter moments that my resentment surfaced gathering an intensity that surpassed my ability to comprehend it in full. The life lessons I learned from my father, mostly during his visits to Madras, came to me in a stream of vignettes. I heard his voice, gentle, yet firm in its plea that I not parade around in fancy silk pavadais while the children of his much poorer older brother were forced to wear skirts of sturdy cotton fabrics expressly woven to withstand multiple washes over long periods of time. His stance riled Amma who balked at his attitude and openly expressed the little sympathy she had for the impoverished conditions of his sibling. "Who asked him to bear so many children if he can't support them?" she retorted. "Why should my only daughter wear pavadais made of bedsheet cloth?" she remarked snidely. Their spat ended quickly with Amma reluctantly giving in. Appa's stay was going to be short and there was no point in making it unpleasant. She saved my silk pavadais for those occasions when she knew for sure that my cousins would not be around. Another heart-rending scene emerged — the little girl and her blind father begging on the doorstep of my grandparents' home on Mahalakshmi Street. Appa, visibly moved by their plight, wanted to pluck her out of her abject poverty and enroll her in school where she rightfully belonged. There was the time when I saw Appa, angry and sad at the same time. We were standing by the gate when a rickshaw driver hauling human cargo passed by. Appa flinched as his eyes followed the rivulets of sweat streaming down his back. He glowered at the passengers and in a voice, loud enough to be heard, cried out, "Walk or take the bus, Vasu but never sit in a rickshaw!"

Each vignette resounded with the same message: have empathy and compassion for those less fortunate and never flaunt your wealth. I saw myself as his star pupil, an exemplar of everything he stood for. My values and belief system had been shaken to the core by the damned dowry. With Appa dead, there was no one to counter

Amma. Now, more than ever, I needed him in my life, to once again hear him coo in my ear, "You are the apple of my eye."

Appa's teachings, deeply lodged in the fiber of my being, made it all the more difficult to justify Amma's concession to foot the bill for Raghu's airfare even if it was for an economy class ticket. I, at times, wondered if her capitulation was an act of desperation driven by a fear that my marriage would not take place. I had come to admire my mother as a woman of great resolve and it was a pitiable sight to witness that resolve dissipate in order to safeguard my future with Raghu. I wanted her to stand up to his parents but, most of all, I wanted her to stand up for me. I could not shake the feeling that I was a damaged piece of merchandise that needed to be off-loaded. Raghu's love and acceptance of who I was had bolstered my self-esteem and inspired in me the kind of confidence that was liberating. My letters of late embodied an unfettered expression of my innermost thoughts, pried loose from the vise-like grip of tradition and over-protectiveness that had dogged me since childhood. I felt utterly diminished by the largess of the dowry. Forced into the role of a bystander, excluded from all conversations, I could only guess at the truth. It riled me even more when I came to know that vindication for such behavior could be found in a well-known Tamil saying, "A thousand lies must be spoken to arrange a marriage."

Under these circumstances, it was difficult to greet the engagement ceremony with the enthusiasm it deserved. I had seen enough rituals to know that the ceremonial trappings would bear similarity: the right mantras would be chanted by a chorus of Vedic priests; the sacred hearth, Agni, made of baked clay, would take center stage fueled by libations of ghee or clarified butter; trays of flowers and fruits would be laid out; reeds made of coir would be dipped into small bowls of water and some kind of milky liquid and sprinkled around the fire at selected intervals; and a group of musicians — when given their cue by the priests would beat the drums loudly accompanied by the blare of the nadaswaram, a non-brass wind instrument, said to be one of the loudest in the world.

The Nichyathartham was conveniently arranged to take place in May, so as not to coincide with my final exams which were scheduled in April. I passed with distinction and was named valedictorian. A nun, who had traveled all the way from the Vatican for the graduation ceremony, presented me with a hard bound edition of Thomas Hardy's Tess of the d'Ubervilles. It was a surprisingly appropriate gift, one that struck a responsive chord in me. The social and sexual hypocrisy of Victorian aristocracy proved to be an equally apt description of the Brahmin community in Madras. I had witnessed first hand the uppityness displayed by Brahmins towards castes they considered inferior and, at the temples I frequented, I had seen the lecherous looks of the priests as their eyes traveled over the curve of my breasts. Cocksure of their anointed status, they intoned the mantras with reverence as their eyes roved licentiously over the gathering of young girls, their heads piously bowed in prayer asking God to forgive their sins.

The Nichayathartham formally announced my marriage to Raghu and, barring any unforeseen circumstances, it symbolized an unbroken pact between the families. The surety of this pledge made it safe to finally share my exciting news with my college friends. I announced my engagement to Raghu to my close circle of friend and, heeding Amma's advice, hid the fact that we had been corresponding by mail. After a chorus of congratulations, I answered the barrage of questions: Who was the boy? What did he do? When was the wedding? Where would it be held? Many envied my going abroad and starting a life free of the pressures and obligations that often came when living with one's in-laws. Much to my surprise, the usual questions about the size of my dowry and the kind of wedding sari I planned to wear never arose and I saw no reason to bring them up. That I had snagged a husband who would take me to America, a land they had come to believe as glamorous and rich from the Hollywood movies that found their way to Madras, was heralded as a marital coup that eclipsed their need to know much else. It struck me as I heard the banter of my friends — a motley crowd comprised of Hindus, Muslims, and Christians — that each and every one of them saw the path to marital bliss originating in a place other than their own. To live in India as a married woman, inevitably in a joint family, was to trade one set of shackles for another.

The festivities for the Nichayathartham were underway. Our house on Luz Avenue had been transformed. A huge pandal, a brightly-colored canopy, hoisted on thick and sturdy bamboo poles, had been erected over the front gate. It signaled to our neighbors and passers-by that a propitious occasion was about to take place. A necklace of bright green mango leaves adorned the archway. Decorative floral designs using powders of various colors, called Kolam in Tamil, had been carefully drawn in the courtyard and in the center of the living room floor. They were thought to bestow prosperity on the house-hold and it was a common sight to see Kolams of different designs grace the entrances of most homes.

Well-ahead of the wedding, four of my five maternal uncles along with their spouses and children had arrived from the major cities of Delhi, Bombay and Calcutta. Bed-rolls, suitcases, and per-sonal paraphernalia cluttered every available space and to make it across a room was like jumping hurdles in an obstacle race. Our fairly sedentary life turned chaotic with all the accommodations that had to be made from the use of the bathrooms to the cooking of all the meals. I welcomed the sudden frenzy of activity, the inces-sant chatter and the spontaneous outbursts of gaiety and laughter. The presence of so many relatives provided a pleasant diversion and kept me from dwelling on the darker thoughts that had plagued me earlier. Most of all, it was a refreshing change to see myself as a bride-to-be rather than a piece of merchandise to be bartered.

The Nichyathartham was an afternoon affair that commenced at an auspicious time pre-determined by the priests summoned for the occasion. They were the first to arrive and in short order the Agni, the sacred fire hearth, was lit accompanied by the chanting of the mantras. It was very much a family occasion with no outside guests. A more public version of the ceremony would be simulated on my wedding day by way of compensation. Raghu's family, along with some relatives I had never met, were the next to arrive and greeted with the kind of reverence reserved for royalty. Two huge platters called thamboolams, each representing the bride and groom's side, were laden with betel leaves, betel nuts, fruits, flowers, and vials of vermillion powder and turmeric. Towards the end of the ceremony, the platters would be exchanged to symbolize the forging of our families. The lagna patrika, a marriage document, perched on this bounty, would be read aloud by a Vedic priest conveying the acceptance of the alliance along with the date, time and venue of the wedding which signified that the agreement was final. The ceremony would conclude with the bride's crossing over to the groom's family.

Much as she did at the bride-viewing, Amma had selected my attire. It was a shimmering sea green sari in the latest style called oosi vanam, which literally meant sparks of needles in Tamil. And indeed, the tightly woven threads of gold that fell like a cascade over the sari looked like a glittering shower of needles. A set of green emeralds from the city of Jaipur, (a pre-wedding gift from my maternal uncle Raghu) was a perfect match for the color of my sari. The jewelry was far too ostentatious for my taste but I dared not offend my uncle who had made it a point to tell anyone who would listen that he had hand-picked the stones to calibrate perfectly in color and size. Dressed to the nines, my hair bedecked in flowers, I exuded an aura of wealth much like the ornately-clad and bejeweled mannequins on display in the shop windows.

My cousin, Urmila, led me to the living room to be presented to the gathered assembly, cautioning me along the way to keep my head bowed like a dutiful bride-to-be. The priest instructed me to sit on a wooden plank decorated with a simple Kolam pattern composed of rice flour, which much to my chagrin, left white blotches on my sari. It made it hard to concentrate on the proceedings which fortunately for me turned out to be short. The lagna patrika was read aloud to the simultaneous beat of the drums joined by the euphonic tones of the nadaswaram, the instrument tilted upwards, as if reaching towards the heavens, crying out to the gods to shower their blessings on this union. The two families rose, their respective platters in hand. Just as the exchange was about to take place, Amma, by some sleight of hand, pulled out an envelope from the folds of her sari and stuffed it under the wedding document. It was filled with cash, the first installment towards the dowry. I winced as I stepped around the Agni and crossed over to the groom's side. It was official. I now belonged to Raghu's family.

Chapter 11

Letters End

The epistolary nature of our courtship was coming to an end with Raghu's imminent departure. The enigma of sex had consumed the content of my past couple of letters and tormented me to the point that I was too exhausted to pursue the matter any further. What I did not know about sex, I would learn from the books Raghu promised to bring. Time was running short. My days of going to the post office to weigh and stamp my letters were about to cease. My last letter was still waiting to be written. It should have been a romantic farewell that charted the trajectory of our growing affection with its culmination in a deep and abiding love that surpassed expectation. Instead, I was weighted down by another concern which caused me as much anguish as my apprehensions about sex and had yet to be resolved. It had to do with the future of my education.

Early in the marriage negotiations, I openly expressed to Amma my one and only reservation. "Raghu must allow me to study after marriage. I want a college education." With her usual tough as nails attitude, she assured me by responding, "If Raghu cannot get you admission at his university, I will keep you with me after marriage, educate you and then send you to him." I had no reason to doubt her veracity. The story of her own hard fought battle with her father to secure her right to a college education, and her subsequent victory, had in repeated tellings become the stuff of family lore. The bravado she displayed by fleeing home in order to achieve her goal, had impressed Amma's siblings more than her championing of a cause which she embraced as a natural birthright. That I should covet the same for myself must have struck Amma as a natural request. Her solution seemed a viable option at the time, but now, my desire to start a new life with Raghu collided with my long cherished ambition of becoming the next Marie Curie. I had just completed my Pre-University program and had received high marks with distinction in all my subjects which placed me in the fifth rank among all the students who had taken the public exams in the state of Madras. I had my pick of colleges to pursue a Bachelor's Degree in Chemistry with the added bonus of a scholarship. To jettison such a golden opportunity without the guarantee of an equal if not better education tested the limits of what I was willing to sacrifice. I was in a quandary and asked myself over and over again, could my thirst for knowledge be sufficiently quenched by my love for Raghu?

I had been distracted by the fledgling nature of our courtship and it took four months into our correspondence before I could summon the courage to raise the topic of my studies. In early January, 1964, we periodically interrupted the flow of the more amorous content of our letters with brief detours into other arenas of our lives. Raghu wrote of his passion for mathematics and how it was the lifeblood of his existence. He was engaged in the kind of research where he posited a theory about some particular phenomenon and took up the challenge of finding a proof. It was an ardent quest for a mathematical truth that both exhilarated and consumed him and appeared to be an essential component of how he defined himself. Much of what he wrote was beyond my comprehension, handicapped as I was by age and the limits of a high school education. He had earned a PhD which I had never heard of and had no idea what the letters stood for except that it was a lofty degree to have been attained by someone so young. Strangely enough, I never asked Raghu directly for clarification nor did I bother to find out from anyone else. I doubted if even Amma knew what a PhD was, although it was a credential she constantly touted when people asked about the qualifications of her future son-in-law.

Compared to the heft of Raghu's resume, mine was gossamer-thin, yet, not without merit. Industrious and competitive by nature, I had garnered many honors in my school days, but, measured against Raghu's achievements, they amounted to a paltry sum. He was an intellectual giant, and I felt like David facing Goliath minus the slingshot. Having outshone my peers, I had no reason to be self-deprecating but I was competing with a child prodigy now and felt belittled in his company. In a tentative hand I wrote, " It would be a real shame to marry such an intelligent person as you, and I remain a veritable dud without even a degree to my name. My mom and dad have Masters degrees and I will have only attended Pre-University." I couched my desire to attend college in the form of a plea hoping it would resonate with a belief Raghu had espoused in one of his earlier letters, namely, that a wife should be equal to her husband. Although he had neglected to elaborate on the nature of this equality, at the time, I was thrilled at the overture he made. It was refreshing to know that I would have a voice in matters and that it would be heard and given due consideration in comparison to the subservience that was demanded of me. The euphoria I had initially felt had abated somewhat on a second reading as I slowly began to mature and ponder more seriously what it meant to be Raghu's equal. I was convinced that a college education was a necessary pre-requisite if I wanted to be the kind of wife Raghu wanted. I asked him to inquire about the admissions process and the length of time it would take for me to get a baccalaureate degree.

I was both heartened and disheartened by Raghu's response. He had contacted the admissions officer at New York University, procured an application and listed the educational records I would need to submit. He would also look into housing close to the college so I would not have to commute. I was touched by his earnest efforts and concern for my welfare but when he wrote that he was dead set on returning to India after two years which would cut short the four years required to get my degree, my heart sank. He softened the blow by suggesting I could continue my education after we settled down. It was a prospect I did not relish. I had experienced first-hand the bureaucratic hurdles endemic to the Indian educational system. Despite my excellent academic record at Good Shepherd Convent and the passing of my matriculation exams with honors, I had been denied admission at the only college to which I had applied, Queen Mary's. It was Amma's alma mater and as a former alumna, she was sure I would be accepted. It was a time of reverse discrimination towards Brahmins and the government had decreed that places be reserved for the underprivileged or, to use their term, the backward castes, no matter how stellar the record of the upper caste students. I was in a panic as I had not applied anywhere else and could not stomach the thought of discontinuing my studies. As a last ditch effort, Amma approached Stella Maris and although the deadline to apply had long passed, surprisingly, they accepted me. I had received a lucky break without resorting to bribery and/or nepotism, necessary evils, if one aspired for an education in India. It was highly unlikely in this climate to expect any college in India to blindly accept two years worth of courses from an American university. Raghu, educated entirely in India, was surely no stranger to these machinations and his response to the dilemma that I would eventually have to face — through no fault of my own — struck me as glib. I discerned an adamantine trait in him as he nonchalantly mapped out his future with only a slight nod in my direction. His preponderant use of the pronoun "I" when writing about the path of his career juxtaposed harshly with the more inclusive "we" he was prone to use when it came to speculating about other aspects of our life together.

I strained to respond in an adult-like manner and make clear that my education claimed top priority and that we should try to probe other alternatives but the words failed me. I reacted instead like a sulky child and privately nursed my disappointment. It was a natural reflex after years of habitual compliance and blighted hopes. Any urges I might have had to resist had been killed over the years by the smell of certain defeat. The recent fiasco with my mother over the dowry issue was still fresh in my mind and stuck out as an egregious example of her calloused indifference to my deep-seated beliefs about such a pernicious practice. I had been bred to conform and to obey and sank into a state of dependency. When I looked at Raghu, it was through this lens. He was six years older than I, mature, independent, responsible, kind and nurturing, qualities that made me trust in his guidance. I felt incapable of acting on my own and had my relationship with Raghu been filial, the wisdom I sought from him would have appeared as the kind of request any child would have made of her parent. I had not consciously thought of Raghu as a father figure — although, subconsciously I was attracted to traits of his personality which bore an uncanny resemblance to that of my father — and saw my reliance on him as another instance in the cycle of dependency that continued to revolve around my life. I was also smitten and did not want to jeopardize the only relationship that nourished the freedom to express myself without restraint. Why dampen his spirits or mine for that matter? I reverted to the cheerful tenor of my previous letters and in a complete volte face wrote, " I am prepared to sacrifice my studies for you darling. One can learn throughout one's life if one wants to. I could learn from you, couldn't I, my love? Anyway, we'll cross that bridge when we come to it."

I let four months slip by preoccupied more with the exigencies of the present than the uncertainties of the future. The month of April was a frenzied period with one final exam after another, followed by the graduation festivities. Now that my engagement ceremony had taken place, the wedding invitations had been printed and ready to send out. There was a certain protocol that had to be observed when it came to inviting people for one's marriage. Paternal relatives and close friends would take offense at receiving a mailed invitation and custom dictated they be invited personally. In most cases, maternal aunts and uncles on the girl's side were recruited for the task and served as stand-ins for the bride whose presence was neither expected nor required. Amma, in consultation with her siblings, had drawn up a list of invitees which was checked and double-checked several times to insure no one of import had been inadvertently omitted. This select group was divided amongst her siblings who would begin their rounds invitations in hand. So great was the risk of insult, that in a few instances, a second or third trip was warranted if no one had been home the first time. A simple phone call would have obviated the need of multiple visits but it was only people of means who could afford the luxury of owning a telephone and there were very few on the list.

My request to invite my closest friends in person was greeted with relief by my tired and leg-weary relatives and since they all had telephones, we were able to quickly arrange a meeting on the campus of Stella Maris so I could hand deliver my wedding invitations and use the occasion to commune one last time before being deluged by pre-wedding preparations. We had all matriculated the same year from Good Shepherd Convent and had now completed another rite of passage by earning our Pre-University degree. We had opted for different tracks, according to our interests, which spanned various disciplines in the Humanities, Physical Sciences or Natural Sciences, but found common ground in our elective courses which allowed us to cement the camaraderie forged in earlier times. The PU degree was conferred after a year and its goal was to prepare us for the rigor of specific subject areas at a college level. We competed with one another much like our school days but always in an atmosphere of genuine bonhomie that characterized our shared history. We were a new breed of young Indian women eager to enter the work force as professionals. There was no doubt in our minds that a college education was the ticket to success and, if our marks on the final exams turned out to be as high as we had hoped, there was a good chance of staying on at Stella Maris for the Bachelor's Degree. Considered to be one of the most prestigious colleges in Madras, we would be recipients of an elite education that uniquely qualified us to enter a vocation of our own choosing.

In what had become a common ritual, we gathered under our favorite tree and congratulated ourselves on a job well done. We could finally call ourselves Stella Maris girls and laughingly recalled the first day of convocation when Mother Superior, with a radiant smile on her face and with arms outstretched as if she were about to hug us to her bosom, said in a voice pregnant with hope, " You will all become stars of the sea and carry the name of our college wherever you go." Those words, we had initially dismissed as empty rhetoric, had in the short span of a year acquired a gravitas that would come to define how we saw ourselves and how we intended to direct our future.

We formed our usual circle, a familiar setting for our conversations both serious and trivial. The topic, uppermost in everyone's mind save mine, was the pursuit of their undergraduate education. I lowered the hand that clutched my wedding invitations and hoping no one would notice, I casually draped my sari to shield them from view. I stepped back slightly, a creeping sense of distance beginning to take hold and watched and listened as each one in turn boldly proclaimed her ambition with a markedly blithe unconcern should an unforeseen contingency arise. "No doubt I'll continue maths here at Stella," said Rama, who, since our days at Good Shepherd Convent, had evidenced her prowess in the subject by acing every exam. Viji, my best friend, chimed in next. " I'm going in for literature and who knows, maybe I'll replace Miss Prema, our English teacher. You all know she's getting married and had to give up her job." Janet, the rebel of Good Shepherd, who had always seemed more interested in the boys from Loyola College than in her studies, surprised us all by announcing, "I plan to be a doctor. It will be a grueling course of study but I'm confident I'll make it." Lastly, came Bridget, Janet's more shy and retiring sister. She had been held back a grade when she started at Good Shepherd Convent and wound up in the same class as Janet despite being older. This had made her a target for merciless taunts by her fellow classmates who cruelly referred to her as the "dumb sister." It was no different at Stella Maris. Her marks were always lower than Janet's and she was considered a least likely candidate to pursue a college education. It was quite a shock to hear her say quietly, in a voice full of conviction, " I'm going in for Tamil studies and want to be a teacher. I'll apply to as many colleges as I can. I'm bound to get in somewhere."

My usual garrulous self ached in silence. The triumphant spirit of my classmates made the deflation of my own hard to bear. It seemed incongruous that only weeks ago, I had addressed them as their class valedictorian, a sterling example of someone who was destined to go to college, only to find myself on the margins playing eavesdropper to aspirations that were beyond my reach. It had taken five years to shed my status as the foreign-returned girl and earn my citizenship among this circle of friends as a bona fide Indian, yet, once again, I stood apart from them, an anachronistic figure who belonged to an older generation. As the only one in the group to have readily submitted to an arranged marriage at the age of fifteen — considered to be young even at the time — I knew deep in my heart that my friends saw my future to be a sad repetition of the lives of their own mothers who were forced to give up their education, in some cases, while in elementary school, the minute their marriages were fixed. In countless conversations stemming from our days together at Good Shepherd Convent, they had railed against the practice of child marriage and with fierce determination had latched onto their dreams of becoming professional women. Although they had not ruled out the possibility of marriage, it was of secondary importance when it came to carving out their careers.

I would have done anything to recover a fraction of the tenacious spirit that had guided my friends through the Pre-University year and continued into their future. But the premature death of my father and the quick arrangement of my marriage a year later, had snuffed it out. I had not noticed its loss until now. Standing in this milieu suffused with excitement and enthusiastic outbursts, I was ashamed to be a bride-to-be. The exuberance of falling in love, the elation of my upcoming wedding day, and the joy mixed with fear of starting a new life in a country, thousands of miles away from a place which I now called home, quickly evaporated. My ambition to be a good wife, a perfect domestic partner for Raghu, now appeared as a trivial goal, a betrayal of the beliefs I had once espoused. What hurt most was that I had let down my friends in the worst possible way. I tightened my grip over the wedding invitations and would have crumpled them if I could, had they not been the reason I called my friends together in the first place.

What happened next was a ringing testimony to the kind of goodwill that only the best of friends could have offered. In a spontaneous gesture of collective embrace, I was drawn into the arms of my friends. A medley of voices broke through: "So lucky you are Vasundara, getting married and all. No need anymore to study for exams. You will be on honeymoon with your would-be all your life." Their positive spin on marriage would have been laughable under different circumstances, nevertheless, it saved me from the embarrassment of having to tell them that my educational plans were up in the air. I feigned my appearance as a blushing bride-to-be and extracted a promise from each of my friends to attend my wedding as I pressed the invitations into their hands. They knew better than to ask about my college plans. They had seen enough in their young lives to conclude without a doubt that marriage and education were mutually exclusive. I had, in our time together, earned their admiration as a leader be it as captain of the sports team at Good Shepherd or, more recently, as valedictorian, but the roles were now reversed. It was they who were the pioneers, sloughing off antiquated practices to clear the path that lay ahead and it was I who had been left behind.

I bid farewell to much more than my friends that day. They had framed the first five chapters of my adolescent years. It was about to end abruptly as I took on the adult role of wife. They would continue to enjoy a sense of security under the aegis of their parents and the concomitant insouciance that came with being a teenager. Marrying young, robbed me of both those experiences. My initial excitement of carving out a new life in New York was replaced by a deeper malaise at the thought of being separated from my mother, under whose protection, for better or worse, I had lived all these years. The afflictions that plagued me now were chained to reminiscences of my childhood. Taking on the role of surrogate mother to my younger brother at the age of seven had forced me to be mature and forfeit much of the playfulness normal to those years. I had been too young and too obedient to act on the resentment I felt at the time and what had been bottled up then spilled into my present when I realized that my adolescent years were soon to be truncated in a similar way. At age sixteen I would assume my role as wife. The romantic tableau I had pictured for myself began to blur when I gave serious thought to what I might have to sacrifice by way of my education.

These thoughts and many more troubled me on the bus ride home. I was haunted by a different sense of dislocation that went beyond the travails of assimilation. I had succeeded in reinventing myself over the past five years, oftentimes painfully, in my adoption of and adaption to rites, customs, and cultural nuances and in the process had subsumed my personal desires and ambitions. Unlike my friends, who felt entitled to a college education and were optimistic in their pursuit of it, I had let uncertainty dictate my future. I began to question if Amma's assurances to educate me were genuine or merely her way of appeasing me. I was even more perplexed by the contradictions that surfaced when I took a hard, dispassionate appraisal of some of my mother's attributes that drove her own desire to become a well-educated woman.

Born into the same generation as that of my friends' mothers, she stood apart from them in her refusal to get married at a young age and not before acquiring a college degree. Her act of defiance was leveled not only at her father but also at the prevailing attitudes at the time where marriage and not education was the end goal for most young girls. It was this iconoclastic spirit in my mother that distinguished me from my fellow classmates who constantly bemoaned the fate of their own mothers whose education was often stopped midway once they were engaged to be married. These were women who would never know their intellectual potential nor could they ever hope to resurrect it in the future. The only measure of their talent that had counted for anything lay in their ability to produce children, preferably boys, and in running a household to their husband's satisfaction. The anger expressed by my friends was unmistakably audible as was their sadness as their voices tapered off into disappointment and pity replaced what should have been pride as they recalled the lives of their mothers. Nevertheless, they were a gutsy lot and when the focus shifted to their own aspirations, they vehemently declared, " We will never be cowed into submission." Sympathetic as I was to the concerns of my friends, I felt none of their anxiety. I was so confident that a mother like mine would never yield to so inimical a practice as child-marriage and certainly not at the cost of throwing away my education. I could not have been more wrong.

Amma had always gone against the tide and met with success. Had she thought I would do the same and not let marriage stand in the way of my own education? Did she have more confidence in me than I had in myself? Her past wove into my present, threads of hope crisscrossing threads of despair. I had tasted none of the independence that had fed my mother over the years and at age sixteen, I was unsure I could match the audacity she had shown while in her twenties. She had overthrown the barriers that had impeded her progress and had paradoxically reinstated them in my life. Instead of joining my peers who had poised themselves on the cusp of modernity, I had been hurled into a past inhabited by women, not only of my mother's generation, but of the one preceding it as well. The fact that I would be married after reaching puberty and, not earlier like both my grandmothers, was a distinction of little import. It was an uneasy time and place to begin a new chapter in my life. I had long discarded the book of my American childhood and written myself into a new narrative that was distinctly Indian. Despite the pitfalls, Indian culture had a seductive hold on me. I was reluctant to escape its grasp. Carving out a new life in America with Raghu filled me with trepidation. What I saw before me was a rocky road to maturity and, instead of taking a big stride forward, I would start my journey one baby step at a time. The reinvention of myself was about to begin as I hurried home to pen my very last letter to Raghu.

" About the application," I began, "I'll be able to get all my certificates, Matriculation and PU, only after June 2. The principal is away right now. This is very troublesome as I want to get everything settled before we get back. Will July be too late for submitting my records? I do hope everything turns out alright and am very worried as I earnestly want to study." It was a sharp detour from the obsequious tone I had adopted previously and it felt strangely satisfying. I threw in a couple of hastily scribbled paragraphs indicating my excitement over Raghu's arrival and signed off with what now had become stock expressions of my love for him. I dashed to the post office and paid the exorbitant but well-worth price of express mail. It was a lovely thought to start off our marriage in an ambience of togetherness, but it was even lovelier to see myself as a young woman who had taken her first bite at independence.

Chapter 12

Anticipation

In a matter of weeks, May 15th to be exact, Raghu would be leaving New York and arriving in Madras on May 17th well in time for our wedding on June 5th. We crammed in as many letters as time would allow barely able to contain the surge of passion we felt for each other. Our growing love for one another, limited to pen and paper over the past eight months, screamed to be expressed in person. We imagined our first kiss. I confessed to being shy and naive and asked Raghu how a kiss started and whether it was proper for us to kiss before marriage. He admitted that what little knowledge he possessed about kissing came directly from Hollywood movies. He dismissed my doubts as silly and assured me that a kiss was a natural expression of love between two people that required no particular technique nor the sanction of marriage. "If there is such a thing as a perfect kiss, we will discover our own version of it," he concluded. With a touch of humor, he suggested we indulge in short "kissing sessions" every weekday evening followed by ones of longer duration on the weekends until we were thoroughly exhausted and fell asleep in each other's arms.

Our thoughts raced ahead to his arrival at Madras airport and we speculated as to how we would react on seeing each other in person. We wrote of our desire to be swept up in each other's arms, planting kisses on each other's lips. However, in the following sentences, we were both quick to shoot down our love-fueled fantasy with a more sober description of what would actually transpire. We were painfully aware that such a public display of affection could never take place with our families looking on and resigned ourselves to the fact that at best we could exchange a smile and maybe, on the sly, manage a squeeze of the hand. "You can rest assured," Raghu wrote "that at a later time, when we are alone, nothing in the world can stop me from kissing my lady love."

As our letter-writing days drew to a close, I had graduated from pen pal, to girlfriend, to soon-to-be wife. With a sense of abandon, I shamelessly expressed my physical longing for Raghu finding in the written word a safe outlet and a kind of emancipation I had never known. The end of our letters also meant an end to my adolescent musings on love. In a month's time, I would become his wife, a role I felt ill-equipped to handle. It was one thing to let loose on paper the passion I had towards Raghu, and quite another to translate those thoughts into action. My knowledge of romantic love had always been vicarious, drawn primarily from pulp fiction and the movies. I had absolutely no experience in real life to serve as a guide and felt inadequately prepared to assume my new status as his wife. I began to fret. I reflected on my past letters where I had bandied around with the term, "wife." I wrote easily of my willingness to do all the household chores as if it were my duty to be Raghu's caretaker. It was a notion, deeply embedded in my childhood role as my younger brother's guardian along with being my mother's little helper. At other moments, I elevated the status to include myself as Raghu's partner and lover with no clue as to what this entailed except that it sounded sophisticated on paper. I also prayed he would never become an absentee husband like my father. The pain of abandonment that had plagued me most of my life had already left deep scars. I wanted to bury that part of my past and look to the future with renewed hope.

Time was running out with Raghu's imminent departure, leaving only a small window to pen my remaining letters. Jittery and desperate, I decided to be upfront with Raghu and lay bare my doubts and ignorance about what it meant to be a wife. In a show of honesty, I readily admitted that I had no expertise in the culinary arts and asked him to give me a run down of what he ate for each meal. Except for dinner, his breakfast and lunch fortunately consisted of ready-made foods like bread, cheese, milk and orange juice. On the other hand, when he mentioned rasam and sambar were the main staples of his evening meals, it sent me running to Amma for a crash course in Indian cooking. Busy with the wedding preparations, she palmed me off on her younger sister, my aunt Sasi, instructing her to take me in for a week and teach me the basics of South Indian cuisine. Eager to be a quick study, I spent the first few days following my aunt around the kitchen, notebook in hand, trying to jot down with great precision the exact amount of each of the ingredients required for the various recipes. It was a wasted venture. My aunt, noted for being a top-notch cook, never measured anything out. When I pressed her to tell me the quantities in terms of teaspoons and tablespoons, she laughed and said, "I learned to cook by observing my mother. There were no spoons in our house. We measured everything by hand." Seeing that my palm was of a similar size to my aunt's, I created a table of equivalencies for myself: 1 teaspoon = a quarter palmful; 1 tablespoon = half a palmful. I carefully tabulated the required amounts of dry ingredients for each recipe. However, an ingredient like tamarind pulp posed a problem. An essential base for making both rasam and sambar, too much tamarind would render the dishes overly sour and too little would make them bland. Measurements in terms of teaspoons and tablespoons were of no help in gauging the right amount of the gooey paste. The best advice my aunt could offer was to make a ball of the tamarind paste equivalent in size to that of a lemon, specifically an Indian lemon. "Now, remember Vasu," she cautioned me, "that's half the size of those big lemons I hear you have in America." By week's end I could make not one but two kinds of rasam and two kinds of sambar. I could now safely guarantee a few good dinners for Raghu.

Once I returned home, I dashed off a letter to Raghu to let him know of my recent culinary accomplishments. His reply was a touching one: " Please don't take your role as a housewife too seriously. My dearest angel, I love you as you are and if you are ignorant about a few facts of life, I really don't mind. We will learn together on how you can be a housewife and I can be a house husband (if there is such a thing)." His unreserved acceptance of me and willingness to be my domestic partner comforted me greatly. Learning how to cook no longer appeared a daunting task and I crossed it off my checklist of wifely duties. I was beset by more serious concerns which I could barely articulate to myself let alone in writing. They hung in limbo as I struggled to find the vocabulary that would make them more tangible. It was the fortuitous arrival of Raghu's next letter that both spared and saved me from having to address the matter directly.

Dated May 2, 1964, exactly two weeks before his departure, Raghu wrote of a growing "funny feeling," inside him. " I feel impatient and slightly uneasy, uneasy because I have always been somewhat irresponsible. And now, I have to change my way of life. I don't mind it in the least as long as you are with me." His next few lines struck at the core of my angst as if we had become telepathically linked over the course of the last eight months. In near textbook fashion, and in a clinical tone, he wrote, " Regarding sex matters, my education is now more or less complete. I have finished two books and they have now given me a precise knowledge whereas earlier I was only vaguely informed of various things. It does not take much time to learn these things and once we are married, we will have plenty of time to learn. Please do not worry." However, I did worry.

Raghu's allusions to "sex matters," and "various things," gained no clarity despite my repeated efforts to parse their meaning. That he had acquired competence in the subject of sex only exacerbated my own ignorance. I implored him to bring me the books hoping a crash course before the wedding would put us on an equal footing. In the interim, I scoured my brain for any tidbit of information that might have lodged itself in my memory that dealt with sexual matters. The first thing I turned to was my collection of romance novels leafing through the pages of each one while I scanned for passages that described moments of physical intimacy between lovers. Without exception, in what appeared to be a collective act of plagiarism, every romantic encounter was rendered in similar terms. There were plenty of "heaving bosoms," and "ardent passionate kisses," culminating in a grand finale where the heroine got swept up in the arms of her hero as he carried her towards the bedroom. What happened next was left to the imagination of the reader, only in my case, my imagination stretched no further than the words on the page.

The few Hollywood movies I had occasion to see, most of them of the Rock Hudson-Doris Day variety, barely alluded to what Raghu called "sex matters." The bedroom scenes presented a sanitized version of sex, much like my romance novels. I fared no better with my steady diet of Tamil films. The Central Board of Film Certification, popularly known as the Censor Board, banned kissing between the sexes in all cinema. Lovers were often shown in a close embrace and just as their lips were about to touch, the camera quickly cut to a scene either of bees pollinating flowers or of merging waves crashing towards the shore. The deeper symbolism of such imagery escaped me at the time and signified nothing more than what I believed to be a true meeting of two minds and two hearts.

A feeling of helplessness crept over me. I had never conversed about sexual matters with any of my girlfriends either here in Madras or in Parkway Village. I often thought that my parents' decision to uproot me from America was deliberately timed to quash any interest I might have developed in the opposite sex. The quick and sudden immersion into Indian culture under the strict guardianship of my paternal aunt and uncle sealed off all contact with the male species. Where in this sheltered existence could I even remotely hope to get an education on sex?

I began to take stock of my own feelings about the opposite sex, feelings I considered to be genuine, unencumbered by parental authority or societal rules. I recalled the childish crush I had on Sergio Quimper, the tall and handsome Peruvian boy, several grades ahead of me at the UN School. I ogled him from afar without receiving so much as a glance in my direction. No other boy in Parkway Village captured my interest neither had there been any opportunity to cultivate a relationship with someone new. My mother made sure of that. After all these years I could still taste the bitter disappointment of being forced to drop out of the UNIS swim team because it meant competing with teams from other schools where according to my mother, "strange boys would be present." Similar reasons governed her ban on my attending "mixed" birthday parties, namely, parties, where boys were invited. Filled with resentment over my mother's behavior which I saw as grossly unjust, I lapsed into daydreaming about boys. I imagined myself in the arms of a boy, dancing cheek to cheek, just like the couples on Dick Clark's American Bandstand. It was painfully obvious that this would never come to pass yet I continued to dream. I found sustenance in these scenarios of romance and as I reflected upon my past, I realized with a new found clarity that my notions of love had been derived solely from the fictional world of books and movies.

I would have remained content with these self-concocted fantasies but for the intrusion of two ugly encounters which confirmed my mother's worst fears about strange boys wanting to do me harm. I dredged up the incident of the boy in Parkway Village who had tried to pull off my underwear although I still had no idea what he would have done had he succeeded. But what hurt me more, now, as it did then, was my mother's reaction. By dunking me in a tub of scalding water and admonishing me to scrub myself clean, I, for the first time, saw my body as an appendage, too dirty to be worthy of scrutiny. I was afraid to see myself completely naked in the mirror and was not in the least bit curious as to what it would reveal. I became overly meticulous about keeping my body clean and washed my private parts with the kind of dispassion I reserved when tackling a sink full of dirty dishes. Very little had changed since that incident. My body still remained a mystery to me.

The more recent jeep incident with the military drunks, and my narrow escape, had injected a certain amount of fear in me. Again, it was the lack of empathy on my mother's part that further estranged me from my body. Her concern as to whether I had been defiled in some way overrode her concern over my mental well-being. As before, she ordered me to bathe immediately except this time I did not need her to scrub me clean.

I wandered back in time to the days of my arrival at my grandfather's home on Mahalakshmi Street. The sudden shedding of my western clothes followed by an equally sudden shift to the half-sari made me more aware of my body than ever before. I had barely noticed that my breasts were beginning to develop and could not comprehend the cultural imperative to keep them covered. They became a source of embarrassment and I developed a nervous habit of adjusting and re-adjusting the folds of my half-sari, particularly in male company, only to find them staring at my breasts with a sly look that I was too young at the time to decipher but knew intuitively was the wrong kind of look to cast in my direction.

My first menstrual period reinforced the idea that my body was polluted. Its natural tendency to ovulate was seen as an abnormal process, one that demanded three days of isolation. My aunt's public manner of purifying me by the well in the backyard was a cruel baptism and I could still feel the shame of standing half-naked in a thin cotton towel while the boys next door ogled my body.

More shame followed when Amma shipped half a dozen Maidenform bras along with her usual quota of Kotex napkins. Excited at the prospect of wearing my first bra, I thought of Ann Wald, my close friend in Parkway Village, who was the first one in our group to wear a bra and the mischievous delight we took in peering down her blouse. I knew not to expect a similar reception here. No one I knew wore a bra. I, much like the girls next door, wore a shapeless piece of cloth resembling a sleeveless vest with hooked clasps running down the front as an undergarment. My breasts looked like flattened pancakes. It would be a welcome relief to restore their shape in my new Maidenform bra.

My uncle, who ordinarily deferred to my aunt when it came to the female aspects of my upbringing, asserted his authority in the matter of my wearing a bra. The pointy cups and thin straps that were bound to be visible under my blouse was immodest attire, he said, for a young Brahmin girl. Yet, he was answerable to my mother who was bound to ask me in her next letter if the bras were of the right size and fit comfortably. My uncle's solution was to have me wear the usual cotton vest over my bra to mitigate its seductive features. Forced to compromise, I went to school sweltering under all the extra padding. As I stood in line during assembly, my blouse soaked in perspiration, the girl behind me whispered, "Your bra is showing." Afraid of being caught by Mother John, the headmistress, for talking in line, I could not offer a rejoinder. Just as assembly was about to end with The Lord's Prayer, I felt the tip of a pen on my back as the girl behind me hurriedly traced the outline of my bra straps. Branded, much like Hester Prynne in The Scarlett Letter, with the inked sketch of my bra clearly visible to one and all, I was forced to endure the derisive laughter and jeers of my classmates who thought it was ridiculous to cover up my bra when the whole point of wearing it was to display my femininity. It was yet another cruel inauguration that left me ashamed of my body.

As I reflected on these memories, I concluded that to come of age in India was fraught with contradictions. Whether covered up or half-naked, a girl's body simply did not belong to her. Underlying all that Brahmin orthodoxy was an inviolable assumption that the female body was inherently seductive to men and needed to be contained. To give it free reign would yield only perilous results. Ironically, it was the men who came across as the weaker sex. Impotent to control their sexual urges, they were the ones in need of the utmost protection.

"What's past is prologue," wrote Shakespeare in The Tempest and in ruminating on the more regrettable circumstances of my upbringing, was I deluding myself into thinking I could start anew? Was this why I had deliberately omitted mention of the boy in Parkway Village and the jeep incident in my letters to Raghu despite our growing intimacy? It was a sad introduction to the awareness of my own physical being that had left an indelible taint in its wake. I would have never indulged in all this self-examination were it not for Raghu who chose to bring up the topic of sex just as our letter-writing phase was coming to an end. The exercise was a painful one. Its revelations provided no cathartic relief whatsoever and only made me more agitated. In my letters to Raghu, I had painted myself as innocent and pristine in keeping with what I imagined a young bride ought to be. That portrait now appeared punctured by the stabs of tradition and the vagaries of human nature.

I could not shake these misgivings. Although I no longer was subjected to the rigid rearing by my paternal aunt and uncle, Amma, albeit less orthodox, imposed her own set of rules. She did not insist on isolating me for three days during my menstrual period and I was free to roam around the house save for the kitchen area and puja room where she performed her daily prayers. It was customary to first offer our daily food to God before we ate and the presence of a menstruating female in the cooking area was considered a sacrilege. Now, the fourth day purification took place in the privacy of my bathroom and not by the well, although we had one in our backyard. There were other rules as well. I was never to come out of the bathroom with just a towel wrapped around me. Except for my sari, which could easily get wet, I had to emerge practically fully dressed in my underclothing, petticoat, and blouse with the damp towel draped over my breasts.

Amma continued to buy and select my attire much as she had done throughout my life. The crisp, cotton saris, which I favored, given the scorching heat of Madras, were rejected for nylon ones. "Who is to starch and iron all this cotton?" she asked irritably. "By the end of the day, they will be all wrinkled and make you look unattractive. Nylon saris are much easier to maintain." Amma always chose dark colors with heavily dotted prints and with a matching blouse made of thick cotton, she felt doubly assured that my bra would not show. I often took a ribbing from my college friends who called me "The Grim Reaper," and thought my clothes made me looked dour and old womanish. My bra remained hidden but I was grateful to be rid of those awful shapeless vests my uncle had forced me to wear.

It was a time of daring experimentation in fashion as far as the conservative crowd of Madras was concerned. Less cosmopolitan than the larger cities of Delhi and Bombay, the new more liberating styles were slow to catch on. Popularized by the female stars of Tamil cinema, "glass nylon saris," aptly named for their see-through quality, were worn by the intrepid few who braved the risk of being labelled as sluts. Blouses had gone sleeveless or were stitched "boatneck" style which seductively bared the curves of one's shoulders. It was a foregone conclusion that Amma would never approve of me wearing a glass nylon sari or a sleeveless blouse. How could I forget her arduous undertaking to comb the stores of Paris until she procured the mauve bathing suit with sleeves? In a moment of irrational optimism, I begged her to have just one boat-neck blouse stitched for me. I bolstered my plea by rattling off the names of the girls in my college, with careful mention of the Brahmin ones with mothers as strict as mine, who, without the slightest compunction, took readily to the new fad. It held no sway with Amma. Her refusal hit me hard and the words she uttered stung. "You might as well go naked," she retorted.

It was impossible to negotiate with Amma. Her sense of decorum was so rigid and combined with my proclivity to be malleable, it prevented me from developing a taste in clothes, either in color or style, that I could uniquely call my own. I could see myself only through her eyes and, in more ways than I cared to admit, I adopted not only her aesthetic sense, but also her sense of propriety.

I enjoyed none of the excitement of shopping for my wedding trousseau since Amma had picked the inopportune time of my final exams to make most of the major purchases. I was often asked to bring in the stack of sari boxes when her close women friends came calling. One sari after another was closely scrutinized for the size and design of its border, the weight of its gold threads and, finally, the ornateness of its pallu. No one oohed or aahed at the array of morose colors; there were only polite murmurs of approval. Even the wedding sari, the star of the collection, elicited a muted response. Instead of the customary bright red, Amma had chosen a rust-color with gold checks which in her opinion had just the right touch of sophistication and elegance. Amma's sisters, however, were more vociferous in their comments. They insisted that the reception sari, which was yet to be bought, be of a bright color. "Come on Babu," they said calling her by her pet name, " Vasu is too young to wear such dark colors. They may be fine for you but this is her wedding and she should wear cheerful colors." Goaded into submission, Amma reluctantly bought a red Benares tissue sari heavily brocaded in gold and silver threads. Its effulgence had a blinding effect and was way too gaudy for my taste. How I wished Amma had not relented. On one or two occasions, I did get to accompany Amma to buy a few silk saris for my daily wardrobe after marriage. The shopkeeper, on learning I was soon to be wedded and shortly after live in America, excitedly pulled out his supply of hot pink and parrot green saris. "Madam, these are in fashion. Everyone in America will marvel at these colors," he exclaimed. I, by now, needed no prompting from Amma, and immediately grimaced at the riot of color spread before me. I angrily shoved the saris aside much to the shopkeeper's chagrin and grew annoyed at his persistent efforts to convince me that these colors were all the rage among brides-to-be. When I finalized my selection, he became downright despondent. "Why, Madam, all these sober colors?" he asked in a mournful voice. I proudly eyed my new collection of saris in dark maroon, navy blue, bottle green and basic black. His opinion hardly mattered when I saw the look of approval on Amma's face. There was a self-congratulatory air about her. Her only daughter had become a mirror image of herself.

Until now, I had never passed judgment on the new trends in fashion and given Amma's recalcitrant personality, I knew I would always be reduced to being a mere observer as styles came and disappeared. What I did not anticipate was the sense of moral rectitude I had come to acquire when it came to sartorial etiquette. I asked our family tailor to lengthen my blouses so as to cover my midriff that had always been modestly bared and I had my neckline raised to insure maximum coverage of my cleavage. I imposed my own decorous standards on others and began to look down on the Brahmin girls who abandoned the sari and chose instead to parade around in the North Indian pant-shirt combination called salwar and kameez. Their manly appearance desecrated the sanctity of the sari which I saw as my duty to preserve. The trousers, tapered tightly from the knee down, revealed the curvature of their legs and the flimsy scarf-like dupatta, meant to cover their breasts, was often thrown carelessly over the top and functioned more as an accoutrement. My cousin, Urmila, who had arrived from Delhi well-before the wedding, was another source of irritation. Her very presence brought back unpleasant memories of my childhood vacations in India, during which time, Amma's siblings constantly compared our looks. Urmila was the fair-skinned beauty while I suffered from a darker complexion. I had borne the brunt of their criticism knowing full well that my stay in India was short-lived and that I could safely retreat to my home in America. Now that India was my permanent home, there was no escape. Urmila strutted around our home in a sleeveless blouse, exposing her armpits, impervious to the presence of all the relatives who had descended on our home including my maternal grandparents who, in my opinion, deserved more respect. Her boat-neck blouses were a cruel reminder that my recent request to wear the same had been dismissed outright. I seethed with envy but could not rightfully chastise her without chastising myself. I resorted to sneering behind her back by telling myself she had pudgy shoulders. I found it hypocritical to hear some of my aunts, who denounced the new styles publicly, refer repeatedly to Urmila as stylish and modern and in the same breath mock me for being a country girl. I had hoped as the bride-to-be to take center stage but felt humiliated yet again to play second fiddle to my cousin. Their false show of conservatism aggravated me no end and I manufactured every excuse possible so as not to linger long in their company. The only way I knew to retaliate was to wear my modesty like a badge of honor, a sign to anyone who laid eyes on me that I was a virtuous girl. I recalled what I wrote in my very first letter to Raghu when he asked me to describe myself. "I'm a simple girl," I responded, " with high moral principles." Eight months later, with our wedding only a month away, I began to question my new found sense of sanctimony.

Just reading the word sex in Raghu's letter was enough to wrest me from my moral universe. Without warning, it had infiltrated my vocabulary without definition or contextual clues to assess its meaning. Unlike Raghu, who could boast of his mastery on the topic, I was devoid of access to a single reference, be it a book or a person. Indeed, I had never uttered the word to myself nor committed it to writing. I could only look to my own body for an answer. My earlier visions of physical closeness with Raghu grew beyond passionate kisses and tight embraces. I was aroused at the thought of him fondling my breasts and indulged in the sensation savoring it as one would a guilty pleasure. Whether by instinct or intuition I could not tell, but I suspected that something else was supposed to happen once our bodies met. At this point, my thoughts came to a sudden halt and I could visualize nothing further. What I did know was that, for the first time, my body was desirous of touch and, in turn, desired by another.

This new perception of my body with all its visceral complexity was a radical change from anything I had ever known. The particular shibboleths of Brahmin culture had forced me to view the physical transformations of my body from the development of breasts to its natural function to ovulate as aberrations that needed to be contained. With no overt mention of sex, every gesture, every item of clothing, down to every movement had been imbued with sexual innuendos. A female had to be constantly on guard when it came to men. It was true that I had experienced strange men as threats but I had also fallen in love with a man who was a stranger to me a mere eight months ago. Raghu had promised to allay my fears in a spirit of togetherness while recognizing my innocence. It would be a gentle start to my education in sexual matters at the age of sixteen. I could finally anticipate the liberation of my body from the prison that had been its home.

Chapter 13

Dating Indian Style

At long last, the waiting, the letter-writing, and the flights of imagination that had consumed the better part of the last eight months of my life, was over. It was Sunday, May 17, 1964, and Raghu's flight was due to arrive at 7:30 am. It was an hour's drive to the airport and Amma, afraid of being late, hurried me into getting ready. I wanted to look my best for Raghu but could barely make out my face in the dimly-lit bathroom mirror. Nervous with excitement, I broke into a sweat in spite of the coolness of the pre-dawn hours and hastily daubed myself from top to bottom with talcum powder. I smeared a little EyeTex on my index finger and applied the kohl paste to my lower eyelid and with a shaky hand attempted to draw a circular bindi in the center of my forehead but it wound up looking more like an ellipse. I peered into the mirror and even the poor lighting could not mask the fact that I looked like a ghost with raccoon eyes. I wiped the powder, which had now begun to streak, off my face and quickly dressed in a dark-colored light silk sari. Whether it was a deep navy blue or black was hard to tell. I could hear Amma urging me on and told myself that this would have to do. Besides, Raghu loved me for who I was and not for my looks.

It should have been me and not Amma who first spotted Raghu as he walked across the tarmac towards the arrival area. I hardly recognized the slim man in a sporty striped blue and white short-sleeved shirt that grazed the waist of his dark blue slacks. I had imagined him as I last saw him — a bit chubby with scant attention to sartorial concerns, his eyes radiating kindness along with a warm smile that made him unconventionally handsome. I was pleasantly taken aback by his suave appearance and, as I reveled at the sight of him, Amma cast a disapproving eye in my direction and sneered, " Look at Raghu! He has transformed himself into a gorgeous looking groom. I wonder if he'll still want to marry you. You've become so dark under all this sun. It would be a miracle if he takes you as his bride!" For a split second, I came close to hating my mother. Her caustic remarks lacerated my heart and drained the joy out of me. I struggled to fight back the tears and never felt more ugly than I did at that moment. Why, I asked myself, would Amma choose this day of all days to crush my self-esteem. Was it too far-fetched an idea to think she was jealous of my happiness? I was at a loss for answers and did what I could to quickly regain my composure. I no longer cared if my skin was dark, or if my bindi was lopsided, or if my face was splotched with talcum powder. In a matter of minutes, I saw Raghu heading straight towards me, his jet-weary eyes sparkling with familiar kindness. He inched closer to where I stood and broke into a smile without uttering a word. His mere presence was enough to comfort me. I looked into his bespectacled eyes; floating in an aqueous pool was a beautiful reflection of myself.

We spoke to each other for the very first time when I softly asked him in Tamil, "Sowkyama?" to which he replied, "Sowkyam." It was a standard greeting, an ordinary exchange of the "how are you-I'm fine," variety. We both knew it would have to suffice what with his father and uncle and my mother and my uncle watching our every move. A surreptitious squeeze of my hand which he had mentioned in one of his letters was a nigh impossibility as our families crowded between us like human shields. Baggage in hand, Raghu was about to depart for his home but not before asking my mother if he could come by in a day or two and take me out. Much to my surprise, she said yes. I was baffled by the mercurial nature of Amma's temperament never knowing with any certitude whether a favor would be withheld or bestowed. Nevertheless, I was grateful for the least bit of indulgence she threw my way much like a hungry dog snatching at a bone.

I was beginning to feel the effects of the frenetic pace of the morning and had hoped the one hour car ride home would allow me to wallow in a state of pleasant lassitude in the company of the foremost thought on my mind — my first date with Raghu. Instead, I was held captive to Amma's continuous gushing over Raghu's new look as if she were the bride-to-be, which I would have been willing to tolerate had she not compared me to him in the most unflattering terms with the same refrain of being too dark and too thin and the miracle it would take to transform me into a half-way decent looking bride. Her incessant harping blunted my spirits and the excitement that had greeted this long awaited day sunk to a low ebb. I curled up in the back seat like a wounded animal and wished with all my might that the dead could speak so that once again I could hear Appa whisper in my ear, "You're the apple of my eye."

The attention I had received from Appa over the years until his death had sufficed in large measure to offset what often seemed to me a deliberate effort on Amma's part to not issue any compliments where I was concerned. In moments of self-doubt, a favorite quip of Appa's echoed in my head like a personal mantra, "Beauty and brains often don't go together except in your case, Vasu." What had sustained me in the past had lost its potency with his passing. It was to Amma I turned, hoping against hope for the slightest form of approval, be it a smile or a glint of admiration in her eyes. I would scour her face, peer into her luminous brown eyes and wish those pursed lips would crack a tiny smile. All that was rendered was a judgment in stone.

At times, I rationalized Amma's behavior in terms of a trait I found peculiar to Indian culture: no one dished out personal compliments. I remembered an incident soon after my return to India when I remarked to my Aunt Saroja that the girl next door looked beautiful. I was totally unprepared for the admonishment that followed, "Be quiet! Don't say such things! You'll cast an evil eye on her." This was such a radical change from my upbringing in America where compliments flowed so effusively that it was hard to tell if they were genuine. At the UN School and in Parkway Village, we were all exotic, and by extension beautiful, and members of a mutual admiration community. Appa, unlike Amma, had embraced this ethos, was at ease in both giving and receiving compliments, and was insistent that my brothers and I display a similar politesse. Amma, who rarely said "please," or "thank you," to us indulged in these niceties only with her American friends and reverted to being more reserved in the company of Indians. It was more of a passing observation and I was too young at the time to dwell on it further.

My aunt's attitude was by no means exceptional and I noticed that my friends at school were equally withholding in handing out compliments towards each other. On the few occasions that we were allowed to dress out of uniform, the closest thing to a flattering comment was couched in oblique references like "Your sari is beautiful," or "That's a lovely color you are wearing." I began to understand Amma's reticence to say I looked beautiful directly to my face. After all, no mother would want to cast an evil eye on her own daughter. But for her to maintain a stone cold silence without so much as a favorable aside in my direction went beyond the dictates of culture. It pained me to speculate that her attitude had nothing to do with the superstition of the evil eye and had more to do with the stark truth — which I was loath to admit to myself — that Amma never found me beautiful in the first place.

With the wedding barely two weeks away, Amma went full throttle as she frantically summoned her five sisters-in-law and her younger sister, my Aunt Sasi, and begged them to somehow transform me into a beautiful bride, one worthy of standing next to her soon to be ever so handsome son-in-law. Each of my aunts, equipped with her personal arsenal of remedies, scrutinized me from top to bottom and devised a regimen of treatments that, according to them, were guaranteed to work miracles. Every morning a thick impasto of ground turmeric root and sesame oil was smeared all over my face, arms and legs. Serving a dual purpose, it acted as a depilatory and acne preventer but even after several rinses, the yellow dye of the turmeric stubbornly coated my skin. Instead of being rewarded with a healthy glow to my face, it resulted in a jaundiced patina that showed no signs of fading as the day wore on, and made me look sickly. To make matters worse, my bras, all white in color, were permanently stained and neither were my colored blouses spared unless I happened to have been wearing a yellow one.

My skin, a natural almond color, had darkened over the last few months as a result of commuting to college under the scorching rays of a Madras summer. My aunts, who easily dismissed some of my flaws like the peach fuzz on my arms and legs or the occasional break out of pimples as inherently curable, were relentless in their efforts to whiten my skin, the primary target being my face. I had learned from experience that a fair skinned complexion was a mark of beauty in India no matter how unattractive one's features were. Throughout my childhood, I had been unfavorably compared to my whiter than white cousin, Urmila, despite the fact that she had a lopsided forehead, a crooked nose and overcrowded teeth in sharp contrast to my even forehead, aquiline nose and even teeth thanks to orthodontic treatment. It was rumored that well-known dark-complexioned actresses went to bed with their pancake make-up and would rather be caught dead than be seen au naturel. In a culture, purposely averse to giving compliments, criticisms, on the other hand, were dished out easily. The worst greeting one could ever receive was, " Oh dear! You have become so dark!"

I was hyper-sensitive about the color of my skin since the days I had been reviled as a "brown-faced monkey," at PS 117. At the UN School, my teachers prettified everyone's color with a slew of adjectives referring to white skin as being the color of ivory or alabaster and to darker skin as being chocolate or cocoa colored. In my case, I was painted in hues of amber and dark honey. Once I moved to India, friends and relatives often described me as being "maaneeram," literally the color of mangoes. It was a descriptive term that lacked verisimilitude as my color bore no resemblance to the yellow-orange flesh of the fruit. What it was meant to designate was a person who was neither too dark nor too fair. I had often been cautioned by my mother to stay out of the sun, but I was unwilling to compromise my love for outdoor sports like netball and badminton.

I now had to suffer the repercussions of my indiscretion as my aunts examined my face in the harsh sunlight and unanimously came up with a solution that the only way to bleach my skin in a hurry would be to slather my face in a mixture of olive oil and lemon juice. Olive oil was an expensive commodity and Amma dispensed with it sparingly, but given the exigent circumstances, she handed over the entire bottle to my aunts hoping it would do the trick. The acidity of the lemon juice overpowered the soothing effects of the olive oil and my face stung. My aunts assured me that this was a desirous effect, an indication, they collectively chimed, of its whitening property at work. A daily inspection of my face proved disheartening. I had a distinctly yellow pallor to my skin from the constant application of turmeric and a few additional pimples had cropped up due to the excessive use of the olive oil. My aunts, however, blind to the actual results, took great pride in their handiwork and were convinced that they had successfully changed the proverbial ugly duckling into a swan. Amma, caught up in the frenzy of last minute wedding preparations, barely noticed any change in me and with an unsentimental eye tersely remarked, " I guess this is the best that can be done. It will have to suffice."

I prayed Raghu would look past my physical appearance as I got ready for our first date but just to be sure I dabbed a bit more talcum powder than usual on my face to mask the yellowish tinge and darkened my eyes with an extra touch of kohl for a heightened effect. Clad simply in a printed nylon sari I dashed downstairs as I heard the doorbell ring and stood discreetly out of sight on Amma's orders while she and a couple of her brothers welcomed Raghu into the alcove that served as a sitting room. After a few minutes, Amma escorted me in and with my head slightly bowed, I greeted Raghu in Tamil with the standard opening word, "Sowkyama?" meaning "How are you?" He replied he was well and when I lifted my head up to get a good look at him, the first thing to catch my eye were the rivulets of perspiration streaming down his cheeks and then I noticed that his eyes, small to begin with, looked smaller and bloodshot as he pulled out a limp, sweat-soaked handkerchief to wipe his glasses. I felt a surge of sympathy for Raghu for having braved the heat of the mid-afternoon. It was about a forty-five minute ride by commuter train from his home to the station closest to us followed by a twenty-minute ride by auto-rickshaw. I was overly appreciative of the effort he had taken and saw it as an affirmation of his love for me. My current disenchantment with the way I looked ceased to matter. Why should I care if my skin was too dark, or too yellow, or too hairy, or too pimply? Raghu could not take his eyes off me.

We were both eager to set out on our first date and be alone for the first time but Amma, in keeping with tradition, insisted that Raghu partake of the afternoon tiffin that had been especially prepared for him. Much like I did at the bride-viewing, I served him hot bajis (vegetable fritters), followed by kesari, a sweet semolina concoction, and coffee. Some light banter ensued, mainly between Raghu and my two maternal uncles, Raghu Mamma and Gidi Mamma, who happened to be staying with us. I shuttled nervously between the kitchen and the alcove and caught snippets of their conversation, but felt intimidated by the presence of Amma and her brothers to join in. I had the entire evening ahead to have my first real conversation with Raghu. It was time to leave but not before Amma had a chance to issue her dictum. Addressing Raghu directly, she made it emphatically clear that I was to be brought home by seven in the evening. "There is absolutely no staying out after dark," she added in a stentorian voice, as if we were schoolchildren under the thumb of a headmistress. Raghu vouchsafed my return by the appointed deadline. Perhaps it was the manner in which Raghu spoke, the sincerity in his voice, that dissipated any qualms Amma might have had in agreeing to our going out in the first place. She gave us permission to leave without being chaperoned, a bold move for a mother who had been overly protective of her daughter.

As soon as we cleared the corner of my street, Raghu extended a tentative hand towards mine while his eyes darted furtively in all directions to see if anyone was in sight. I was about to reciprocate the gesture when I suddenly turned back and espied my Uncle Raghu a few yards away. "Carry on, carry on," he shouted, "I'm just on my way to the market." It was hard to tell if he had followed us of his own accord or had been sent by Amma who may have had second thoughts about us being alone. We broke into laughter at his obvious subterfuge and continued walking, our hands respectfully apart. Although my uncle was well out of earshot, his close proximity proved unnerving and we maintained an uncomfortable silence. Once we reached the bus stand, Raghu suggested we go to Elliot's Beach, a secluded spot located at the end-point of the much larger Marina Beach. Named after Edward Elliot, a colonial governor of Madras, it had acquired a certain notoriety for being a place where foreigners went skinny-dipping with no hint of shame and where lovers often held romantic trysts. It was a daring choice on Raghu's part and the clandestine atmosphere of the place both excited and intrigued me. I had been tethered to tradition far too long and the lure of going to a place, considered taboo, tasted of sweet revenge.

We parked ourselves on the sand with the sound of the waves as our only company and began our first ever conversation chit-chatting about the most innocuous topics, many of which were re-soundingly similar to the ones covered in our early letters: movies, books, his work, my schooling, his friends, my friends, his family and my family. Curiously absent was any utterance from either one of us of the profligate expressions of love that characterized our last letters. What had flowed so easily from pen to paper got caught in our throats and neither one of us knew how to get the words out. Raghu picked up a twig and started to doodle on the sand. My first thought was that he might be drawing a heart inscribed with the words, "Raghu loves Vasu." Instead, it was a cluster of math equations that made him exclaim, "I think I finally found the proof!" Knowing next to nothing about the kind of math he did, it was difficult to exult over his discovery. Still, I did manage to say I was happy for him. Inwardly, I laughed and told myself that if anyone asked about our courtship, the incident would make for a comic an-ecdote. I could see myself recounting my very first date with Raghu and how he solved a math problem, his bride-to-be by his side, in one of the most romantic spots in all of Madras.

The oncoming darkness emboldened Raghu to make the first move. He clasped my hand and held it to his lips. He then turned my face towards his and kissed my mouth, his tongue, salty from the sea air, caressing mine. He slipped one hand under my sari and cupped my breasts giving them a gentle squeeze. I moistened at his touch, my panties wet and sticky, and was grateful to be swaddled in the multiple folds of my sari to avoid being embarrassed. We quickly drew apart afraid that an unsuspecting stranger might creep up on us and realized that the deadline of my curfew was approaching. We held hands as we hastened towards the bus stop and quickly unclasped them as we neared a throng of awaiting passengers. No sooner did we alight at the stop near my home and turned the corner of Nageswara Rao Park, than my Uncle Gidi cropped up, seemingly from nowhere, to greet us. A few minutes later, he was joined by my Uncle Raghu whose presence was equally miraculous. It was as if they were lying in ambush to catch us in an uncompromising situation and I strongly suspected Amma had sent them on a scouting mission to insure my safe return. Raghu and I suppressed an urge to laugh at their feigned attempts to convince us that this was nothing but an accidental encounter. We had hoped to steal a kiss before parting but now that we had a small entourage accompanying us, it was out of the question.

Amma, a bit reluctantly, gave into Raghu's request for another date. "It wouldn't be proper," she said, "if both of you were caught seen together just before the marriage ceremony. People will talk and I have to protect Vasu's reputation. After marriage, you can do what you like." The authoritative tone in Amma's voice was unmistakably clear and it was futile to bargain for a few more outings.

We decided to see the movie, "Stalag 17," based on its popularity, plus the fact that it was being screened in one of the few air-conditioned theaters in Madras. As the lights dimmed, Raghu inched his hand closer to mine and held it in a tight clasp. A kiss would have been too daring a move in such a public space. The plot with all its intrigue of American POWs in a German camp trying to ferret out a spy was enough to rivet our attention and the catchy closing tune of "When Johnny Comes Marching Home Again," had everyone in the audience including us singing along. The words stuck with us in the years immediately following our marriage and we often hummed them together. It was a lovely memento of the very first movie we had watched on our second and last date.

As we emerged from the theatre, a voice rang out, "Vasundara, is that you?" I turned around and saw my mathematics teacher, Miss Shakuntala, eyeing me suspiciously as her gaze wandered towards Raghu who immediately lowered his head which made him look all the more sheepish. Flustered and embarrassed, not quite knowing how to respond though the look on her face clearly demanded a response, I nervously introduced Raghu as my fiancé. " Going out before marriage and having fun are you?" she replied which sounded more like a reproach than a question. A bit angry at the intrusion yet mindful of her teacher status, I came up with a quick and what I had hoped would be a satisfactory rejoinder and said, "No Miss, nothing like that. Amma gave me permission to go." She seemed slightly appeased as she waved us away on a more encouraging note by saying, "Carry on, carry on. Have a pleasant afternoon." We scuttled towards the exit and I dared not look back for I knew in my gut that she was scrutinizing my every move. As an afterthought, I wished I had told her that I was marrying a mathematician and a brilliant one at that. Surely, she would have taken a kinder approach in knowing that she and Raghu shared a mutual love for the same subject.

I stewed about the encounter to Raghu and fretted over the possibility that Miss Shakuntala might gossip about me to some of my other teachers. I further dreaded the possibility of such gossip reaching Amma's ears. Raghu, however, in true mathematical fashion, logically explained away my fears by reminding me that my college was closed and that the probability of Miss Shakuntala running into any of her colleagues, most of whom were likely to be on vacation, was slim to nothing. That Raghu could come up with a rational answer to what he perceived to be my irrational fears was comforting, yet, oddly enough, I was a bit disconcerted. There was something cold and calculating in the way he chose to placate my anxiety. There were no tender expressions of concern for my plight and despite his well-meant intention of which I had no doubt, to allay my fears, his lack of empathy disturbed me. His very logical and very rational approach had recast my emotional state as if it were a math equation that could be easily solved. My tormented thoughts suddenly appeared trivial and I never felt more child-like. It was too early in our relationship to know for sure but I sensed that Raghu did not particularly care for emotional outbursts no matter what the circumstances, be they silly or serious.

The sky threatened rain and with a couple of hours to kill before my curfew, we hastened towards Kwality Restaurant on Mount Road, a high-end venue for the best ice-cream and afternoon snacks in Madras. We shared a plate of vegetable samosas and vegetable cutlets, two favorites of mine, and ended our meal with chocolate sundaes. Our conversation revolved around the movie we had just seen with added mention of some of the ones currently playing. As we savored the food, the topic shifted to dishes we liked and disliked until it was time to leave. Nothing of an intimate nature was broached by either one of us although we had enough privacy to do so, seated as we were in a semi-enclosed booth. Since Raghu had initiated our first kiss, I thought it only natural for him to take the lead and steer the conversation towards more personal matters. Being younger than him, and much more unworldly, I chose to remain deferential and wait for his cue. Yet, nothing was forthcoming much to my puzzlement. It was as if Raghu had exhausted his vocabulary of the lovey-dovey terms that had peppered his letters and had seen no need, or perhaps even no purpose, in having to voice them aloud. The proof of his love for me was evident in his letters, I told myself, by way of consolation. Yet, how I wished he would whisper, "I love you, Vasu," so I could follow suit and breathe life into the words that I had penned again and again. I was dying to say" I love you too, Raghu." A quick flashback to that moment of physical intimacy on Elliot's Beach brought into stark relief that, while in the throes of that passionate embrace, neither one of us had uttered a word.

A heavy downpour had caused the buses to be filled beyond capacity and they zoomed by without stopping. We waved down every auto-rickshaw and taxi to no avail and I became increasingly agitated when I realized I had passed my curfew. Drenched to the bone, ankle-deep in debris-laden water, we finally hailed an auto-rickshaw driver who agreed to take us but not before exacting a much costlier fare.

The look on Amma's face was grim and it was plainly evident that she was annoyed at us. "Where have you both been?" she barked. "Do you realize how late it is? Raghu, I did not expect this kind of behavior from you. I told you clearly that Vasu has to be home by seven. It's now eight o'clock and getting dark." We simultaneously explained the difficulty of finding transportation in such inclement weather and apologized profusely for our lateness but Amma remained unconvinced. Much to my consternation, she practically shooed Raghu out the door, caring little that he had a long commute back home. She then turned the full force of her anger towards me. "Where were you really and what were you two up to?" she demanded in an accusatory tone. "We went to the movie and then to Kwality for a snack. Nothing else, Amma. Like I told you, the buses were full and did not even stop, no taxi was available, and after much bargaining we finally got an auto-rickshaw," I replied, standing my ground. " All I can say, Vasu, is that this is not proper behavior on your part or Raghu's. He is older, he should have known better. Thank God, there will be no more going out before the wedding. Go now, dry yourself off and change your sari. Eat something if you're hungry or go to bed," she said in a huff.

I crawled into bed rankled more by Amma's abrupt dismissal of Raghu than by her string of accusations. My anger at her inhospitality, almost downright uncouth, quickened and I was surprised by my readiness to defend and protect Raghu as if he were already a part of me. It was Amma who came across as the enemy. Once again, her tongue, her standard weapon of choice, like a poisoned quill, bled all the joy out of my last date with Raghu. I was in part thankful that no such inquisition took place after my first date. Amma would have been mortified had she known that the daughter whose chastity she had taken great pains to guard all these years, had been titillated by her first kiss and had at long last experienced a sexual awakening, a burgeoning sensation that was hard to quell despite the indoctrination into a culture which took elaborate pains to render women asexual beings. I slept fitfully not knowing if Raghu had reached home safely and wished I could have called him to find out, but, sadly, there was no phone connection in his home.

I awoke the next day, my head heavily laden with the disquiet wrought by yesterday's events. I wasn't sure if Raghu would call but I needed to be near the phone in case he did. Ordinarily, I would have sat on the sofa in the alcove, burrowing my nose in a book I had no intention of reading, at the ready to pick up the phone when it rang. But the space had now been taken over by the numerous relatives who had descended on us for the wedding. Aunts, uncles, and their assorted progeny occupied every inch of every room and our modestly-sized house, rather than buckling under their collective weight, grew more expansive to accommodate them all. Worse yet, lacking a phone of their own, they eyed the instrument as a novelty and vied with one another to see who would get to it first each time it rang. Mustering up a voice that made them sound like office attendants, they would shout into the receiver, "Narayanan residence. May I have your good name please?" My chances of beating them to the punch were slim and hovering over the phone would have aroused suspicion and opened up questions which I would have preferred not to answer. I gave in to their idle chatter on sundry topics, an activity which they would have gladly prolonged when the phone rang. My Uncle Gidi got to it first and on hearing that the caller's good name was Raghu, he asked in a booming voice, "Hello Mapillai, (the Tamil word for groom), how are you?" After a brief exchange of pleasantries, he handed the phone to me and gestured towards the others to leave the room but neglected, perhaps intentionally, to close the door behind him. There was no way for me to do it discreetly without appearing rude. After all, they had retired to the adjacent room and I would have had to face them directly. Besides, this was a culture where there was no expectation of privacy. One's business was everyone's business and a private conversation between Raghu and me was bound to set the female tongues wagging. I could well imagine what my aunts would say: What was the need for Vasu to say something to Raghu that we should not hear?; Do you think there is some problem before the marriage? They can talk privately after marriage, why do it before? Such behavior would have never been tolerated in our time. We only spoke when spoken to.

Erring on the side of caution, I was guarded in my comments to Raghu who had the luxury of chatting freely while safely ensconced in the privacy of the phone booth. In hushed tones I told him I was fine after last night's encounter with Amma and that she was too busy with wedding preparations and attending to all our relatives to stay angry with me. I was relieved to hear he had made it home without incident and how he had been fussed over by his mother who had stayed up beyond her usual bed-time just to pour him a tumbler of warm milk from the silver thermos purchased exclusively for his use since he was a child. I was both happy and envious of the close bond he shared with his mother and chose not to tell him that I went to bed hungry and mad as hell with my own mother. I was about to lower my voice further and tell him how lucky he was to escape censure for coming home late when he blurted out that he had received a scolding from his father earlier that morning. On learning that he and I had taken tiffin together at Kwality's, his father had turned livid. Unbeknownst to both of us, it was apparently taboo for a couple about to be wed to partake of a meal together, even a light meal like a snack, before marriage. It must have been a rule observed only by ultra-orthodox Brahmins since Amma made no mention of it. It was an irreversible transgression and the only recourse, according to his father, was to make sure no one else got wind of it. Raghu did not sound too perturbed and made light of the situation when I asked how he felt. "I was ignorant of this custom," he replied, "and it's too late to do anything about it." Once again, his disposition to deal with problems logically highlighted my own inadequacy. My tendency was to fret and dissolve into a state of self-recrimination at the slightest hint of trouble. I hoped I wouldn't be too much for Raghu to handle.

So it was that our second and last date ended on a miserable note. Verbal grenades from both sides of our family had been hurled at us for different reasons. Innocent and in love, we had inadvertently violated certain codes of behavior by indulging in a harmless outing to the movies followed by a trip to the ice-cream parlor. It would take years of living in America and our subsequent adoption of its more laissez-faire attitudes to recount our second date in a more humorous vein. Our teenage sons found it amusing when they heard our date had to end by the 7 pm curfew. Their date nights went into the wee hours of the morning. As for getting yelled at for eating together before marriage, the boys thought it wasn't such a bad custom. "Hey Dad," they said, patting him on the back, "it certainly makes for a cheap date."

Chapter 14

Prelude to the Wedding

It was Wednesday morning, June 3, two days before the wedding, when I realized how woefully ignorant I was of the proceedings that were soon to take place. I picked up an invitation from a small stack of the extras that lay strewn on the coffee table and saw in big, bold, print that the Muhurtham, the auspicious time period designated solely for the performance of the wedding rites, was to commence at the ungodly hour of 6:00 am and be completed by 8:30 am. "Aiyai Yo," I shrieked, using a Tamil expression that often accompanied the receiving of bad news. "I'll have to get ready so early in the morning," I groaned, much to the shock of my relatives who were about to enjoy their morning coffee. " You should not talk like that, Vasu," they admonished me in unison. "The priests have selected that time based on your and Raghu's horoscope so you can begin your life together under the most ideal of circumstances. You will have to grin and bear it and sacrifice a good night's sleep. You can rest all you want after the wedding."

I did not want to jinx what was intended to be a blessed beginning of my life with Raghu and apologized for my outburst but inwardly I still chafed. I turned my attention once again to the invitation. I had barely glanced at it when it was first printed a few weeks ago. Caught up in the excitement I felt at the time, my eyes had remained riveted on the elegant gold lettering that announced that Sow. Vasundara was to be wed to Chi. Srinivasavaradhan (alias Raghu) on Friday, June 5 at the A.V.M. Rajeshwari Kalyana Mandapam, located in Mylapore, not too far from our house on Luz Avenue. I had glossed over the various events printed in smaller type at the bottom, all of which were to take place before the Muhurtham. In fact, the first event, the Janavasam, also called "Maapillai azhaippu," where the groom is taken in procession through parts of the city, was to take place the very next evening.

I was glad to have the English version of the invitation in hand and not the Tamil one. I found the script in the latter to be totally incomprehensible as it used a more formal version of the language which bore little resemblance to how it was spoken. In the past five years, I had learned to speak Tamil without committing too many gaffes but I could barely read or write my own native language. Although it bore the weight of tradition and authority, according to the priests and the elders in the family, I adopted a rather cavalier attitude towards the Tamil invitation. Wedding announcements in any other language had none of its legitimacy but, as far as I was concerned, I wanted my wedding to be proclaimed in a language I knew well and cherished. Besides, the Tamil invitation, a dull pink on the outside and a ghastly neon yellow on the inside, was visually unappealing and looked like every other invitation to a Brahmin wedding.

I cared little that the English invitation was viewed as inauthentic, a western import, more for show than for substance. It was more expensive to print and sent a message that the girl came from a wealthy family. Amma, may not have seen herself as rich but she certainly saw herself as sophisticated. Widowed or not, she would always be known as the wife of a UN diplomat and, in keeping with that status, she moved among the more wealthy and powerful circles of Madras. Nothing less than a gold embossed invitation would do to announce the wedding of her only daughter. The Tamil invitation would have been too parochial and commonplace for such company.

I laughed out loud when I saw the prefix, " Sow." before my full name, Vasundara, and the prefix, " Chi." before Raghu's given name, Srinivasavaradhan. "What's so funny?" asked Raghu Mamma, Amma's favorite sibling and confidant. " Why is there a Sow before my name? I thought a sow was a female pig and isn't Chi a word we use when we dislike something?" I asked, still laughing. " What an ignorant girl, you are," he retorted and began to elaborate. "Sow. is short for Sowbhagyavati and it's a term affixed to the name of the bride-to-be and essentially means she who is filled with good fortune. For the groom, Chi. is short for Chiranjeevi, and means he who is blessed with a long life. Both attributes combined will make for a harmonious union. It's time you learn about these things."

Sanskrit in origin, the true meaning of both words, and the symbiotic connection they implied surprised me. It was heartening to know that the Hindu scriptures had separately endowed the bride and groom with a special attribute that contributed equally to the well-being of one another. It was a pity that the kind of equality bestowed at the start of one's married life was short-lived. In my years of growing up in India, I had seen my married aunts cater to their husbands hand and foot. Whatever good fortune they had brought to the marriage had quickly become the provenance of their husbands.

As I pressed Uncle Raghu to fill me in on the nitty-gritty details of what was to transpire over the next few days, it was becoming exceedingly clear that this type of obeisance was expected of me. My Uncle was closest to Amma among all her siblings. In many ways his relationship to her echoed the one I shared with my younger brother, Ranga. At my birth, he had stood in for my father who was away in Indonesia and had held Amma's hand through her difficult labor. In the ensuing years he guided Amma through the many travails following my father's death. When Amma asked him to give me away in marriage, I could think of no one more suitable to take my father's place. Her decision, however, was antithetical to the dictates of custom and created a bit of a stir among her own siblings. I knew better than to give my opinion on what was an adult matter but the heated discussions that took place at home were loud enough to be overheard. "What will people say?" said my Aunt Sasi. "Your husband has an older brother and is it not his duty to give the bride away? Even if he had no brothers, the shastras, or rules of conduct, say the eldest of his male relatives can assume this role." "The girl's maternal side has nothing to do with this part of the ceremony, only the paternal side," added my Uncle Gidi. Amma, not in the least bit cowed, angrily replied, " Do you think I can forget the way my husband's family treated me right after he died? How they threw me and my children out of the house in front of all the neighbors? No one in his family has the right or deserves to give my only daughter away." An ominous silence filled the room only to be broken by another of Amma's tirades. " Just so you all know, I have only invited his sister Yasoda and his older brother Aravamudhan along with their children to the wedding. They may not have stopped what went on but at least they did not directly participate. Even my father-in-law, the elder of the family, is not invited."

There was no mistaking that Amma's decision was final. Looking directly at my Aunt Sasi, she lashed out. " You talk about the shastras and the correct way one must do things but did you know that the shastras also say that if a childless couple gives away a virgin bride they will be blessed with a child of their own? Raghu and his wife, Vimala, have been childless for years. Can any of you give me one good reason why should they be denied this blessing?" Beaten into submission, not the slightest peep escaped anyone's lips. It was inconsequential that most of us knew that the likelihood of Raghu Mamma and Aunt Vimala having a child so late in life was extremely slim if not downright impossible. But the shastras, for all its rigid rules on matters secular and arcane, had also cleverly devised loopholes to prepare for any contingency that might arise. In Amma's case, it had provided her with enough ammunition to save face. If the ancients believed that a barren couple would be graced with the miracle of birth, why shouldn't we?

I secretly admired Amma's bold stance and her fiery spirit and was relieved that this thorny issue had been settled weeks before the wedding. With the start of the various ceremonies just a day away I inched closer to Raghu Mamma to gain his undivided attention. Gratefully, the living room was slowly emptied of the rest of my relatives and I welcomed the peace and quiet. Amma was nowhere to be found; I guessed she was off somewhere to attend to last minute details. In any case, she had neither the time nor patience to clue me in on anything that had to do with the wedding. "Just follow what the priests say and don't ask any questions," was her terse advice. I didn't mind being an obedient bride but I had no intention of being an ignorant one.

I was not a total stranger to the goings-on at South Indian weddings and had in the past attended a few, mostly at Amma's urging, and not of my own volition. The rituals were interminably long and, unless the bride or groom was someone I knew, I was usually impatient to leave. I often sat quietly by Amma's side while she gossiped with acquaintances, many of whom I hardly knew. The only time I felt noticed was when someone inquired if Amma had any intention of marrying me off. " She's only fifteen and has yet to complete her Pre-University degree. Still too young for marriage," Amma replied. Neither of us could have foreseen that my marriage would be fixed a few months later. For the most part, I found these Brahmin weddings to be joyless affairs and had no reason to think my wedding would be any different. However, at the risk of being ridiculed for my youthful optimism, I still thought it was possible to rescue a little bit of fun amidst the elaborate and oftentimes dreary rituals.

The Janavasam, slated for the next evening, seemed a perfect opportunity to have a few laughs albeit at Raghu's expense. I wanted to see the look on Raghu's face as he was being paraded around in a jazzy convertible. Knowing him to be shy and reserved, and generally unflappable, I wondered how he would bear up to being under the spotlight surrounded by a gawking crowd of onlookers. Unkind as it was of me, I took a perverse delight at the thought of catching the ever-sensible Raghu off-guard. The first thing I had to find out was whether it was at all possible for the bride to observe the Janavasam and knew Raghu Mamma would have the answer.

I would have preferred a concise explanation of the ritual but Raghu Mamma, a born teacher, since the days he tutored me in algebra, decided to turn my query into a history lesson. I learned that the purpose of the Janavasam was to allow the public at large to scrutinize the groom and report back to the bride's family if they had knowledge of unsavory details about his character. The wedding could be stopped if such information came to light.

"I hope Raghu passes the test," I said jokingly.

"Have no fears Vasu. Raghu is a gem of a boy and everyone we asked thinks of him highly. Your mother, for some reason, likes this event and I think she wants to proudly display her son-in-law to be."

"Can I attend too? I would love to see Raghu all decked out sitting in a fancy car."

"Usually, the bride is not present at the Janavasam. You are supposed to wait in the wedding hall for his arrival so that the more formal engagement ceremony can take place."

"I'm going to plead with Amma to let me see the Janavasam. Maybe I can hide in the background somewhere so no one sees me. Anyway, thanks Mamma for filling me in. I'm sure there will be others to guide me if I don't know what to do. And, of course, I always have you to turn to," I replied as I slowly rose and gave his shoulder a gentle squeeze.

Most of the day passed in a blur of excitement. Whatever anxiety or nervousness I might have felt was swept up in a hurricane of activity. Saris, blouses, petticoats, and jewelry, both real and fake, were strewn across every room downstairs as my aunts traded opinions on what outfits to wear for the Janavasam and Muhurtham. Except for my wedding and reception sari, I had no idea what Amma had chosen for the other occasions. As always, I would have to rely on her taste and could only hope that the colors were not too sombre. As the bride-to-be, I was fussed over by my relatives, each in turn scurrying to the kitchen to fetch me coffee or snacks without my having to ask. I wasn't permitted to lift a finger and was exhorted to conserve my energy as the next few days would involve a grueling exercise of standing and sitting for long periods of time while the priests intoned the various mantras. I was warned that the wedding hall lacked air-conditioning and I would have to settle for a hand fan which was of minor consolation given the sweltering heat. I soaked up the loving attention and in many ways welcomed the diversion. I did not want to think about the separation from my mother and brothers after marriage and, most of all, I did not want to mourn the absence of my father on the biggest day of my life. I had noticed that the large picture of him that usually hung on our living room wall was missing. It had been carted to the wedding hall and would be propped up on the dais where the wedding rites were to be performed. My gaze wandered upwards to the empty space on the wall and a fulgurating sadness coursed through my veins. I saw myself seated on Appa's lap, his arms tightly wrapped around me, and felt his grip loosen, almost begrudgingly, as he offered me to Raghu on my wedding day.

I was at the point of bursting into tears, the pent up feelings I had managed to suppress so far, threatening to spill out. I fought the urge to cry afraid to appear unhappy in front of my relatives who had gone to such great efforts to brighten my spirits. I quietly slipped away unnoticed while my aunts and uncles busily gossiped amongst themselves. I sought out my Patti, my maternal grandmother and found her sitting quietly on the front porch, legs outstretched, staring at nothing in particular.

"Patti, what are you doing out here?" I asked.

"I'm just sitting idly. Your mother has seen to all the arrangements and has a lot of help from your uncles and aunts. There is nothing for me to do," she replied, sounding apologetic.

"It's about time you get a rest. You have been taking care of everyone all your life, cooking and cleaning all day long," I said stroking her hands softly.

"But I'm so used to that way of life and now your mother won't even allow me in the kitchen," she lamented.

"I don't want you in the kitchen either. We have hired two cooks to feed everyone so just relax and eat well," I responded, hugging her close.

"The festivities will begin tomorrow evening. What a pity that your father's life was cut short and he won't see you get married," she sadly remarked. "Raghu is a good boy. He would have approved of him were he alive."

I buried my head in Patti's lap and finally let the tears flow.

"There, there, Vasu, why would you cry before your wedding day?" she whispered in my ear.

"Oh Patti, I'm scared to live in Raghu's house after marriage. His parents are so orthodox and I know nothing of their ways. There will be no one around to guide me. What if I make a mistake and do something improper?" I sobbed.

" You have nothing to worry about, Vasu. You will slowly learn and, if you make a mistake, they are not the type of people to yell at you. After all, you are their one and only daughter-in-law. Did you know that Raghu's father is my cousin? His family and mine are from the same village of Sathamangalam and I remember him as a quiet reserved person. Your mother-in-law may be a bit fussy about doing things the right way, so just observe her closely and follow whatever she says. In any case, you are not going to be with them for too long and will be leaving for America in August," she replied.

Her last remark dredged up another fear that I had fought hard to suppress — the fear of being separated from Amma and my brothers, especially Ranga who had looked so forlorn these past few weeks. In all the excitement of Raghu's arrival and the pre-wedding plans, I had paid him scant attention and deeply regretted my actions. We had been joined at the hip as far as I could remember and to leave him behind was akin to self-amputation.

Patti must have sensed the wild beating of my heart and, much as she did when I was a child, she began to knead my arms, pressing her fingers gently into my flesh, as if she were squeezing out every drop of sadness that had gathered in a pool around my heart.

Maybe it was the softness of Patti's cotton sari, or the softness of her touch, or their combined effect but I suddenly yearned to be a child again. Now, more than ever before, I wanted to recapture those moments in my childhood when I was allowed to be and act my age. I brushed aside all memories of growing up in Parkway Village where I had to shoulder so many responsibilities that I often felt like a miniature adult. I preferred instead to think of my summer visits to India, the times spent with both my grandmothers, who in many ways were the saviors of my at times troubled soul. They each knew how to ease the awkwardness and loneliness I felt in my new and strange surroundings. Neither had censured me for my American mannerisms but had chosen rather to guide me patiently and happily through the myriad customs that framed their daily existence. My childhood had been sacrificed at the altar of responsibility during the better part of those twelve years spent in America and were it not for both of my grandmothers, it would have eluded my grasp forever. Every little moment in their company, every small activity we shared, every snippet of conversation, every caress — all these and much more were their gifts to me.

Curled up in Patti's lap, it was hard to believe that the bony figure protruding from her sari had withstood the ravages of physical abuse by my Thatha to say nothing of the mental abuse that went with it. There was a quiet strength in Patti which I silently hoped, through some kind of osmosis, to absorb and thereby fortify myself for what lay ahead. Her gentle spirit and her magnanimity had remained unbroken in light of her untold suffering and I could think of no better way to repay her than by adopting those qualities into my own life. The maelstrom of emotions that had sent me reeling towards her slowly began to quieten down. I saw in Patti a small reflection of myself — a child-bride, albeit a bit older, who had been forced to grow up too fast. The tests of endurance I would have to face paled in comparison to hers. It felt safe and secure to be huddled against Patti, the child in me tethered to her body and soul. But the time had come to let go of these tendrils of the past and, however shakily, begin my journey as a bride.

The Janavasam was to take place on Thursday evening, June 4 around six o'clock. I had slept fitfully the night before, unable to quieten the thoughts that raced ahead to the events that were about to unfold in the next few days. I can barely recall how I passed the day except to say that it was fraught with activity: relatives were scurrying around from one room to another; flower sellers, bangle sellers, ribbon sellers, had invaded the front courtyard lured by the decorative pandal at the entrance, a stretch of colorful cloth hoisted on bamboo sticks that signaled an auspicious event was about to take place; coconuts, betel leaves, betel nuts, flower garlands — items required for some of the ceremonies — were being loaded into cars loaned to us by friends to be transported to the wedding hall. To add to the hustle bustle, my older brother Ramu, had chosen that particular day to summon his male friends who rode up to the front gate in gleaming motorcycles with the engines revved to a deafening roar in a swaggering display of their machismo. There was neither a quiet moment nor a quiet place to be had anywhere at home and the distractions succeeded in keeping my mounting nervousness at bay.

The time had come to get dressed for the inaugural event, the parade of the groom around the city. Amma, whose daily make-up routine consisted of a few dabs of talcum powder and the application of a bindi, knew next to nothing when it came to primping and preening a bride-to-be. She gladly left the task to a team of my aunts who converged on me as a lion about to devour its prey. The wedding ornaments, each one aglitter with a variety of precious stones, beckoned eagerly for their touch. My aunts could barely believe that the gems were real until Amma told them that her close friend, whom we affectionately called Jaya Mammi, had insisted on loaning out her personal collection for such a prestigious event. Imitation gems, much cheaper in cost, were usually preferred for what was a once-in-a-lifetime occasion, but Jaya Mammi had chided Amma for even considering such a purchase. "Paste is too tacky for someone of your status," she told her. Jaya Mammi, the wife of an extremely wealthy industrialist magnate, overlooked the fact that we were of modest means. In her eyes, Amma was a cosmopolitan woman, a foreign-returned wife of a now deceased prominent UN official, credentials that more than sufficed to enlist her as a member of Madras' elite. It would have been downright unthinkable that a bride of such pedigree be trotted out in ersatz jewelry.

With great efficiency, each aunt tackled a different part of my body. My Aunt Sasi, took charge of my hair. She neatly parted it and once it was braided she tied the end with a kunjalam, a kind of pom pom with silken tassels, which kept the plait from unraveling. My aunt was about to reach for the ruby-studded rakkudi, a circular ornament used to adorn the hair near the soft spot of the scalp, when Amma, who had been standing by quietly, suddenly cried out, " No, no rakkudi for Vasu! Ever since the fan accident, that part of her scalp is sensitive and cannot bear the weight of all these stones. It will only hurt her." There was a note of tenderness in Amma's concern for me that brought me to the brink of tears. That horrible day that had robbed me temporarily of my memory, and which I later had consciously chosen never to revisit, had, however, not been forgotten by Amma. I was taken aback at its recall at this particular moment when my nerves were on edge. I knew Amma cared about me and often thought her withholding personality kept her from translating her caring into actual words. To hear her now, speak up in a fiercely protective tone, made me want to stay with her forever. The trepidations that had haunted me the day before, while lying in my Patti's lap, returned in full force. I wished this evening would never happen and wished even more that tomorrow would never arrive. I also wished my aunts would disappear so I could wallow in my emotions and let Amma know that I would rather live with her than go off to America and live with Raghu. Alas, my thoughts remained merely as thoughts, unexpressed and bottled up.

The rakkudi was put away much to the disappointment of my aunts. " Surely, Vasu can endure a little pain for one evening," they beseeched Amma in a last ditch effort which fell on deaf ears. After much cajoling, they managed to convince her that the diamond netti chutti — a thin long piece of jewelry that lay on the parting of the hair with a small pendant that dangled on top of the forehead — was light enough in weight. Still worried that one hair ornament was one too many for me to bear, Amma had my aunts step aside and decided she would be the one to tuck the flowers in my hair. She picked up the tightly woven strings of jasmine and roses, feeling their weight in her palms, and starting with the lightest one she gently and cautiously began to weave one after another through the strands of my hair, pausing after each tuck to ask me if it felt too heavy. I was soothed by Amma's touch and thought back to the time when she had last adorned my hair with flowers. It was the day she and Appa had presented me with my first sari. Now, on the eve of my wedding, I caught a glimpse of my Amma as she was then, caressing my hair, my very being, with the kind of love that needed no words.

I did a few head rolls to make sure everything was in place and assured Amma that I could get through the evening with no major discomfort. My aunt Veda, wife of Uncle Gidi, was in charge of my make-up. Her notions of beauty were based on the screen images of the major Tamil actresses, especially in their roles as brides, and she was determined to make me look like them with whatever cosmetics were at hand. After dusting my face with sandalwood powder, she applied the kohl to my eyes extending the line near my bottom lashes just a tad to give the appearance that my eyes, naturally big, were even bigger. Instead of the usual round bindi, she designed one that looked like a large teardrop, its curvature outlined in sandalwood paste with a small red line made of kum-kum paste drawn in the center. "If only you could wear lipstick," she said, "you would look like a movie star." On hearing her comment, Amma winced and curtly replied, " Natural beauty is real beauty. There is no need for embellishment." It would have boosted my spirits if Amma had just come out and said I was naturally beautiful but the generality of her remark only confirmed what I already knew. No matter how gussied up I was in all this bridal paraphernalia, she could not find it in herself to pay me a compliment. I had swallowed the hurt before and would do so again.

With climactic flourish, Amma whipped out the last of the jewelry — a dazzling pair of diamond earrings and an equally dazzling two-tiered diamond necklace with a diamond pendant. The aesthetic design and brilliance of the stones were so mesmerizing that my aunts and I were rendered speechless. "It's part of Vasu's dowry," Amma said in a voice that betrayed little emotion. The diamonds had been purchased on a trip to Amsterdam. Appa, who had nothing but disdain for any display of wealth, had, after much pestering by Amma, caved in and told her to craft whatever jewelry she liked with the stones. A private jeweler had designed a beautiful necklace which Amma sadly never got to wear as Appa died soon after. When Raghu's parents insisted that a pair of diamond earrings and a diamond necklace be included in the dowry, Amma was forced to dismantle the necklace and reset the stones.

I looked at the earrings and necklace but this time with contempt. Amma had pointed out with pride that the diamonds were of the Blue Jagger quality, nearly flawless, but all I saw were stones contaminated by avarice. My rancor only increased when I watched my aunts drool over this luminous display of wealth while trading envious looks with one another. I was nothing but a showpiece to them, a vehicle that carried a loud and clear message that I was no ordinary bride but rather one of substantial means. My side of the family could boast that the groom had married up. Raghu's side, in turn, would crow over what a good catch he was and worth every cent or by Indian currency standards, every naye paise. It boiled down to a game of one-upmanship that I found utterly tasteless and petty.

The nearly two-carat earrings had such thick posts that even with a dab of Vaseline, I struggled to insert them in the holes of my ears. The weight was still too much for my thin lobes and a diamond mattal, courtesy of Jaya Mammi, had to be used. The chain, with a small hole at one end, was looped over the post and a hook at the other end clung to a few strands of hair above my ears. I fared no better with the diamond necklace which proved to be too tight and threatened to choke the breath out of me. I slipped on the bangles Amma handed me, a hodgepodge of gold, rubies and emeralds and stood still while my Aunt Vimala, draped the golden-hued sari with a royal purple border over my body. She meticulously adjusted the pleats in front to look perfectly creased and gathered up the pallu, pinning the folds to my blouse so it would hang gracefully over my left shoulder. I looked in the mirror and could barely recognize myself. I had been turned into a mannequin studded with diamonds, amounting to little more than window dressing.

Amma was to drive me to the wedding hall where I would await the arrival of Raghu at the end of his procession around the city. As we headed towards the car, Amma, as though she had read my mind, asked if I would like to see the Janavasam. Nothing could have made me happier, but I was still concerned. " Won't people talk if they see me there? I thought the bride was not allowed to watch the groom being paraded around town," I replied somewhat cautiously. "Oh, who cares about tradition? It will be lots of fun and we can stand in a place where no one can see us," Amma said excitedly.

Amma, suddenly appeared years younger. The mischievous glint in her eyes, her conspiratorial manner, joined us more as equals than as mother and daughter.

It was the first time in the past few weeks that I had Amma all to myself and with the busy itinerary that lay ahead, I wasn't sure if such an opportunity would present itself again. Emotions of fear overlapped with welling gratitude. I wanted to thank her for all she had done, tell her how scared I was to be apart from her and how much I would miss her. I wanted her to comfort me, to impart some words of wisdom and to assure me that I would have a happy life. One thought chased another vying to be expressed only to converge in silence. After all these years, I still did not know how or where to begin when it came to baring my soul to Amma. I glanced in her direction hoping for an opening, a small word, perhaps, even a light-hearted comment, but her eyes remained firmly fixed on the road.

If I were to freeze-frame this moment, I would have realized that my impulse to open up to Amma and expect her to respond in kind was irrational as much as it was unnatural. Through all the upheavals of the past few years, and amid the many turning points in my life, we had never indulged in heart-to heart chats with each other. The love we showed one another was expressed in deeds, not words. My abject obedience to all her directives was sufficient proof that I was the daughter she expected me to be. Amma's cloak of protection, which she wrapped around me like a second skin, coupled with her sense of maternal duty indicated the depth of her love for me. Yet, on the eve of my wedding and facing a future without Amma by my side, I yearned to forge a closeness with her unlike anything we had shared in the past. I knew we would miss each other terribly but neither of us could summon up enough courage to say the words out loud. These precious moments in the car, alone with Amma, were rapidly slipping away as we neared the venue of the Janavasam. I had allowed them to be irretrievably lost and cursed the emotional paralysis that afflicted our relationship. Just once, before I became Raghu's wife, I longed to be a different kind of daughter to Amma, one who was unafraid to utter the words, "I love you."

Amma parked her blue compact Fiat on a dimly lit street, not too far from the Hanuman Temple where the procession of the groom was about to take place. Partially hidden in the shadow of a street lamp, I had a clear view of the temple's entrance from which Raghu would soon emerge after seeking the blessings of the god. A throng of people, mostly relatives on both sides of our families, intermingled with the local residents. Curious passersby had begun to gather around the gleaming white convertible bedecked with flowers. The marching band in their red and white uniforms struck up the music with much fanfare as soon as they espied Raghu. " I can't see Raghu's face, Amma," I whined. "Why is he keeping his head down?" "He's probably shy," Amma said with a laugh. I could see from the look on Amma's face that she was enjoying all the hoopla. I recalled her telling me that there had been no Janavasam at her own wedding, just a quick ceremony since my father at the time, a war correspondent at The Hindu newspaper, had to report to duty.

Once Raghu was seated, the crowd converged on the car and were quickly shooed away by the wedding photographer who was desperately trying to get a shot of Raghu with his face towards the camera. For an instant, Raghu looked up into the blinding glare of the flashbulb and then promptly lowered his head again. Raghu, spiffily dressed in a crisp, long-sleeve, white shirt and dress pants, was a handsome groom. I had a sudden urge to rush towards him and prop his face up so everyone could see what a great catch he was. It was a sultry evening without a hint of breeze, typical of Madras at this time of year. Raghu looked hot and bothered and kept fidgeting with the rose garland that rested heavily around his neck and shoulders. His discomfort only worsened when he was suddenly bathed in a hot circumference of light by a group of men carrying kerosene lamps atop their heads. Commonly known as Petromax lamps, they emitted hot blue flames of such intensity that it was a wonder that nothing or no one was incinerated. The procession had barely started and there was poor Raghu, squirming uncomfortably, as the stares of familiar and unfamiliar faces rained down on him. I watched him with a small measure of pity and a larger measure of amusement. There was an odd comfort in knowing that my normally unflappable Raghu could on occasion buckle under pressure.

"What if someone knows something bad about Raghu, Amma? Will the wedding be stopped?" I asked jokingly. " Nothing like that will ever happen, not after all the digging your uncles did into his background," replied Amma in a light-hearted vein. " We better hurry and get to the wedding hall before Raghu arrives."

Of all the wedding rites, it was the Janavasam I would come to treasure the most. Thanks to Amma, I had had a bit of fun at Raghu's expense. But the real highlight of the evening was to watch Amma vicariously enjoy the inaugural event of my own wedding and imagine it as the one she had never had with my father. I would look back at the Janavasam as our pre-wedding gift to each other, a mutual exchange that expressed the love between us in the only way we knew.

The wedding hall was a feast for the eyes. Strings of technicolor bulbs were intertwined with long ropes of fresh flowers dangling from the ceiling. The dais where the rites were to be performed had been draped in white cloth and propped up on a small table, off to the side, was a framed photograph of my father, garlanded by a string of roses. I waited in the bride's quarters with my aunts while Amma scurried off to greet the arrival of the guests. The furious beating of the drums signaled the arrival of the groom and the excitement mounted when it came time to lead me to the dais. "Keep your head bowed at all times and take small steps," counseled my aunts as they steered me towards the main hall. Through the corner of my eye, I saw that Raghu had changed into traditional attire, a silk dhoti wrapped around his waist. We stood side by side, our eyes cast downward, while the priests reenacted the engagement ritual that had been privately performed weeks ago. The public nature of the event allowed the numerous relatives and friends who had gathered that evening one last opportunity to thoroughly scrutinize the groom and launch any objections they might have about his character and suitability. In reality, I had never heard of a wedding that had been stopped at this juncture, but it must have been reassuring for the bride's family to know that such a safeguard was in place.

The ceremony was thankfully short given the early hour of the Muhurtham the following day. Following the exchange of the thamboolams, or plates, I was presented with a new sari from Raghu's parents and asked to quickly depart and change into it. Once again, I had my Aunt Vimala assist me. In what must have been record time, she had me draped and ready to be ushered back to the dais. I barely noticed the color and design of the sari except that it was bottle green with gold stripes. There had been no time to fuss with my appearance, let alone check myself out in the mirror. The priests, a rather humorless bunch, were punctilious about every detail. There was a strict adherence to the span of time in which an auspicious rite was to be performed. Delays of any kind were not tolerated. I recalled a wedding I had attended where a male guest had suffered a heart attack and died. The families of the bride and groom, more worried that the odor of death had contaminated the wedding, were afraid the proceedings would be halted. The priest, however, dismissed the tragic occurrence as a minor intrusion and insisted on completing all the rituals. His only request was to keep the news of the death as private as possible, a ludicrous piece of advice given that the elderly gentleman had keeled over right in front of the wedding dais!

The closing act was about to take place. The Tamil invitation was read aloud while Raghu and I garlanded each other. We touched and locked eyes for a few seconds before again turning our gaze downwards. His face was bathed in perspiration and he looked fatigued. Maybe the Janavasam had taken its toll on him. Bedecked and bejeweled I stood before him and wondered if he found me beautiful. There was no way to know. We were like puppets on a stage, our every movement choreographed to the tunes of an ancient tradition.

Our Wedding Picture

Chapter 15

The Bride of Good Fortune Weds the Groom of Long Life

It was 3:00 am in the morning and pitch dark when Amma roused me out of a deep sleep on my wedding day. What an ungodly hour to usher in such an auspicious occasion. Bleary-eyed, annoyed, and irritable, I craved for a few more hours of sleep and greeted what was to be the happiest day of my life with a scowl instead of a smile. There was no time to dillydally, and after a quick cup of coffee followed by a quick shower, Amma and I drove to Jaya Mammi's house where arrangements had been made to adorn me from head to toe in bridal ornaments and bridal make-up. Jaya Mammi, in anticipation of the marriage of her own two daughters in the near future had amassed an array of wedding jewelry, all set in genuine stones. Unlike the Janavasam where I had worn a modest amount of jewelry, some from her collection, nothing but a full blown display of various trinkets would do for my wedding day. There would be no compromise and even the rakkudi which Amma feared would be too weighty on my scalp was cleverly pinned to the flowers. Working with great speed and efficiency, a group of women specifically hired for their expertise in all things nuptial, had me looking like a bride in one hour. With the Muhurtham fast approaching, I barely had time to soak in my reflection and had but a brief glimpse of myself in the mirror. Everything about me dazzled from the gold-mustard sari to the brilliance of the precious stones. that framed my hair and face. I took a few gingerly steps just to check if I could bear up to the additional weight of all this paraphernalia and looked expectantly at Amma to offer some comment. "Now, at last, you look like a bride," was all she could manage to say.

Amma whisked me through a side entrance of the wedding hall and led me to the bride's quarters where she handed me over to my aunts. She scurried away to attend to Ranga, whose Upanayanam or coming of age ceremony, had been slated to take place before my wedding rites began. Amma saw no point in holding the event as a separate occasion and re-inviting the same crowd already assembled at my wedding. Poor Ranga was forced to take second billing with none of the fanfare that accompanied Ramu's thread ceremony a year earlier. I felt sorry for Ranga and sadder still that I could not witness his special day as I was under strict orders to stay put in the bridal room. I sat stiffly as if rigor mortis had set in while my aunts pampered me no end: They took turns fanning me; my sari pleats were creased and re-creased multiple times; a deft touch of a comb kept my hair neat and flat; and gentle dabs of talcum powder kept me looking fresh. They chattered away though I paid little attention to what they said. When the time came for me to make my debut, they declared with great joy, " This is exactly how our weddings are meant to be. All brides should be as young as Vasu. Once they get older, they lose their innocence." Nervous, excited, scared, and a bit sad to leave that innocence behind, I bowed my head, partly out of deference to tradition, but mostly to hide the tiny drops of tears that clung to my lashes.

I stood on the sidelines and watched Raghu perform the Kasi Yaatrai where the groom tells the bride's family that he is about to embark on a journey to lead the life of an ascetic and shun all worldly pleasures including marriage. Standing under an umbrella, a palm leaf fan in one hand — to keep him cool on his trip — and the Bhagavad-Gita — which he was supposed to study — in the other, Raghu made a show of walking away. At that precise moment, Raghu Mamma took me by the hand and dangled me in front of Raghu like the proverbial carrot and pleaded with him to stay. " Postpone your spiritual pursuits and take Vasu as your wife. She will stand by your side always," he implored. Everyone knew the entire enactment was a sham; no groom had ever refused a bride. I found the whole scene comical and could not help but whisper in Raghu

Mamma's ear, " If he wants to go, let him. Ultimately, it's his loss." My uncle suppressed a smile as he placed Raghu's hand in mine. The softness of his touch, the warmth of his gaze, and the impish grin on his face was assurance enough that we would stand by each other's side forever.

The Maalai Maatral, or exchange of garlands was playful in nature. In the old days, when the groom and bride were little more than children, they would be hoisted on the shoulders of their maternal uncles and as they attempted to garland each other, one side or the other would pull away. It was a contest to see who would garland whom first. Although not quite as entertaining, Raghu and I did manage to reap some fun as our uncles jostled us towards and away from each other. In the end, I couldn't be sure if I was wearing Raghu's garland or he mine. We held hands again and made our way to the Oonjal, a huge mahogany swing that hung from the ceiling. It was the women's turn to fete the bride and groom. Aunts on both sides softly sang lyrics to ward off the "evil eye," and for added measure, they placed a small ball of rice soaked in vermillion paste in their right palms and drew a circle around us in a clockwise direction before throwing the rice ball off to one side. We each were fed an unappetizing gummy mixture of bananas, milk and sugar, meant to provide a little sustenance given the lengthy duration of the marriage rites that were soon to take place. Swaying gently, our right hands loosely clasped, Raghu and I rose from the swing bathed in a halo of goodness so luminous; it eclipsed all that was dark and evil in the world.

The wedding dais, thick with smoke from the ritual hearth, smarted my eyes; the incessant pouring of ghee into the flames made it only worse. I had to sit patiently on the wooden plank while Raghu, at the behest of the priest, repeated various slokas, short Hindu prayers, invoking the gods to guarantee us a life of eternal bliss. In the interim, a tray with my wedding sari and Mangalasutra, the gold wedding chain, was passed among the guests to receive their blessing. Once it made its way back to the dais, the tray was placed in the hands of Raghu's parents who offered it to Raghu Mamma and his wife, Aunt Vimala. To the roar of beating drums and high-pitched pipe music, the wedding sari was then given to me. This marked a turning point in the ceremonies wherein the bride leaves to don her wedding sari and re-emerge for the grand finale, the tying of the wedding thread and the placement of the Mangalasutra around her neck by the groom. The priest was quick to remind me that the Muhurtham time was closing in and at his urging my aunts rushed me towards the bridal quarters.

The rust-gold wedding sari was as beautiful as I remembered it but unlike the standard sari which was six yards in length, it was of the traditional kind, nine yards long, specifically worn for auspicious occasions. The draping of the sari in and of itself was a daunting task in need of an expert hand, or several expert hands for that matter. With little time to spare, I unraveled the sari I had been wearing, changed my blouse, and stood like a wooden doll while my aunts went to work. A petticoat could not be worn with a nine yard sari as it was a hindrance to the numerous tucks and ties that held the material in place. I reluctantly took it off and felt vulnerable and half-naked in my underwear. I noticed a vaguely familiar presence in the room and realized it was Raghu's cousin, Rajamma, his mother's sister's daughter. I had last seen her at my engagement ceremony and wondered why she was peering at my body so intently. I discovered later from my aunts that it was customary for the groom's sister — in this case, Raghu's cousin, as he was an only child — to inspect the body of the bride for any skin ailments or defects. The appearance of anything suspicious was sufficient cause to stop the wedding. I must have passed muster for she did not linger too long and left as silently as she had entered. After a lot of acrobatic twists and turns, I was finally wrapped and warned not to fiddle around with any part of my sari. One inadvertent tug in the wrong place was all it would take to unfurl the entire nine yards. I was cautious in my movements and took a few baby steps at a time. Despite the hastening hour, I could only manage a slow shuffle towards the podium.

The capstone ceremony, the Kanyadanam or giving away of the virgin bride, was about to take place. I sat on Raghu Mamma's lap, his wife alongside him, when in a sudden panic I called out for Amma. I had not seen her since she dropped me off at the bridal room and had been too distracted and absorbed by all that was going on to notice her absence. The most crucial moment of my life was about to occur and Amma was nowhere in sight. I was ready to leap off Mamma's lap and go in search of her but it was too late. Somewhere, a voice, which sounded like one of the priests, rang out, " There can be no further delay. Tell the bride her mother cannot be here during the Muhurtham. She is not allowed to witness this auspicious moment." Everything happened within seconds of one another. The priest gave Raghu the signal to tie the wedding thread and place the Mangalasutra around my neck. The musicians, right on cue, created a din with their percussion and wind instruments supposedly to drown out any unwanted and unwelcome sound. We were pelted by a hail of raw rice to the chants of a long and happy blessed life. My cry for Amma went unheard. I looked up at Raghu trying to hide the ache in my heart with a forced smile. I had officially become his wife and by extension his family was now mine. From this day forward, I was no longer my mother's daughter and the only parent to witness my wedding was the lifeless portrait of my father. What should have been an euphoric culmination to all the preceding events ended on a bittersweet note. Among the swarm of relatives who had inched closer to witness the ceremonial tying of the knot, I saw neither my mother nor my two brothers. Much like every other Indian bride, I was a prop at my own wedding.

Raghu stooped down and caught hold of my right big toe as I took seven steps otherwise known as the Sapthapadi, around the sacred fire. Each step constituted an oath made to each other as husband and wife. My foot was then placed on a grindstone with an accompanying mantra that asks the wife to be firm as a rock so that the family can depend on her. At that very moment, I lost my balance and clutched Raghu's arm. I burst out laughing and told the priest that it was I who needed to depend on my husband and not vice versa.

Next came the prostration of the elders, a necessary but tedious exercise which involved incessant crouching and stretching at their feet as they showered their blessings on us. We began by bowing before my father's picture followed by Raghu's parents and the elders in his family. We stepped down from the dais and Amma appeared seemingly from nowhere. In her blessing she asked Raghu to take good care of me. "She is just a child," she said wistfully as if she regretted marrying me off at tender age. I pulled Amma aside and asked almost in a whisper why she wasn't at the Muhurtham. "There is no place for widows at auspicious events, Vasu. We are considered bad omens, women who are spoilt, and cannot be near the holy fire. I had no choice but to obey the priest." "But you are my mother," I protested. "How can you not be there?" Amma, not wanting to prolong the conversation, evaded my question and propelled me towards her friends and a few of the special guests to receive their felicitations. I noticed a sadness in her eyes. Appa's absence must have weighed heavily on her soul, and although she found Raghu to be a perfect match for me, I knew she wanted to hold onto me, perhaps not forever, but maybe for a little bit longer.

It was barely mid-morning and I was already exhausted. A look at Raghu's face indicated that he fared no better. Ramu, whom I hadn't laid eyes on until now, climbed onto the dais to perform the rice giving ceremony. He placed some puffed rice into my hands which I threw into the sacred fire while Raghu poured the ghee into the flames. This was a special offering to the gods to bless not just Raghu and me but also the generations to come. It reiterated the importance of the maternal home of the bride to the well-being of the groom and his family.

There were still numerous guests to greet and it was a social imperative that each and every one of them be invited personally to partake of the specially prepared wedding repast. To overlook an invitation even unintentionally, was tantamount to a slap in the face, an inexcusable slight that would be long remembered and for which there was no atonement. The onus of ushering each guest to the dining hall fell on the bride's family and I could see a platoon of my relatives scurrying back and forth to insure everyone was fed properly. It was a long wait before Raghu and I had our first meal as husband and wife. Far from being a leisurely affair, a particular set of protocols had to be followed when it came to the order in which each dish was served and which ones were to be consumed first. Banana slices dipped in sugar were purposefully placed on the right corner of the plantain leaf, the left corner being taboo, and had to be eaten at the start. It was a symbolic gesture meant to indicate a sweet beginning to our married life. A team of servers trotted out dish after dish none of which could be refused and had to be tasted even if it meant a small bite. At one point, midway through the meal, surrounding relatives on both sides of our families, teased us into feeding each other. Raghu and I exchanged bites of a diamond-shaped cake of sugar and flour which I never relished but felt compelled to eat. A parade of desserts followed, each one soaked in jaggery — a concentrated form of sugar cane and date palm — sweet enough to induce a diabetic coma! At long last, a mixture of curds and rice arrived. Often thought of as a digestif after a rich meal, it mercifully brought the affair to an end and I scooped it up with gusto.

Sapped of energy, my belly achingly full, I would have done anything to rid myself of my glad rags and all my jewelry and be able to crawl into bed. There was, however, one last ritual remaining before the evening reception, the Nalangu or wedding games. Meant to be an ice-breaker for the newlyweds, it was a series of light-hearted competitions between the bride and the groom. Raghu and I, seated across from one another on straw mats, were each given a cup of sandalwood paste. The goal was to see who would be the first to smear it on the other's feet. As I attempted to do so, he quickly eluded me by retracting his feet under his dhoti to the delight of his relatives. When it was his turn, I wasn't as quick. He managed to snatch my feet, and egged on by his cousins, slathered the mixture over my ankles and toes with an air of triumph. Having lost round one, I was determined to gain the upper hand in the next game which involved the rolling of a coconut between us. We began by gently gliding the coconut back and forth, when, at the urging of my cheering gallery, I clamped my hand over the coconut and dared Raghu to wrest it from my grip. He nearly succeeded but smarting from my previous loss, I suddenly pinched his hand really hard and he was forced to let go. "Vasu is a clever girl. You better watch out!" cried his side while mine jubilantly replied, " You'll never get the better of Vasu. She is too smart for you." I gloated over my win and derived an immense satisfaction in knowing that I could best Raghu at something even if it happened to be a trivial game of coconuts. His status as a child prodigy, his brilliance as a mathematician, and his overall maturity put him on a pedestal in my eyes. I was too young to gauge my future but sufficiently ambitious to tell myself that one day I might be standing on a pedestal of my own. My small victory that afternoon, minuscule by all accounts, nevertheless made me believe that in the years to come I would become Raghu's equal.

The frivolity of the Nalangu was a fitting denouement to the austerity of the morning activities. It had generated a convivial atmosphere that finally gave in to the lassitude brought on by the warm afternoon and still- heavy stomachs. Most of the guests had left, the priests, having done their part, slept by the kitchen and Raghu and I retired to our respective quarters for a much needed rest. We had but a few hours to get ready for the reception. I hurriedly changed into a simple nylon sari and with the help of my aunts divested myself of all the ornaments except for the wedding thread and wedding chain. "You should never take these off," I was warned. It was a needless warning for I knew all too well that once a woman became a widow, the very first act to be carried out was the removal of her wedding chain. A painful memory of what Amma had to undergo as Appa was being cremated surfaced. I pressed my new wedding chain against my heart and prayed that God grant Raghu a long life.

I stretched out on a cotton rug, too dazed by everything that had transpired to savor the happiness of being wed to Raghu. A numbness set in that made me oblivious to everyone around me.

Voices nearby receded in the distance. I had had my fill of people, of noise, of smoky hearths, of mantras, of food, of flowers, of jewelry, of guests, of prostrating everyone and of everything else that had been required of me. I had sailed through my performance as a dutiful bride without any missteps yet I felt neither pride nor joy. The moral fulcrum around which spun a complex array of marital laws and customs had drained me of all emotion. I craved for solitude, to be far away and free of all this cultural claustrophobia. It was a pipe dream. The call to ready myself for the evening reception rang loud and clear.

The richly brocaded red sari hung heavily on my slim frame, held in place by a gold belt girding my waist. I sagged under the weight of it all. I begged to keep the jewelry to a minimum amidst the protestations of my aunts for whom the reception was a grand finale to the day's events, a last opportunity for the newly wedded bride to dazzle everyone with her cache of diamonds. I was on the verge of giving in, when in what must have surely been an act of providence, Amma popped in and upon seeing me visibly discomfited shooed everyone away and took charge. She first put aside the hair ornaments and in a comforting tone said, " You wore enough of these today. I don't want your scalp to hurt." Her renewed concern tied to the fan accident of my youth would never leave her. She clasped the diamond necklace above my wedding chain, slipped a few bangles on my wrist and once I screwed in my diamond earrings, she eyed my appearance with a sense of self-satisfaction. The weight of the sari and my spirits had suddenly been lifted. With a jaunt in my step I eagerly made my way to the entrance of the wedding hall. There stood Raghu looking debonair in his suit and tie. It was a glorious start to the evening, one that promised to provide some joy on my wedding day.

We stood for hours greeting an endless stream of well-wishers, many of whom, we barely knew. This came as no surprise as most Indian wedding invitations requested the presence of family and friends, a request that was often followed to the letter. There was the added draw of a concert by a famous Carnatic Music vocalist, Ariyakudi Ramanuja Iyengar. Amma had performed quite a coup in snagging him for the reception and it was a pity that we were a good distance from the podium to appreciate the music. In any case, Raghu and I were not the intended audience. The presence of an artist of great renown was clear proof to all the guests that the bride's family were people of means.

I was elated to see my Good Shepherd gang who immediately clustered around me. True to their word, they had shown up in the wee hours of the morning for the Muhurtham, but apart from a cursory nod and smile, I had little opportunity to chat with them. I was eager to introduce them to Raghu. There was Rama, the math genius, who was particularly happy to see me married to a mathematician; my dear friend Viji, mentioned to Raghu that it was her father, who worked at TWA, who had booked his ticket when he left for New York nine months ago; I pointed to Janet and told Raghu that she and her sister, Bridget, had personalities that could not have been more diametrically opposed. I teased Janet about her intrepid stance towards those ogling boys of Loyola College and how she could stare them down until they were forced to flee; in contrast, Bridget was the goody two shoes among us all. I heard myself laugh and it felt good. The photographer asked us to pose and I light-heartedly warned Raghu to keep his eyes on me and not on my girlfriends. Embarrassed by my brashness, or just plain shy, he averted his gaze altogether and tilted his head down staring at nothing in particular.

I met some of Raghu's friends, all mathematicians, none of whom were very talkative. Serious Carnatic music fans, they rushed off to hear the maestro sing. The photographer whispered that a VIP was approaching and that he had to take our picture with him. A small crowd had gathered and we saw Amma escorting Mr. R. Venkataraman, Union Minister of Industries, who happened to have been our old neighbor when we lived on South Beach Road. I knew little else about him and would have never guessed that he would become President of India some twenty years later.

The evening was beginning to wind down. Most of the guests had left after dinner but not before they had received a small plastic bag containing a coconut, betel leaves, a few pieces of turmeric root, areca nuts, a packet of vermillion powder and some sweets — all auspicious offerings. This was a mandatory parting gift and my cousins stationed at the exit saw to it that no one departed empty handed.

I did not know what to expect after our families had dined. Would I be going to Raghu's home that night or spend it at the wedding hall? Neither as it turned out. Raghu's father had insisted that our consummation take place a week later, on June 12, at their home in Tambaram. I gathered from Amma that apparently our stars would be in perfect alignment that evening, perfect enough, according to Raghu's father, to insure the procreation of future offspring. A mere teenager, I laughed at the notion of producing children right after marriage and was taken aback when Amma responded with all seriousness.

"Raghu is their only child, born after nearly 25 years of marriage. They are keen that both of you perpetuate the family line."

"Well, they'll have to wait, Amma. I want to finish my studies first," I answered with indignation.

"Everything will be okay, Vasu. Calm down. Just humor them for now. Don't forget that Raghu promised to educate you."

I strongly believed in the strength of that promise and was too tired to entertain the thought that it might be broken. Besides, I was thrilled at the prospect of having an extra week to spend at home with Amma and my brothers, especially Ranga. They had appeared only intermittently in the midst of all the festivities and I couldn't be sure if my brothers had even witnessed the crucial part of the Muhurtham, the tying of the wedding thread. There was also my ignorance of sex to contend with and finding the proper means to educate myself. It was too daunting a thought to tackle right now. I could barely process the fact that I was a married woman now. All I wanted was the comfort of my bed and a good night's sleep.

Wedding Reception Photo

Chapter 16

First Night

The Shanti Kalyanam or First Night as it was called in common parlance, was to take place as Raghu's parents wished on Friday, June 12, exactly a week after our wedding. What little I knew about the consummation act had been gleaned from Tamil movies where the hoopla surrounding the event took precedence over the event itself. There was the usual song and dance routine, the demur bride pulling away from the groom as he attempts to coax her towards the marriage bed festooned with flowers. This was followed by a more solemn ritual of the wife's offering of milk and fruits to the husband, who after consuming a small portion, feeds her in turn to symbolize their shared future. The wife then prostrates at the feet of her husband, seeking his blessings, at which point he gently picks her up and takes her in his embrace. Soon after, darkness blankets the screen eliciting an eruption of wolf-whistles from the young college boys seated in the designated "Gents Section," with cries of "Kiss her, man! Hug her tightly and don't let go!" Those of us in the "Ladies Section," too embarrassed to look up, lowered our faces, and twiddled with the ends of our saris while trying hard to suppress the mischievous smiles that crossed our lips.

I tried not to think about my own first night, and when I did, it filled me with dread. I had hoped to read the book Raghu promised to bring but in the excitement of the wedding, I had neglected to ask him. I was too diffident now to broach the subject of sex and decided to put my trust in Raghu who had assured me in one of his letters that he had "mastered everything he needed to know about sex."

I had hoped for a quiet outing with Raghu some time before that Friday, perhaps a repeat of our very first date at Eliot's Beach to rekindle the passion between us. It would have greatly allayed my anxiety and given me the perfect segue to approach Raghu with my concerns about sexual matters. Our families, however, saw fit to fill our week up with a series of obligations, none of them particularly pleasant. Amma, who had deliberately shunned most of Appa's family by not inviting them to the wedding, had a sudden change of heart. She singled out Appa's father and two of his brothers and insisted that it was only proper to pay them a visit and seek their blessings. She offered no reason as to why her attitude towards them had softened or why she had continued to exclude another paternal aunt and uncle. As far as I was concerned, they were all equally culpable in their mistreatment of my family. Raghu, who had been told little about the rift that had occurred, readily agreed and, with much reluctance, I too gave in.

I had not entered No. 3 Mahalakshmi Street since the day we had been unceremoniously evicted from its premises. The house looked dark and dingy making it all the more uninviting. Saroja Chitti and Veera Chittappa, the aunt and uncle who had taken care of my brothers and me when we first arrived in Madras, greeted us politely but with cold reserve. My grandfather, as always, was reclining in his easy chair, a permanent scowl lining his face. Too frail to get up, he asked my aunt for the customary kernels of raw rice which he scattered over our heads as we prostrated before him. Without so much as a glance or a word in our direction, he closed his eyes. I was further reminded of the disdain he had for me as a child. We quickly took the blessings of my aunt and uncle, declined their offer of coffee, and left. I could feel the rush of anger palpitating in my heart and vowed to never set foot in that house again. The light that had once glowed within its walls had been extinguished when my Patti died.

We headed towards Ranga Chittappa's home, Appa's younger brother, whom I abhorred as much as my grandfather. I could never forget how close he came to beating Ramu, only to face a wrathful and vengeful Amma. I had no quarrel with his wife, Vijayanti Chitti, in spite of the rumors we heard that it was she who had secretly abetted my uncle in his plans to have us thrown out. Her two daughters, who had joined Good Shepherd Convent when I was still a student, were often given a ride in our car and my aunt, by way of thanking me, usually had me stay for tiffin. I enjoyed the chit-chats with my aunt and found her to be youthful in body and in spirit. Slim and attractive, she wore saris in the latest design, brightly colored printed silks that made me envious when I thought of my sombre collection. Her blouses were daring, tailored to the latest fashion — an assortment of sleeveless and boat-necked ones, and even some with buttons down the back that made relatives titter in private, "Surely, it must be her husband who does her up." Next to her, I looked and felt dowdy in my high-cut, long-waisted and long-sleeved blouse. To boot, the white uniform sari with its narrow striped red border did little to enhance my appearance. Not the least bit orthodox or conservative, she earned the dislike of her father-in-law and sisters-in-law who were quick to deride her for being modern. My envy extended to her daughters who got to dress in North-Indian attire, the pant-shirt salwar-kameez, which looked both comfortable and chic. Not once did I hear Amma voice her disapproval of either my aunt or her daughters and, in fact, she was quite effusive when it came to complimenting them on the way they looked. It hurt to see her tolerate in them what she would never tolerate in me. These short teas with my aunt were a refreshing change to the entrenched orthodoxy that awaited me in my grandfather's home and I lingered as long as I could in her company.

I could not conceal my affection for my aunt when Raghu and I entered her home. The bad blood that had formed a wedge between us vanished in our spontaneous embrace of one another. As for my uncle, I could only manage a nod. Raghu became the center of attention as they appraised his looks and fawned over him as if he were a busy dignitary who had taken time out of his schedule to grace their home. Over sweets and coffee, my uncle grilled Raghu about his education and professional prospects in America while my aunt and cousins asked me news of Amma and my brothers. Raghu was not the least put off by my uncle's questions and slipped into the conversation with ease. I, on the other hand, had nothing but scorn for my uncle and could barely make eye contact. I chafed whenever Appa's sisters looked at him and with great pride exclaimed that he was the spitting image of my father. Nothing could have been farther from the truth. I was hard put to detect an ounce of compassion in this man let alone accept him as Appa's brother, an accident of birth, in my opinion. It irritated me further when later in the car, Raghu remarked, " I really like your Uncle. He comes across as a nice and friendly person." I was tempted to tell Raghu about the ugly encounter three years ago, but thought better of it. I wasn't sure if he had been told by his parents why they had not been invited to the wedding or if he knew who my father's siblings were. In any case, I did not want to dredge up the past. I also did not want to spoil his first impression of Appa's side of the family even if that impression happened to be false.

There was one last stop to make, a request by Raghu's parents to visit his maternal uncle. It was, however, a request fraught with high drama which I came to know of shortly before Raghu arrived at my home that morning. Amma had counseled me to hold my tongue in the presence of my aunts and uncles and make no reference to the acrimony that had strained our relations with them. When it came to Raghu's uncle, she hurriedly filled me in on why he had been banned from attending the wedding. Amma had heard a rumor, later confirmed to be true, that the husband of Raghu's mother's sister had leprosy. Livid that his condition had been deliberately kept secret during the many months of negotiations between both our families and only brought to light days before the wedding, Amma had threatened to stop the proceedings were he to be invited. The shame that accompanied the disease, along with the fear of contagion from oozing sores, had prompted Amma to take such a drastic step and after a tense battle of words, she won out. Fearful of the disease, I grimaced at the thought of seeing him and begged Amma to spare me this one obligation. At this stage, her concession to Raghu's parents came across as illogical and irrational, yet she had agreed. " It will be okay, Vasu. Just listen to me and do what I say." She reeled out a list of cautionary measures: Do not partake of any food that is offered. Do not touch or sit close to him or anyone in his family. Make sure to keep your hands and legs covered at all times. My faith in her warnings was shaky at best so I said a quick silent prayer asking God to forgive any sins I might have committed and pleaded for his protection.

My skin tingled the entire ride over to Raghu's uncle's place and I envied Raghu's calm disposition. Surely, he knew about his Uncle's condition and must have inquired about his absence at the wedding but he said nothing. He had been a good sport in fulfilling Amma's requests and it seemed only fair that I reciprocated accordingly, although, I told myself, none of Appa's relatives suffered from such a dire affliction. In any case, it was too late to back out.

If there was ever a time to appreciate the Indian way of greeting people, it was now. I could breathe easy — and stick to Amma's directive — knowing there would be no American style hugs and pecks on the cheeks or any other kind of physical contact. A simple nod of acknowledgement and a slight smile would do. I sat in the farthest corner of the room, a good distance away from his uncle, and brought my pallu around to cover my arms and kept my feet tucked under the edges of my sari. It gave me the appearance of a shy and reserved newly-wed. Raghu, with no qualms, sat near his uncle who had taken extra pains to hide the ravages of his leprosy by covering his arms with a hand towel and his legs with his dhoti. I could hear Amma's voice in my head and wondered how I would avoid the sweets and savories that were bound to be offered. It would be a grave insult to refuse. I excused myself by feigning a bad case of indigestion and stomach cramps and exaggerated my condition much to the consternation and ensuing disappointment of Raghu's relatives. Raghu threw me a sharp glance which made me feel worse. He ate everything off his plate with relish and asked for seconds. It was a mean way to rub more salt into my wound, but it failed to change my mind. I sincerely hoped he was free of contagion. As soon as we left, I expected an earful about my lack of cordiality, but Raghu was either too well-mannered or too squeamish to start off our marriage on a bad note.

What little hope Raghu and I had of a few hours of privacy vanished quickly as the week progressed. One by one, the hordes of relatives began to leave and it would have been rude not to see them off after the time and expenses they incurred to attend our marriage. My only contact with Raghu was by phone and we were often too busy to engage in a long conversation. Amma, in anticipation of my impending departure to New York had me go through my wardrobe and make a list of any additional saris or blouses I would need. There was barely time to think ahead to Friday, though when I did, often before going to sleep, a chill washed over me. Apart from hugging and kissing Raghu, I had no idea what else was expected of me.

It was late Thursday evening when Amma marched into my room and thrust what looked like a thick college textbook into my hand, saying, "Read this before tomorrow night and educate yourself." She then turned her back to me and abruptly left. The stark black cover, free of lettering, was as grim as the title etched along the spine. It read "Ideal Marriage: Its Physiology and Technique," by TH. H. Van de Velde, M.D. The cover page carried a terse quote from Honore de Balzac, "Marriage is a science." How unromantic, I thought. The very word, "physiology," reminded me of the aversion I had for biology, a subject I had never studied in school and had opted out of when in college. To see it paired with the word, "anatomy," in practically all the chapter headings, particularly the one entitled, "Specific Anatomy and Physiology of Sex," did not forebode well. I jumped to the illustrations in the appendix and grew more petrified when I saw the schematic representations of the male and female genital organs, each part numerically labeled with its corresponding Latin name at the bottom. All those years of Latin classes at the UN School failed me miserably as I tried to identify which of my private parts was a glans clitoris, labia minora, or ostium urethrae, to name but a few.

When it came to the diagram of male genitalia, I laughed out loud at the term vas deferens and punned to myself, yes, there is indeed a "vast difference" between men and women!

Where on earth had Amma found this book but, more importantly, why had she, at the eleventh hour no less, deserted me when I needed her most? Curious as to its provenance, I checked for a library stamp but there wasn't one. When I saw that the publisher was Random House, New York, I wondered if the book had been part of the collection Amma had shipped when we moved to India in 1959. But then I saw that it had been printed in 1963 which made it a recent acquisition. It was a good guess that she had purchased it at Higginbotham's, on Mount Road, the oldest bookstore in India, well-known for its vast number of textbooks on every subject imaginable. Bored at the very start by the introduction which promised to provide "data on the technique of sexual congress without prurience or mock modesty," I tossed the book aside. My sense of isolation evoked in me an old sadness. It harkened back to the time of my first menstruation where the only comfort I received from Amma was a box of Kotex napkins shipped from Geneva accompanied by directions for its use. What had made Amma buy this book for me in the first place? Devoid of marginalia or markings of any sort, the book looked pristine, its pages too crisp to have been touched by a previous hand. It was obvious she had not read the book, but it was hard to believe that she had selected it without thumbing through its pages. Did the vapid prose with its clinical bent conform to her own stance towards sex? Did she really believe that sexual union was as passionless as the book made it out to be, reduced to nothing but physiology and technique? Why oh why had Amma dumped this book on me? How could she be this cruel? Marriage had turned me into an adult overnight so why did Amma treat like a child?

I thought long and hard about all these questions but not before a fierce urgency forced me to take another stab at the book. Perhaps, somewhere, buried in those tedious scientific passages, I could find a section with less technical jargon to help me prepare for my first night with Raghu. I leafed through the three hundred or so pages and came across a chapter I had previously missed on prelude, love-play, and sexual intercourse. My eyes jumped from paragraph to paragraph, and, then suddenly, I came upon the first mention of the erotic kiss which described in detail the very same sensations that went through my body when Raghu and I shared our first kiss on the beach. At last, a ring of the familiar! My interest was piqued again when reading about 'mammary stimulation' and the role of breasts in love-play, yet another experience I could recall on that first date with Raghu. With a great deal of trepidation I ventured further, towards the subheading on sexual intercourse, thankfully free of obfuscating Latin terminology. In straightforward language, the author defined sexual intercourse as, "The insertion of the penis into the vagina and its culmination in ejaculation of semen." Much like the grammar exercises of my schooldays, I attempted to parse its meaning, isolating the words I knew, penis, in this instance, and the ones that confounded me like 'vagina' and 'semen.' In addition, there was the unfamiliar context associated with the word, 'ejaculation.' To my knowledge, it was an exclamatory utterance indicating surprise. I went back to the appendix and pored over the picture of the vagina, a dark black circle with a small dot protruding from center, with no clue to its location on the female body. It resembled a mushroom cap that had been plucked from its stem and, on a second look, it could have easily been mistaken for either a bicycle or calling bell. I took stock of what I had learned so far. If the vagina was going to be penetrated, it must be a hole of some kind and the only orifice I knew I had that was different from men, was the one that excreted blood during my menstrual cycle. The very idea that a penis would find it inviting repulsed me. By now my patience was exhausted and I lacked the will and energy to fathom the meaning of semen and its ejaculatory trajectory. It had something to do with the penis, part of Raghu's anatomy, not mine. So why worry about it? I had made infinitesimal progress in teaching myself about sex and what little I had managed to glean dashed all my dreams of a romantic first night with Raghu.

I blamed Amma for my ignorance and was angry, resentful and sad that we were no closer than we were when I was a child. She had withheld so much from me while I was growing up, including herself. Under the guise of protection, I was denied the simplest of pleasures. She performed what she thought of as her motherly duties beyond reproach and mistakenly perceived my gratitude as love. I had hoped for a turning point in our lives where we could converse freely and openly, where sentiments we had for each other could be expressed and not inferred, where thoughts that popped into our heads came out of her mouths uncensored, where a spontaneous gesture of affection spoke louder than words and where the umbilical cord that had been snipped at birth could be sutured to the womb from whence it came.

I tucked the wretched book under my pillow, a miserable substitute that contaminated the very spot where I hid Raghu's letters. I dug out one of the more recent ones he had penned with its outpouring of passionate phrases urgent with desire. I savored each and every word. " My dearest Vasu, I will hug you, encircle you in a tight embrace, and kiss you full on the mouth until we forget everything. It will be an entirely new world where only we exist, where the only words in our language will be love, happiness and pleasure." The book be damned! I was not going to let it deaden my anticipation. I was ready for a night of rapture just as Raghu promised.

Amma and I studiously avoided one another the next day. The door to open any kind of personal exchange on such an intimate topic as sex had been permanently shut. Amma had let the book do the talking for her and exiled me to its content. We found our separate ways to kill time. The house, now bare of most of my relatives, bore the vestiges of excess and had to be thoroughly cleaned and put in order, a big task that required Amma's supervision. I spent a large part of the day with Ranga, recapturing our favorite pastimes and revisiting the favorite haunts of our childhood in Parkway Village. There was an innocence in the pleasures we took: the bike rides to Alley Pond Park, our make-believe names as the travel agents, Jani and Kanakula, our Sunday jaunts to Carvel with Appa and how lucky I was to return to New York and eat Pizza again. It would be hard to let go of my baby brother, more my child than Amma's. I would miss him the most.

We were expected at Raghu's home around 7:00 o'clock that evening. Amma had asked her younger sister, Sasi, to accompany us so she wouldn't have to make the drive back alone, especially at night. She was my favorite aunt, a staunch ally, and surrogate mother, who had given me a few crash courses in cooking and treated me to the movies over Amma's protestations. Despite the vast age difference between the sisters, she stood up to Amma and chided her for being so strict with me. Given the chill that had set in between Amma and me, I could not have asked for a better buffer. I took extra care with my personal hygiene and put on my cleanest bra and underwear. I would have loved a spritz of Amma's Chanel No. 5 but felt too embarrassed to approach her. Instead, I settled for Pond's Sandalwood powder and sprinkled it liberally all over my body. Raghu's parents had selected a pink sari for the First Night, a color, unbecoming to my taste and to the pallor of my skin. It did not succeed in turning me into an alluring bride which became painfully evident when my Aunt Sasi, who was not one to mince words, cried out, " That sari is so ugly! It looks awful on you!" She immediately tried to placate me, but her unkind remark still stung. My first night with Raghu appeared to be doomed from the start and there was no telling what else was in store.

I felt awkward the minute I stepped foot into Raghu's house. There were no men to be seen, not even Raghu, and save for a small group of three women who were introduced as neighbors, we were welcomed by my mother-in-law and Raghu's cousin, Rajamma. I remembered her from the wedding as the relative chosen by the groom's family to inspect my body for any obvious abnormality while I was being draped in my wedding sari. For a moment, I thought she might have been solicited again for the same purpose, to make doubly sure that I was fit for consummation but thankfully that was not the case. I found her to be warm and friendly, someone I could trust and possibly turn to if I ever needed help. I sat quietly, disinterested in the conversation which for the most part involved news of relatives known to both our families. My mother-in-law seemed to relish her role as match-maker and became quite animated while inquiring about suitable prospects for so-and-so's daughter or son. Amma and my aunt played along, more out of politeness I suspected, as they rarely engaged in this sort of topic. My attention wandered to the neighborhood women who were milling around the foot of the staircase. I could hear them egging one another on, " You go first, then I'll go." " No, I'm too shy to look, you do it," until finally one of them caved in and ascended the stairs. A short ten minutes later, she came bounding down the steps, her impassioned gesticulations conveying both excitement and despair. Breathless, she struggled to get her words out: "Oh, what a beautiful bed! So many flowers! Will my daughter ever be this lucky? I'm praying for the day she gets to sleep on a bed just like this." Her boorish outburst came as a shock to Amma, my aunt and me, and before we could make sense of the situation, we were further aghast to see my mother-in-law chuckle in delight and assure the woman that one day her prayers for her daughter would be answered. Raghu's cousin, Rajamma, seeing how we reacted, turned away flush with embarrassment. Amma squirmed, struggling to keep her composure. Knowing full well that my mother-in-law was hard of hearing, she leaned into my aunt and whispered very softly,

"How uncouth of Raghu's family to invite these women for this kind of an occasion!"

There was a look of instant regret in Amma's eyes. She absolutely abhorred what she referred to as the barbaric practices of Hinduism such as the forced tonsure of widows and the isolation of menstruating women that turned them into pariahs. This egregious custom of putting the wedding bed on display to neighborhood women was as new to her as it was distasteful. Her educated background and dignified life as the wife of a diplomat had put her in a stratum of society a cut above most Indian families, not just socially and economically, but also in terms of her modernist views. She was well aware that she had married me into a family that was decidedly old fashioned and conservative, but Raghu was such a prize, a better than good prospect, no matter the cost to her long-held beliefs. That I might have to suffer the occasional indignity was mere collateral damage. Amma saw my future as being tied to Raghu and not to his family. We would soon depart for America and I would be spared the problems that often plagued new brides in an extended family.

It was getting late. Amma and my aunt rose to leave. I had a sinking feeling in the pit of my stomach as I walked them to the car. It was a night of many new beginnings: my first time alone in a home other than my own which from now onwards I was to embrace as my only home; a brand new family to take the place of the one I had since birth; and my first time to be completely alone with Raghu as his wife. Amma was impatient to leave and chided my aunt to hurry up and let go of my hand. I edged towards the passenger side window as Amma turned on the ignition. My eyes begged her to take me back home. I lingered by the gate, too scared to enter this unfamiliar house that felt nothing like home. I stayed long enough to hear the last words that fell from Amma's lips: " Poor, innocent, child! God help her! She knows absolutely nothing." The life I had known for the past sixteen years retreated in a cloud of dust.

The sudden realization that I was fully independent for the first time unnerved me. The transition had occurred so abruptly with no preparation whatsoever. The world before me was dark and strange, uncharted territory with not so much as a compass to point me in the right direction. I stared at Raghu's house with a sense of foreboding and summoned what little courage that remained to cross the threshold and face up to my future. My mother-in-law took me by the elbow and urged me to make my way upstairs. "Don't forget that you must give Raghu the warm milk first, after which, you can take a few sips." I resented the subservient role she expected me to play and knew from the start that if there was any hope of gaining an equal footing in this house, I would have to battle hard. I braved the steep climb of the narrow winding staircase and clutched the banister tightly as I mounted each step. I turned off the voices pounding in my head and told myself that this was my first night, mine alone to possess. I was not going to let Amma or my mother-in-law or tradition stand in my way. I would do what came naturally to me and become a woman on my own terms.

Jittery and nervous, I stumbled as soon as I hit the landing. Raghu was nowhere in sight as I pulled myself together and having never visited this portion of the house, I was unsure where to find him. Directly in front of me was the bedroom, most of its space taken up by the much talked about Marriage Bed that had sent that poor lady into a swoon. Apart from a few scattered rose petals that were beginning to wilt and a technicolored bedspread, there was little else that made it special. Certainly, nothing to make a fuss over and a far cry from the sumptuously adorned bed pictured in Tamil movies. A closer look revealed that two single beds had been fused together to give the appearance of one large bed. I prayed I wouldn't toss and turn and fall through the gap. The only sign of an attempt at opulence was a bowl of apples and plums — fruits not native to Madras and clearly imported at some expense — along with a silver kuja of milk, a uniquely Indian pitcher with a screw-top and two small tumblers stacked one inside the other along the neck. Most kujas were made of brass and it must have cost a pretty penny to have one crafted in silver. The extravagance was oddly out of place in the cheap surroundings. Why splurge on fruit and a silver kuja and not on the marriage bed where the act of consummation was to take place? I should have known that the consumption of fruit and milk on one's wedding night held more significance. As symbols of fertility, they served an utilitarian purpose. The real joy and ultimate goal of consummation was not the fulfillment of carnal desire, but rather to produce progeny. I eyed the fruit for a completely different reason. They were my favorites and I was famished.

I turned left towards a few short steps that led to a small hall beyond which lay a balcony. Leaning against the parapet, his back towards me, stood Raghu, lost in thought. I whispered his name and when his eyes looked into mine, they brimmed with kindness much like the very first time we met at the bride-viewing. I knew without a doubt that there was nothing more to fear. Clad in a brand new dhoti and a crisp new shirt, both white, he was the picture of virginal purity. I felt a bit ridiculous in my garishly pink sari which made me appear as if I were a temptress out to beguile a poor unsuspecting soul. He seemed not to notice as he led me by the hand to the bedroom. We blushed at the sight of the rose petals and proceeded to pluck them off the bed before turning on the ceiling fan. I sat on the edge of the bed, my back taut, and felt the beads of sweat, drop by drop, slither down my spine, greedily absorbing every molecule of the sandalwood talc I had lavishly applied only hours earlier. I stewed inwardly to no avail as the sweat gathered momentum. "Don't be afraid," Raghu said, his voice calm and sympathetic while he unscrewed the kuja and offered me the milk in a tumbler. "You're supposed to drink first and then give it to me," I responded, a bit surprised that he was unaware of the custom. "Whatever we have, we will share it together, Vasu. It doesn't matter who drinks first." Yet, it mattered to me. For all my bluster about wanting to be treated as an equal, I was unable to relinquish my long accustomed role as a dutiful girl and guided the tumbler to his lips. I looked on admiringly as Raghu deftly carved the fruit with the skills of a surgeon, extracting the pit and seeds with such precision so as not to damage the flesh. We fed our hunger, turned off the lights, and reached for one another in the darkness. Our shared passion, long contained in the reams of pages that connected us from afar, was finally unleashed. I finally fell asleep in the safety of Raghu's outstretched arms.

Departure to New York 1964

Glossary

Agni: God of Fire symbolized by the ceremonial hearth around which rituals that accompany marriage, birth and death, to name a few, are performed.

Atthai: Father's younger sisters.

Chittappa: Father's younger brothers or the husband of mother's younger sisters.

Chitti: Mother's younger sisters or the wife of father's younger brothers.

Choli: A short blouse worn under a sari that bares the midriff.

Dhoti: A traditional men's garment, mostly worn in southern India. It is a rectangular piece of unstitched cloth, about 5 yards long, that is wrapped around the waist and legs and knotted at the waist.

Iyengar Brahmins: Tamil Brahmins who follow the Sri Vaishnava tradition where worship centers around the Vishnu pantheon of gods.

Iyer Brahmins: Tamil Brahmins who follow the Smarta tradition where worship centers around five key deities — Shiva, Vishnu, Shakti, Surya and Ganesha.

Mamma: Mother's brothers.

Muhurtham: The time set by the priests for the start and end of the marriage ceremony. The bride and groom's horoscope along with the alignment of the sun, moon and stars are calibrated to select the time that is most auspicious for the tying of the marriage thread.

Nichayathartham: Formal engagement ceremony where the official date and time of the wedding is announced. Families of the bride and groom exchange plates filled with fruits, flowers, and other auspicious items. A cash dowry is given to the groom's family.

Pallanguzhi: An ancient mancala game, using cowrie shells; popular among girls in Tamil Nadu.

Pallu: Loose end of the sari that is often woven in ornate and intricate designs.

Pavadai: A traditional long skirt in South India, especially in the state of Tamil Nadu, worn by young girls until they reach puberty.

Pavadai Davani: Also called a half-sari, it's a three-piece item of clothing that includes a long skirt, a short blouse called a choli, and a three-yard strip of cloth that is draped across the chest. It is traditionally worn by young Tamil girls after they reach puberty.

Periappa: Father's older brothers.

Poonal: A rite of passage for young Brahmin boys where they receive a sacred thread and become eligible to learn the teachings of the Vedas and other sacred texts. Also known as the Upanayanam Ceremony.

Puliyankottai: A game that involves the juggling and catching of tamarind seeds without dropping a single seed; popular among girls in Tamil Nadu.

Rahu Kalam: A certain period of every day that is considered inauspicious for any new venture due to the influence of the powerful and malefic planet, Rahu.

Rasam: A thin soup of southern India, typically made with tomatoes, tamarind, and various spices including turmeric, coriander, cumin, and red chilies, often served with steamed rice.

Sambar: A thick lentil soup of southern India with a tamarind base to which vegetables and spices are added.

Theetu: Being in state of pollution. For females, it occurs during their menstrual cycle where they are isolated for three days. It also applies to mothers over a ten-day period after childbirth.

Tiffin: An Indian English word, possibly coined from the words, tea and muffin, or from an old British slang word, "tiffing," meaning to take a little drink. In southern India, it can be a light snack between meals, or an early morning breakfast.

Acknowledgments

I owe an immeasurable debt of gratitude to Carol Bergman, who helped me from start to finish in bringing my memoir to life. Writer, teacher, mentor, and friend, I struck gold the day I stepped into her Creative Non-Fiction Writing Seminar. Still grieving from the loss of my son, Gopal, in the September 11 attacks, Carol extended a gentle hand with a firm grip. Her astute critiques and ear for language honed my writing skills. But, most importantly, Carol forced me to confront my inner voice and translate it onto the page. The sorrow of losing a child will always persist but a sense of hope and a chance to renew one's spirit are the gifts I received from Carol. For this, I am eternally grateful.

I was fortunate to have gracious and supportive colleagues at the Gallatin School of Individualized Study who read drafts of the memoir in its early and late stages. A big thank you to Michael Dinwiddie, Lise Friedman, June Foley, Victoria Blythe, and Scott Hightower. I couldn't ask for better friends than Lee Bell, Uma Puri, Ed Burns and Samidh Guha who took the time to read my work and encouraged me all the way to the finish line.

Memories of the past are the raw material with which I had to work. At times, I had to grapple with the chronology of events and turned to my younger brother, Ranga, the memory-keeper in our family. His razor-sharp recall of events down to every detail was of immense help and we shared many a moment reliving our past. Over the years, I drew closer to my older brother, Ramu, and to this day we be-bop to the rock and roll music of our childhood. Lastly, I would like to thank my husband, Raghu, who abandoned his study and gave me a room of my own.

Photo by S.R.S. Varadhan

About the Author

Vasu Varadhan holds a PhD in Media Studies from New York University where she is currently a member of the faculty at the Gallatin School of Individualized Study. She has taught a wide range of interdisciplinary seminars on media theory, identity in a multi-cultural world, ancient Indian literature and South Asian literature with a special focus on emerging Indian writers in the diaspora. She is the featured subject of the documentary, *Knowing Her Place,* by Indu Krishnan, which chronicles her struggle with "cultural schizophrenia" as an Indian American woman searching to forge her own identity. Her writing has been published in two of India's leading newspapers, *The Hindu* and *The Indian Express,* in the *South Asian Review* and in the online publication, *The Pythians.* She lives in New York City.

Made in the
USA
Monee, IL